ROBERT J. MARZANO

JULIA A. SIMMS

Coaching Classroom Instruction

Marzano Research Laboratory

with TOM **ROY**

TAMMY **HEFLEBOWER**

PHIL **WARRICK**

THE **CLASSROOM** STRATEGIES **SERIES**

555 North Morton Street
Bloomington, IN 47404

888.849.0851
FAX: 866.801.1447

email: info@marzanoresearch.com
marzanoresearch.com

Visit **marzanoresearch.com/classroomstrategies** to download reproducibles from this book.

Printed in the United States of America

Library of Congress Control Number: 2012910133

ISBN: 978-0-9833512-6-9 (paperback)

16 15 14 13 12   1 2 3 4 5

Editorial Director: Lesley Bolton

Managing Production Editor: Caroline Wise

Copy Editor: Rachel Rosolina

Proofreader: Elisabeth Abrams

Text and Cover Designer: Amy Shock

MARZANO RESEARCH LABORATORY DEVELOPMENT TEAM

Director of Publications

Julia A. Simms

Marzano Research Laboratory Associates

Tina Boogren

Bev Clemens

Jane K. Doty Fischer

Maria C. Foseid

Mark P. Foseid

Tammy Heflebower

Mitzi Hoback

Jan Hoegh

Russell Jenson

Jessica Kanold-McIntyre

Sharon Kramer

David Livingston

Pam Livingston

Beatrice McGarvey

Margaret McInteer

Diane E. Paynter

Debra Pickering

Salle Quackenboss

Laurie Robinson

Tom Roy

Phil Warrick

Kenneth Williams

CONTENTS

Italicized entries indicate reproducible forms.

ABOUT THE AUTHORS IX

ABOUT MARZANO RESEARCH LABORATORY XIII

INTRODUCTION 1

    How to Use This Book 2

CHAPTER 1

RESEARCH AND THEORY 3

    History of Coaching 3

    Clinical Supervision as the Foundation of Coaching Teachers 4

    Research on the Benefits of Coaching 5

    Aspects of Coaching 7

    Requirements for Effective Coaching 9

    Coaching Models 12

    Virtual Coaching 16

    Translating Research and Theory Into Practice 18

CHAPTER 2

A FOUNDATION FOR COACHING 19

    Establishing a Model of Effective Teaching 19

Using a Scale to Measure Teachers' Progress 23

Conducting a Self-Audit 24

Establishing a Coaching Perspective 30

Summary 35

Chapter 2: Comprehension Questions *36*

CHAPTER 3

NOT USING (0) TO BEGINNING (1) 37

Lesson Segments Involving Routine Events 38

Lesson Segments Addressing Content 41

Lesson Segments Enacted on the Spot 49

Summary 58

Chapter 3: Comprehension Questions *59*

CHAPTER 4

BEGINNING (1) TO DEVELOPING (2) AND DEVELOPING (2) TO APPLYING (3) 61

Coaching Is Not Necessarily a Linear Process 62

Lesson Segments Involving Routine Events 63

Lesson Segments Addressing Content 75

Lesson Segments Enacted on the Spot 112

Summary 153

Chapter 4: Comprehension Questions *154*

CHAPTER 5

APPLYING (3) TO INNOVATING (4) 155

Integrate Several Strategies to Create a Macrostrategy 155

Adapt a Strategy for Unique Student Needs or Situations 156

Lesson Segments Involving Routine Events 157

Lesson Segments Addressing Content 165

Lesson Segments Enacted on the Spot 186

Summary 208

Chapter 5: Comprehension Questions *209*

CHAPTER 6

ASPECTS OF COACHING 211

Coaching Systems 211

Differentiating Coaching 213

Coaching Behaviors 217

Virtual Coaching 219

Summary 221

Chapter 6: Comprehension Questions *222*

APPENDIX: ANSWERS TO COMPREHENSION QUESTIONS 223

Answers to Chapter 2: Comprehension Questions *224*

Answers to Chapter 3: Comprehension Questions *226*

Answers to Chapter 4: Comprehension Questions *227*

Answers to Chapter 5: Comprehension Questions *228*

Answers to Chapter 6: Comprehension Questions *229*

REFERENCES AND RESOURCES 231

INDEX 251

ABOUT THE AUTHORS

Robert J. Marzano, PhD, is the cofounder and CEO of Marzano Research Laboratory in Denver, Colorado. Throughout his forty years in the field of education, he has become a speaker, trainer, and author of more than thirty books and 150 articles on topics such as instruction, assessment, writing and implementing standards, cognition, effective leadership, and school intervention. His books include: *Designing and Teaching Learning Goals and Objectives, District Leadership That Works, Formative Assessment and Standards-Based Grading, On Excellence in Teaching, The Art and Science of Teaching, The Highly Engaged Classroom, Effective Supervision, Teaching and Assessing 21st Century Skills,* and *Becoming a Reflective Teacher.* His practical translations of the most current research and theory into classroom strategies are known internationally and are widely practiced by both teachers and administrators. He received a bachelor's degree from Iona College in New York, a master's degree from Seattle University, and a doctorate from the University of Washington.

Julia A. Simms, EdM, MA, is director of publications for Marzano Research Laboratory. She has worked in K–12 education as a classroom teacher, gifted education specialist, teacher leader, and coach. Additionally, she has led school- and district-level professional development on a variety of topics, including literacy instruction and intervention, classroom and schoolwide differentiation, and instructional technology. She received her bachelor's degree from Wheaton College in Wheaton, Illinois, and her master's degrees in educational administration and K–12 literacy from Colorado State University and the University of Northern Colorado, respectively.

Tom Roy, PhD, a lifelong educator, is presently in private practice working with schools and districts to improve student learning, assessment, and school leadership. He has worked with schools and nonprofit organizations nationally and internationally on issues of leadership, curriculum, assessment, and organizational effectiveness. As an MRL associate, Dr. Roy uses Marzano's model of effective teaching as a vehicle for teacher improvement in both coaching and evaluation formats. He has served as a science and mathematics teacher in elementary, middle, and high schools, as well as in school administration. Dr. Roy earned his PhD in curriculum and instruction from Boston College, a master of science in education from Elmira College, and a bachelor of science education from the State University of New York.

Tammy Heflebower, EdD, is vice president of Marzano Research Laboratory in Denver, Colorado. She has served as a classroom teacher, building-level leader, district leader, regional professional development director, adjunct professor, and national trainer and has experience working in urban, rural, and suburban districts. She began her teaching career in Kansas City, Kansas, and later moved to Nebraska, where she received the District Distinguished Teacher Award. She has worked as a national educational trainer for the National Resource and Training Center at Boys Town in Nebraska. Dr. Heflebower has served as president of the Nebraska Association for Supervision and Curriculum Development and was president-elect for the Professional Development Organization for Nebraska Educational Service Units. She was president-elect of the Colorado Association of Education Specialists and legislative liaison for the Colorado Association of School Executives. Recently, she was named Outstanding Alumni from Hastings College. She is a contributor to *The Teacher as Assessment Leader*, *The Principal as Assessment Leader*, and *Becoming a Reflective Teacher* and a coauthor of *Teaching and Assessing 21st Century Skills*. Her articles have been featured in the monthly newsletter *Nebraska Council of School Administrators Today* and in *Educational Leadership*. Dr. Heflebower holds a bachelor of arts from Hastings College in Hastings, Nebraska, a master of arts from the University of Nebraska at Omaha, and an educational administrative endorsement from the University of Nebraska-Lincoln. She also earned a doctor of education in educational administration from the University of Nebraska-Lincoln.

Phil Warrick, EdD, is associate vice president of Marzano Research Laboratory in Denver, Colorado. He was an award-winning school administrator in Waverly, Nebraska, for nearly twelve years. Dr. Warrick has been an adjunct professor at Peru State College since 2005. In 2003, he was one of the first participants to attend the Nebraska Educational Leadership Institute, conducted by the Gallup Corporation at Gallup University in Omaha; in 2008, he was named campus principal at Round Rock High School, a school of nearly three thousand students in Round Rock, Texas; and in 2010, he was invited to participate in the Texas Principals' Visioning Institute, where he worked with other principals from around the state to begin identifying model practices for Texas schools as they educate students in the 21st century. He is a past regional president for the Nebraska Council of School Administrators (NCSA). In addition, he served on the NCSA legislative committee and was elected chair. Dr. Warrick was named 1998 Nebraska Outstanding New Principal, 2004 Nebraska Secondary School Principals Region One Principal of the Year, and 2005 Nebraska State High School Principal of the Year. He earned a bachelor of science from Chadron State College in Chadron, Nebraska, and master's and doctoral degrees from the University of Nebraska-Lincoln.

ABOUT MARZANO RESEARCH LABORATORY

Marzano Research Laboratory (MRL) is a joint venture between Solution Tree and Dr. Robert J. Marzano. MRL combines Dr. Marzano's forty years of educational research with continuous action research in all major areas of schooling in order to provide effective and accessible instructional strategies, leadership strategies, and classroom assessment strategies that are always at the forefront of best practice. By providing such an all-inclusive research-into-practice resource center, MRL provides teachers and principals with the tools they need to effect profound and immediate improvement in student achievement.

INTRODUCTION

Coaching Classroom Instruction is part of a series of books collectively referred to as the *Classroom Strategies Series*. This series aims to provide teachers, as well as building and district administrators, with an in-depth treatment of research-based instructional strategies that can be used in the classroom to enhance student achievement. Many of the strategies addressed in this series have been covered in other works, such as *Classroom Instruction That Works* (Marzano, Pickering, & Pollock, 2001), *Classroom Management That Works* (Marzano, 2003), *The Art and Science of Teaching* (Marzano, 2007), and *Effective Supervision* (Marzano, Frontier, & Livingston, 2011). Although those works devoted a chapter or a part of a chapter to particular strategies, the *Classroom Strategies Series* devotes an entire book to an instructional strategy or set of related strategies.

Coaching pervades our society, most notably in sports, but also in fields such as business and psychology. K–12 education has seen coaching become increasingly popular as a way to help teachers increase their knowledge and skill. While educational coaches fill a variety of roles and perform various functions, the primary purpose of an educational coach should be to help teachers increase their effectiveness. To do this, coaches must help teachers identify areas for potential growth, practice strategies associated with those areas, and adjust their performance in response to feedback. In addition to describing a process for coaching, *Coaching Classroom Instruction* outlines specific components of effective teaching and explains how coaches can help teachers implement and practice those components in their classrooms.

We begin with a brief but inclusive chapter that reviews the research and theory on coaching. Although you may be eager to move right into those chapters that provide recommendations for practice in schools, we strongly encourage you to examine the research and theory, as they are the foundation for the entire book. Indeed, a basic purpose of *Coaching Classroom Instruction* and others in the *Classroom Strategies Series* is to present the most useful strategies based on the strongest research and theory available.

Because research and theory can provide only a general direction for classroom practice, *Coaching Classroom Instruction* goes one step further to translate that research into applications for coaching in schools. Specifically, this book addresses how coaches can help teachers improve their knowledge and skill with 280 classroom strategies related to forty-one elements of effective teaching. We provide a level of specificity that allows a coach to pinpoint specific components of a teacher's knowledge and skill and give helpful feedback.

How to Use This Book

Coaching Classroom Instruction allows coaches to give targeted feedback to teachers and identify specific steps that teachers can take to improve their knowledge and skill. Initially, coaches can acquaint teachers with the model of effective teaching and the five levels of the scale presented in chapter 2. To help teachers advance through these levels and achieve growth goals, coaches can use the 280 detailed classroom strategies provided in chapters 3, 4, and 5. Chapter 6 reviews effective coaching strategies that coaches can use while interacting with teachers throughout the growth process.

Educators can use *Coaching Classroom Instruction* as a self-study text that provides an in-depth understanding of how to coach teachers. As you progress through the chapters, you will encounter comprehension questions. It is important to complete these questions and compare your answers with those in the appendix (page 223). Such interaction provides a review of the content and allows a thorough examination of your understanding.

Groups or teams of coaches and administrators who wish to examine the topic of coaching in depth may also use *Coaching Classroom Instruction*. When this is the case, teams should answer the questions independently and then compare their answers in small- or large-group settings. Groups can also take advantage of the "Role-Play" features at the end of chapters 3, 4, and 5. These dramatizations are designed to be completed with a colleague and provide practice with the knowledge and skills presented in the chapter.

Chapter 1

RESEARCH AND THEORY

With a complex endeavor such as teaching, it is extremely difficult to reach and then maintain the highest levels of performance without help. The most effective help commonly comes in the form of coaching. As Atul Gawande (2011) noted, "No matter how well trained people are, few can sustain their best performance on their own. That's where coaching comes in" (p. 1). Gawande further noted that "coaching done well may be the most effective intervention designed for human performance" (p. 9). Because teacher effectiveness is directly linked to student achievement (Nye, Konstantopoulos, & Hedges, 2004), it is well worth the effort to support teacher growth and performance through coaching.

Coaching also serves as a way to pass along knowledge that has been accumulated over time. Nicholas Emler and Nick Heather (1980) stated that "we are a successful species because we cheat; we tell each other the answers" (p. 145). Bob Garvey (2010) added that "knowledge or experience sharing and advice giving can be an essential part of learning: if we do not do this as a species, we commit the next generation to reinvent the wheel!" (p. 346). Isaac Newton's famous quote, "If I have seen further than others, it is by standing upon the shoulders of giants" (Isaac Newton, n.d.), also echoes this idea. In educational coaching, this knowledge sharing involves helping teachers transfer what they learn in professional development sessions and other experiences into classroom practice. Teachers' needs often stem not from a lack of knowledge, but from a failure to operationalize their knowledge (Joyce & Showers, 2002; Knight, 2007).

History of Coaching

As noted by Perry Zeus and Suzanne Skiffington (2002), coaching is different from consulting, therapy, or mentoring, although it has historically been related to those concepts. According to Stephen Palmer and Alison Whybrow (2007), Coleman R. Griffith began studying the psychology of football and basketball players as early as 1918. In 1926, he published *Psychology of Coaching*, in which he talked about different aspects of athletic coaching and reviewed learning principles that could help coaches better support their players. According to Palmer and Whybrow (2007), Griffith also "questioned commonsense thinking such as 'practice makes perfect'" (p. 5). Griffith's initial efforts to describe the psychology of coaching were soon followed by others.

In two literature reviews, Anthony Grant (2005a, 2006) attempted to provide a history of coaching by examining behavioral-science and scholarly business literature. One of the earliest papers he found was by C. B. Gorby (1937), who described how businesses could use peer coaching among their employees to reduce waste and increase profits. Grant found that this focus on using coaching to maximize profits continued throughout the subsequent business literature, and it was expanded to include coaching to improve executive development and work performance for all employees. Altogether, Grant (2006) located 393 relevant papers published between 1955 and 2005: 79 of them were empirical studies, and the other 314 discussed coaching techniques and theories. Sixty-seven of the empirical studies Grant found were fairly recent (published between 2001 and 2005), revealing that coaching is still a relatively young discipline. This led Grant to conclude that "far more empirical research needs to be conducted. Such research should focus on the impact of coaching at both individual and organizational levels, as well as the establishment of validated, evidence-based coaching methodologies" (2006, p. 369). In agreement with Grant's findings, Lindsay Oades, Peter Caputi, Paula Robinson, and Barry Partridge (2005) observed that "while there are many books on coaching (particularly, books on how to 'do coaching'), there is . . . a paucity of controlled trials on the effectiveness of coaching" (p. 71). The relative newness of coaching as a field and discipline has led to a number of different definitions of coaching and its related terms. Two terms in particular are frequently used when talking about coaching: *coach* and *mentor*.

The term *coach* has its roots in the field of transportation, as Richard Gauthier and David Giber (2006) described:

> Coaching is all about helping transport someone from where he or she is to where he or she needs to be. The verb "coach" derives from the old English noun describing the vehicle for transporting royalty, moving from one place to another via the coach. (p. 124)

Tatiana Bachkirova, Elaine Cox, and David Clutterbuck (2010) further elaborated:

> The word "coach" derives from a town called "Kocs" in northern Hungary, where horse-drawn carriages were made. The meaning of coach as an instructor or trainer is purportedly from around 1830, when it was Oxford University slang for a tutor who "carried" a student through an exam; the term coaching was later applied in the 1800s to improving the performance of athletes. (p. 2)

Although the term has broadened as the popularity of coaching has expanded, the term *coach* generally means helping someone move from where he or she is to where he or she needs or wants to be.

The term *mentor* dates back much further. In Greek mythology, Mentor was Odysseus's friend who watched over his estate and family while Odysseus was away fighting in the Trojan War. Mentor cared for and advised Telemachus, Odysseus's son, and encouraged him to resist the advances of his mother's suitors and seek out information about his father. Additionally, Athena (the Greek goddess of wisdom and the friend of Odysseus) disguised herself as Mentor to visit Telemachus, giving him practical advice and helping him solve problems. The first recorded modern usage of the term echoes its classical roots. In a 1699 book titled *Les Aventures de Telemaque*, French writer François Fénelon expanded on the relationship between Mentor and Telemachus, recounting their travels and lessons together (Smollett, 1997). The modern use of *mentor* to mean a trusted friend, counselor, or teacher is most likely a result of Fénelon's book.

Clinical Supervision as the Foundation of Coaching Teachers

Any discussion of coaching teachers must acknowledge the influence of clinical supervision, which was designed by Morris Cogan, Robert Goldhammer, and Robert Anderson at Harvard in the 1950s and 1960s. As they supervised teachers in Harvard's Master of Arts in Teaching program, Cogan, Goldhammer, and Anderson recognized a flaw in the traditional supervision model they were using.

Supervisors would observe teachers, identify what they thought needed to be changed, and tell the teacher how to change it. This traditional practice failed to consider what issues the *teacher* might think were problematic or what solutions the teacher might want to try.

To encourage "the development of the professionally responsible teacher who is analytical of his own performance, open to help from others, and . . . self-directing" (Cogan, 1973, p. 12), Cogan, Goldhammer, and Anderson developed the clinical supervision model. Described in Cogan's (1973) and Goldhammer's (1969) books, both titled *Clinical Supervision*, the model is designed to help teachers appraise their own performance, identify ways to improve, and evaluate how those improvements affect their overall performance.

There is a respectable research base for clinical supervision (Adams & Glickman, 1984; Glickman, 2002; Nolan, Hawkes, & Francis, 1993; Pavan, 1985; Sullivan, 1980), and the concept has been refined since its inception (Acheson & Gall, 1992; Anderson & Snyder, 1993; Costa & Garmston, 1985; Goldhammer, Anderson, & Krajewski, 1993; Pajak, 1993, 2002). Overall, clinical supervision involves five steps:

1. Preconference between supervisor and teacher

2. Classroom observation by the supervisor

3. Analysis of the results of the observation

4. Postconference between supervisor and teacher

5. Evaluation and critique of the supervision process

Although the clinical supervision process was designed as a vehicle for rich dialogue about a teacher's practice, Robert Marzano and his colleagues (2011) pointed out that "over time, the five phases became an end in themselves" (p. 19). That is, teachers and administrators would move through each stage, but they were not engaging in the "collegial, inquiry-driven quest for more effective instructional practices" (Marzano et al., 2011, p. 19) that Goldhammer envisioned.

Research on the Benefits of Coaching

The efficacy of coaching can be supported from a number of perspectives. Bruce Joyce and Beverly Showers (2002) provided perhaps the most robust synthesis of research on coaching as it relates to educators. Describing their research in the 1980s, Joyce and Showers (2002) commented:

> We found that continuing technical assistance, whether provided by an outside expert or by peer experts, resulted in much greater classroom implementation than was achieved by teachers who shared initial training but did not have the long-term support of coaching. (p. 85)

In their 2002 research, Joyce and Showers found that even when training included demonstrations, practice sessions, and feedback, it did not noticeably affect teachers' transfer of their learning to the classroom (effect size = 0.0). However, they did find that "a large and dramatic increase in transfer of training—effect size of 1.42—occurs when coaching is added to an initial training experience" (p. 77). In other words, coaching provided the most effective means of helping teachers transfer newly acquired knowledge and skills to their classrooms.

Joyce and Showers (2002) found that coaching helped teachers transfer their training to the classroom in five ways:

1. Coached teachers and principals generally practiced new strategies more frequently and developed greater skill in the actual moves of a new teaching strategy than did uncoached educators who had experienced identical initial training. . . .

2. Coached teachers used their newly learned strategies more appropriately than uncoached teachers in terms of their own instructional objectives and the theories of specific models of teaching. . . .

3. Coached teachers exhibited greater long-term retention of knowledge about and skill with strategies in which they had been coached and, as a group, increased the appropriateness of use of new teaching models over time. . . .

4. Coached teachers were much more likely than uncoached teachers to explain new models of teaching to their students, ensuring that students understood the purpose of the strategy and the behaviors expected of them when using the strategy. . . .

5. Coached teachers . . . exhibited clearer cognitions with regard to the purposes and uses of the new strategies, as revealed through interviews, lesson plans, and classroom performance. (pp. 86–87)

Other researchers have also provided useful perspectives on coaching. For example, Jim Knight (2007) emphasizes the importance of coaching partnerships. He compared two approaches to professional learning—a partnership approach (learning with coaching) and a traditional approach (lecture from an expert):

> Teachers reported that in the partnership sessions, they learned more, were engaged more, and enjoyed themselves more than in the traditional sessions. Additionally, they were four times more inclined to implement teaching practices they learned during partnership sessions than those learned during traditional sessions. (p. 39)

Knight (2007) also reported research by Robert Bush (1984), which showed that traditional professional development usually leads to about a 10 percent implementation rate. In response, Knight stated that "our experience has shown that when teachers receive an appropriate amount of support for professional learning, more than 90% of them embrace and implement programs that improve students' experiences in the classroom" (pp. 3–4). In addition to increased implementation of professional development, Anthony Grant, L. S. Green, and Josephine Rynsaardt (2010) reported that coached teachers developed "enhanced self-reported leadership and communication styles . . . reduced stress, increased resilience, and improved workplace well-being" (p. 162).

Allison Kretlow and Christina Bartholomew (2010) reviewed the coaching literature and identified three critical components of effective coaching: "(a) highly engaged, instructive group training sessions; (b) follow-up observation(s); and (c) specific feedback, often including sharing observation data and self-evaluation followed by modeling" (p. 292). They also summarized what an effective coaching process might look like:

> Prior to coaching, teacher educators should conduct at least one observation (e.g., live, video-, or audio-recorded) to determine with which specific skills the teacher is having difficulty. Then, feedback and coaching activities should directly target skills that need to be firmed up. Coaching sessions should include some form of modeling, whether it is during an actual lesson or one-on-one with the teacher. (p. 294)

Michelle Vanderburg and Diane Stephens (2010) identified behaviors that characterized effective coaches. These included facilitating teacher collaboration, supporting classroom instruction, and teaching research-based practices. Susan Neuman and Tanya Wright (2010) emphasized the inherent benefits in the personalized nature of coaching:

> The on-site, individual, and personal nature of coaching created an accountability mechanism that was tailored to helping the teacher enact better instruction. It gave teachers regular feedback that enabled them to make changes in key skill domains. (p. 83)

In addition to the general research on the effects, benefits, and characteristics of coaching, research has been conducted concerning coaching's effects on specific aspects of education, including student achievement and teachers' knowledge and skill.

Student Achievement

There is not a great deal of research linking coaching to student achievement; however, Vanderburg and Stephens (2010) reported on literacy coaching research and found that "the students of teachers who were coached did better on measures of phonological awareness, timed and untimed word reading, phonemic decoding, passage comprehension, and spelling" (p. 142). Although some studies (Garet et al., 2008; Marsh et al., 2008) have shown that coaching had no effect on student achievement, Gina Biancarosa, Anthony Bryk, and Emily Dexter (2010) noted significant increases in student achievement as a result of teacher coaching:

> On average, children in participating schools in the first year of implementation made 16% larger learning gains than observed during the baseline no-treatment period. In the second year, children learned 28% more compared to the baseline data, and by the third year they had learned 32% more. Our analyses also indicate that these results persisted across summer periods as verified through the follow-up of students in the fall of the subsequent academic year. (p. 27)

Although more research on the link between coaching and student achievement is needed, it is reasonable to suggest that effective coaching can have a positive impact on student achievement.

Teacher Knowledge and Skill

The research linking coaching to changes in teacher behavior appears stronger and less equivocal than that linking coaching to student achievement. Kretlow and Bartholomew (2010) reviewed a number of studies on coaching and found "strong evidence for the effectiveness of coaching in promoting the fidelity of evidence-based practices. . . . Overwhelmingly, coaching improved the accuracy of teaching behaviors across studies reviewed" (pp. 292–293). Vanderburg and Stephens (2010) reported the positive effects of coaching on teacher knowledge: "The beliefs and practices of coached teachers became more consistent with best practices as defined by state and national standards" (p. 143). Finally, Kathryn Kinnucan-Welsch, Catherine Rosemary, and Patricia Grogan (2006) reported that coaching helped teachers gain familiarity with the concepts they were teaching, and Susan Cantrell and Hannah Hughes (2008) found that coaching increased teachers' efficacy. In light of this research, it is safe to say that coaching has a positive impact on teachers' knowledge and skill.

Aspects of Coaching

The term *coaching* is used in a variety of ways. Gawande (2011) noted that:

> The concept of a coach is slippery. Coaches are not teachers, but they teach. They're not your boss—in professional tennis, golf, and skating, the athlete hires and fires the coach—but they can be bossy. They don't even have to be good at the sport. The famous Olympic gymnastics coach Bela Karolyi couldn't do a split if his life depended on it. Mainly, they observe, they judge, and they guide. (p. 2)

Different researchers and theorists highlight different aspects of coaching when defining it. Some emphasize the instructional features of coaching. For example, Eric Parsloe (1995) noted that coaching is "directly concerned with the immediate improvement of performance and development of skills by a form of tutoring or instruction" (p. 72). Somewhat in contrast, others de-emphasize the instructional aspects of coaching. For example, Anthony Grant and Dianne Stober (2006) explained that "coaching is more about asking the right questions than telling people what to do" (p. 3). Some researchers stress the importance of feedback and goals in the coaching process. Grant (2005b) noted that "the coaching process should be systematic and goal directed" (p. 4). Finally, some stress the importance of coaching resulting in change. As Anne Brockbank and Ian McGill (2006) noted, "Mentoring or coaching has one clear purpose, the learning and development of an individual, a process that involves change" (p. 9). Just as there are many aspects of coaching, so too are there many views of the goals of coaching. Table 1.1 presents some of these goals.

Table 1.1: Goals of Coaching

To point teachers toward best practices	"As the coach leader 'holds up' the standards and expectations that have been determined from a solid research base of 'what works,' it focuses the work on making decisions and acting in ways that have the potential to most dramatically impact results. When we work from a 'standards based' body of research, the possibility of an aspect of the work becoming someone's personal preference or expectation is diminished" (Kee, Anderson, Dearing, Harris, & Shuster, 2010, pp. 46–47).
To show teachers what good teaching looks like	"Coaches . . . want teachers to know what success looks like and to imagine their own successful handling of situations" (Tschannen-Moran & Tschannen-Moran, 2010, p. 183). "Good coaches know how to break down performance into its critical individual components" (Gawande, 2011, p. 5).
To help teachers maintain their best performance	"The coaching model is different from the traditional conception of pedagogy, where there's a presumption that, after a certain point, the student no longer needs instruction. . . . No matter how well prepared people are in their formative years, few can achieve and maintain their best performance on their own" (Gawande, 2011, pp. 2–3).
To help teachers achieve "flow"	"Flow happens when teachers are fully immersed in the process of growth and change. To reach that state of full engagement, the activity needs to be intrinsically interesting and just within reach of their abilities. If the activity is too challenging, then it is overwhelming and stressful. If the activity is not challenging enough, then it is boring and tedious. The sweet spot—the flow spot—is where the level of challenge perfectly matches the skills, training, strengths, and resources of the performer. . . . Coaches want to assist teachers to enter that state as often as possible while working on their instructional strategies" (Tschannen-Moran & Tschannen-Moran, 2010, p. 218).
To help teachers take risks	"A coach leader is one who will challenge his or her educators to break away from the norm, to be creative, to use their imagination, to initiate something new, to act in new ways. A coach leader is a facilitator of a new mindset that is critically needed in schools today" (Kee et al., 2010, p. 11).

Arguments for the Nonevaluative Nature of Coaching

One strong theme in the discussion of coaching is that it should be nonevaluative in nature. Carl Rogers and Richard Farson (2006), whose work on communication is widely used and well-respected, pointed out that effective communication can only take place in a nonthreatening environment: "The climate must foster equality and freedom, trust and understanding, acceptance and warmth. In this climate and in this climate only does the individual feel safe enough to incorporate new experiences and new values into his concept of himself" (p. 281). Joyce and Showers (2002) emphasized the importance of nonevaluative feedback in their work with peer coaches by encouraging coaches to focus their feedback on inquiry rather than evaluation. Others (Ackland, 1991; Skinner & Welch, 1996) have also emphasized the necessity of nonevaluative feedback in a coaching relationship. Peter Bluckert (2010) stated that "description . . . is more important than interpretation. What this looks like in practice is an emphasis on descriptive rather than evaluative feedback and a more faithful reflection and honouring of the coachees' own words, meanings and subjective experience" (p. 81). Finally, research by Marcus Buckingham (2007) has demonstrated that trying to fix problems by focusing on weaknesses is relatively ineffective.

If administrators coach teachers whom they also evaluate, it is important for them to emphasize learning and growth. Thomasina Piercy (2006) observed that "when leadership is connected to learning, anxiety regarding accountability is greatly reduced" (p. 128). Suzanne Burley and Cathy Pomphrey (2011) suggested a better method, which they term "off-line mentoring." In this type of coaching relationship, neither the coach nor the coachee has "management responsibilities over the other. In short, the mentee will not be mentored by their boss" (p. 66). They went on to explain that this type of nonsupervisory relationship is appropriate "because of the difficulty of being open in a professional relationship where one person has authority over the other" (p. 66).

Nancy Adler (2006) confirmed the importance of a nonevaluative coaching relationship in which both parties agree to keep the content of coaching sessions confidential. She explained, "The privacy of coaching sessions makes it easier . . . to say, 'I'm not certain. . . . I just don't know . . .' Privacy and supportive advocacy legitimize moments of not knowing. Premature certainty and commitment extinguish innovative possibilities" (p. 243). Finally, Arthur Costa and Robert Garmston (2002) suggest that, "should an employer have performance concerns about a staff member, these concerns are best communicated directly outside the coaching process. Coaching should never be about 'fixing' another person" (p. 97).

Requirements for Effective Coaching

Throughout the literature on coaching, researchers and theorists emphasize that effective coaching is not entirely dependent on the coach. Rather, many assert that the person being coached (the coachee or client) is the most important determiner of the success or failure of a coaching relationship. Marshall Goldsmith (2006), who has conducted coaching research with over 86,000 people, stated that "we have learned that the key variable for successful change is *not* the coach, teacher, or advisor. The key variables that will determine long-term progress are the people being coached" (p. 39). Annette Fillery-Travis and David Lane (2007) agree, stating that "overwhelmingly the published work by coach practitioners points to the willingness by the client to change as the primary determinant of the success of the interaction" (p. 63). Specifically, Douglas Reeves (2007) wrote that "the first requirement of effective coaching is that the person receiving the coaching agrees that a change in performance will be useful" (p. 90), and Jenny Rogers (2011) said, "The client needs to be a willing volunteer, open to change, and brave" (p. 342). Edgar Schein (2006) added that, ideally, the person being coached should volunteer and be motivated to learn, grow, and change.

James Prochaska, Carlo DiClemente, and John Norcross (1992) noted that it is important to accept clients where they are: "Probably the most obvious and direct implication of our research is the need to assess the stage of a client's readiness for change and to tailor interventions accordingly" (p. 1110). Similarly, Reeves's (2007) second requirement for effective coaching, "linking learning with performance," (p. 90) emphasized the coach's role in determining a client's current performance and helping him or her learn what is necessary for improvement. Knight (2007) recognized that not all teachers will be willing to work with a coach, and gave guidance to administrators working with reluctant teachers: "Rather than telling teachers they must work with coaches, we suggest principals focus on the teaching practice that must change, and offer the coach as one way the teacher can bring about the needed change" (p. 98).

Trust

Trust is an important aspect of effective coaching relationships and effective schools. In their book, *Trust in Schools*, Anthony Bryk and Barbara Schneider (2002) described their study of twelve elementary schools in Chicago in the 1990s. Their findings emphasized the importance of trust in school communities:

> A school with a low score on relational trust at the end of our study had only a one in seven chance of demonstrating improved student learning between 1991 and 1996. In contrast, half of the schools scoring high on relational trust were in the improved group. Perhaps most significant, schools with chronically weak trust reports over this period had virtually no chance of improving in either reading or mathematics. (p. 124)

One factor affecting the levels of relational trust in a school is the quality of teacher-teacher and teacher-principal relationships. In schools with high levels of relational trust, "teachers . . . value others who are expert at their craft and who take leadership roles in school improvement. Teachers in these schools also typically report that they trust, confide in, and care about one another" (Bryk & Schneider, 2002, p. 95). Additionally, teachers in high trust schools have good relationships with their principals. Bryk and Schneider (2002) stated that teachers in trusting schools "typically describe their principal as an effective manager who supports their professional development. They perceive that the principal looks out for their welfare and also places the needs of students first" (p. 95). Coaching is one way to build the trusting relationships that Bryk and Schneider found in the top-quartile schools.

Knight (2007) pointed out that trust is also important when working with teachers, because most teachers "care deeply about the art and craft of their profession" (p. 26). Writing from the perspective of a teacher, Parker Palmer (2007) observed that "teaching is a daily exercise in vulnerability. . . . No matter how technical my subject may be, the things I teach are things I care about—and what I care about helps define my selfhood" (p. 17). To develop trust with teachers, Bob and Megan Tschannen-Moran (2010) offered several suggestions: "Demonstrate goodwill and genuine concern for the well-being of teachers. Coaches can promote trust by showing consideration and sensitivity for teachers' feelings and needs and by acting in ways that protect teachers' rights" (p. 36; see also Tschannen-Moran, 2004).

Feedback

One of a coach's most important functions is to provide teachers with feedback on their performance. It stands to reason that if a teacher doesn't know what he or she is doing right or wrong, it will be difficult for that teacher to improve his or her knowledge and skill. Joe Folkman (2006) explained that

> feedback establishes a connection between what we think and what we are seen to do, a measure of the gap between our intentions and how others perceive our actions. In the absence of good feedback, we can never know how our behavior may affect others. (p. 71)

In addition to creating a connection between teachers' knowledge and actions, feedback also helps teachers figure out how to accomplish their goals. James Kouzes and Barry Posner (2006) explain that

> people need to know whether they're making progress or marking time. Goals help to serve that function, but goals are not enough. It's not enough to know that we want to make it to the summit. We also need to know whether we're still climbing or whether we're sliding downhill. Therefore, effective leader-coaches also provide constructive, timely, and accurate feedback. Encouragement is a form of feedback. It is positive information that tells us we're making progress, that we're on the right track, and that we're living up to the standards. (p. 138)

Feedback should be specific and honest. Alan Bourne (2007) further stated that feedback should be delivered privately, and coaches should clarify who has access to the feedback (for example, an administrator or the human resources department). Kretlow and Bartholomew (2010) observed that the coaches in their research studies provided effective feedback in several ways, including "the teacher and coach evaluating video recordings of lessons together, direct stating of instructional strengths and opportunities for improvement, reciprocal peer observation and feedback, and in vivo feedback (i.e., coach directly intervenes in a nonevaluative manner during lesson)" (p. 292). Brockbank and McGill (2006) provided guidelines that coaches can follow when giving feedback to teachers:

- Be clear about what you want to say in advance.

- Own the feedback.

- Start with the positive.

- Be specific, not general.

- Give one piece of feedback at a time.

- Focus on behavior rather than the person.

- Refer to behavior that can be changed.

- Be descriptive rather than evaluative. (p. 225)

Effective feedback should specify which strategies a teacher is performing correctly and effectively, which strategies a teacher is using but with errors or omissions, and which strategies a teacher could or should use but isn't.

Choice

The final aspect of effective coaching supported by research and theory is choice. Knight (2007) and W. Timothy Gallwey (2000) both emphasized the importance of choice in a coaching relationship. Knight (2007) explained that

> personal discretion is in many ways the heart of being a professional. Doctors, lawyers, or teachers are professionals because we trust them to make the right decisions, to use their knowledge skillfully and artfully. That is, what makes someone a professional is her or his ability to choose correctly. When we take away choice, we reduce people to being less than professionals. (p. 42)

Gallwey (2000) explained that allowing someone to choose what to work on and how to work on it builds trust and keeps a coaching relationship from becoming manipulative: "In the place of manipulation, there is choice. In the place of doubt and overcontrol, there is trust" (p. 30). Knight (2011) applied the principle of choice directly to education, saying that "coaches who act on the principle of choice position teachers as the final decision makers, as partners who choose their coaching goals and decide which practices to adopt and how to interpret data" (pp. 18–20).

Coaching Models

Since coaching was first introduced as an effective way to help individuals grow and learn, there have been many efforts to formalize the coaching process. A number of coaching models have been developed, each with its own research base and effects. Here we describe several of the more salient models: Cognitive Coaching^SM, the Big Four model, Inner Game coaching, the GROW model, the coaching continuum model, and team coaching.

Cognitive Coaching

Cognitive Coaching is a coaching model created by Costa and Garmston (2002) to facilitate coaching conversations. They described it as "a nonjudgmental, developmental, reflective model" designed to mediate "a practitioner's thinking, perceptions, beliefs, and assumptions toward the goals of self-directed learning and increased complexity of cognitive processing" (p. 5). Costa and Garmston recommended using Cognitive Coaching for conversations that involve planning teaching, reflecting on teaching, or problem solving. They described these conversations as follows:

- The *Planning Conversation* occurs before a colleague conducts or participates in an event, resolves a challenge, or attempts a task. The coach may or may not be present during the event or available for a follow-up conversation.

- The *Reflecting Conversation* occurs after [a] colleague conducts or participates in an event, resolves a challenge, or completes a task. The coach may or may not have been present at or participated in the event.

- The *Problem-Resolving Conversation* occurs when a colleague feels stuck, helpless, unclear, or lacking in resourcefulness; experiences a crisis; or requests external assistance from a mediator. (p. 34)

Cognitive Coaching uses several coaching behaviors to achieve its goals, including reflective questioning, pausing and silence, acknowledging, paraphrasing, clarifying, probing for specificity, and providing data and resources. Costa and Garmston distinguished Cognitive Coaching from three other approaches that might be taken during coaching sessions: evaluation (judging performance), consulting (giving instruction and advice), and collaboration (working together). Kathy Norwood and Mary Ann Burke (2011) explained that Cognitive Coaching grew out of Cogan and Goldhammer's clinical supervision model:

> [Cognitive Coaching] was designed to help administrators support teachers' growth toward self-directed learning by applying humanistic principles in teacher evaluations. This methodology works on changing 'mental models' (Auerbach, 2006)—beliefs about ourselves, other people, and life in general—to arrive at less restrictive ways of thinking. (p. 214)

Ultimately, the focus of Cognitive Coaching is on producing "self-directed persons with the cognitive capacity for high performance, both independently and as members of a community" (Costa & Garmston, 2002, p. 16).

Researchers have found that Cognitive Coaching increases teacher efficacy (Dutton, 1990), collaboration (Alseike, 1997), teachers' satisfaction with their profession (Edwards, Green, Lyons, Rogers, & Swords, 1998), and teachers' reflection (Smith, 1997). With respect to its effects on student achievement, Jeffrey Auerbach (2006) stated that Cognitive Coaching

> has an outcome study research base with positive effects obtained from the students whose teachers had gone through the cognitive coaching program, including significant improvement compared to control groups on the Iowa Test of Basic Skills, reading scores, and math scores. (p. 110)

Cognitive Coaching is widely used in education, and Stephen Palmer and Kasia Szymanska (2007) pointed out that it could be effective in other fields as well.

Big Four Model

Knight (2007) built his model of coaching around what he called the Big Four: "behavior, content knowledge, direct instruction, and formative assessment" (p. 22). Knight suggested that coaches use research-based strategies to help teachers improve in these areas. Table 1.2 describes each of the Big Four areas in more depth.

Table 1.2: Knight's Big Four

Behavior	"Teachers need to create a safe, productive learning community for all students. Coaches can help by guiding teachers to articulate and teach expectations, effectively correct behavior, increase the effectiveness of praise statements, and increase students' opportunities to respond."
Content knowledge	"Teachers need to have a deep understanding of the content they are teaching. . . . Coaches must . . . help teachers translate . . . standards into lesson plans. Coaches can use planning and teaching practices . . . to help teachers unpack standards; plan courses, units, and lessons; and prioritize what content to teach."
Direct instruction	"Instruction is improved when teachers (a) provide an advance organizer; (b) model the thinking involved in whatever processes are being learned; (c) ask a variety of high-level questions; and (d) ensure that students are experiencing engaging, meaningful activities. . . . Many . . . have identified powerful instructional practices that coaches might also share with teachers so that they are better prepared to ensure that students master the content."
Formative assessment	"Teachers . . . need to know whether their students are learning the content and reasoning being taught and whether each student's skills or disposition is being affected by instruction. . . . Coaches can help their teachers form learning teams to become assessment literate."

Source: Knight, 2007, p. 23.

In addition to focusing on specific areas of the Big Four, Knight (2007) encouraged coaches to:

- Build an emotional connection with the teachers they coach

- Help teachers implement research-based practices and strategies

- Help teachers collaborate with their colleagues

- Observe and provide feedback to the teachers they coach

- Use interventions that make change easier

- Partner with the principal of the school where they coach

In 1999, Knight partnered with the University of Kansas and the Topeka, Kansas, school district to begin implementing his coaching model in schools. Since then, the model has gained popularity and is currently used in many schools in the United States.

Inner Game Coaching

Gallwey (2000) created the Inner Game model based on his experiences as a tennis coach. As he coached, he noticed that many of his players' problems were the result of overthinking:

> We have a tendency to get in our own way. . . . Take the simple action of hitting a single tennis ball. The player *sees* an image of an approaching ball, then *responds* by moving into position and striking the ball, producing the *results* of the action. . . . But usually it's not quite so simple. Between the perception and the action, there is some *interpretation*. After the results and before the next action, there is yet more thinking. At each stage, *meaning* is being attributed to each part of the action and often to the performer himself. These meanings can have a huge impact on the player's performance. (p. 8)

Gallwey postulated that simply correcting a player's behavior—an approach he labeled "traditional"—was not an effective way to help him or her improve. Instead, he targeted the player's *perception* of the performance. He created strategies that facilitated the "nonjudgmental observation of fact" (p. 10). For example, instead of asking a player to focus on the proper execution of a backhand swing, Gallwey would ask the player to gauge the height of the tennis ball when it made contact with the racquet. Gallwey discovered that when he asked his players to focus their attention on objective details, their overall performance would improve. He attributed their improvement to increased awareness. Indeed, a basic premise of Gallwey's approach was: "Before you go about trying to change something, increase your awareness of the way it is" (p. 71). Gallwey's theories and methods quickly spread from sports into business, where Gallwey's model led to higher levels of employee engagement and better customer service.

GROW Model

Gallwey's model inspired others to create coaching models, including Sir John Whitmore, an English baronet and racecar driver. In his book, *Coaching for Performance*, Whitmore (2009) described his GROW model for coaching and explained that it targeted "the essence of coaching. Coaching is unlocking people's potential to maximize their own performance. It is helping them to learn rather than teaching them" (p. 10). The GROW model became very popular among business and life coaches because it did not require the coach to have any psychological training. Although the acronym has been adapted by others over the years, Whitmore described the four stages of the process as follows:

> **Goal** setting for the session as well as short and long term.
>
> **Reality** checking to explore the current situation.
>
> **Options** and alternative strategies or courses of action.
>
> **What** is to be done, **When**, by **Whom**, and the **Will** to do it. (p. 55)

Jonathan Passmore (2007) provided questions to help coaches move their clients through each stage of the GROW model. Table 1.3 presents samples of these questions.

Table 1.3: Open Questions to Facilitate the GROW Process

Stage	Possible Questions
Goal(s)	What do you want to achieve? What do you want from this meeting? What do you need to know about . . . ?

Reality	What is happening?
	Why is it a problem?
	What do you mean by that? . . . Can you give me an example?
	What have you tried? . . . What happened?
	How do you feel about that?
Options	What options do you think there are?
	What have you tried?
	What are the pros and cons of this?
	Is there anything else you could do?
Way forward	Can you summarise what you are going to do and by when?
	What obstacles and objections do you expect?
	How will you overcome them?
	Who will you get support from?
	What resources do you need?
	When should we review progress?

Source: Passmore, 2007, p. 76.

According to Passmore (2007), "the four stages are designed . . . to identify the specific behaviours that will lead to improved performance or achievement of a specific, stated goal" (p. 76).

Coaching Continuum Model

As its name implies, the coaching continuum model requires that the coach "learn to flow between the roles of consultant, collaborator-mentor, and coach . . . to stimulate and fuel an accelerated model of learning" (Norwood & Burke, 2011, p. 215). Norwood and Burke (2011) explained that this model is designed to be used with a gradual release of responsibility:

> Teachers are not expected to fully implement new concepts before they have seen the concepts modeled and have practiced with one who is more expert. Four phases progressively build the client's capacity to reflect on his or her practice, increase professional self-awareness, and facilitate self-directed learning. (p. 216)

Norwood and Burke described the four phases as follows:

Phase one. The coach initially serves as consultant and instructs the client in best practices by teaching or directly modeling a concept or strategy for the client.

Phase two. The coach serves as a mentor to the teacher. The mentor and mentee participate as equals in collaborative activities, such as teaching, planning lessons, analyzing student data, reflecting and problem solving, or developing curriculum. The mentor might coteach with the mentee, and together they debrief the lesson and look at student learning.

Phase three. The coach *coaches*. This stance is a "non-judgmental mediation of thinking and decision-making" (Lipton, Wellman, & Humbard, 2003, p. 21). A coach will provide opportunities for a planning conference, observation of the lesson, and a reflection conference with the client as she practices new teaching behaviors.

Phase four. The coach and client celebrate and share concise feedback for a job well done. The client is now practicing the new best-practice behavior independently and successfully. (p. 216)

This model acknowledges that less experienced teachers may need explicit guidance and teaching from a coach. As a teacher gains experience and background knowledge, the coach shifts into mentoring and then more traditional coaching roles.

Team Coaching

Although individual coaching can be highly effective, sometimes coaching is needed on a larger scale. Clutterbuck (2010) explained that "coaching an individual without attempting to influence the immediate human systems in which they operate reduces the impact of the coaching intervention" (p. 272). For this reason, Skiffington and Zeus (2000) recommended team coaching, a model where the coach "facilitates problem solving and conflict management, monitors team performance and coordinates between the team and a more senior management sponsor" (Clutterbuck, 2010, p. 272). Team coaches can help groups avoid negative emotions, such as criticism, anxiety, and anger, replacing them with positive emotions that contribute to productivity and allow progress to be made (Kauffman, Boniwell, & Silberman, 2010).

Virtual Coaching

Most of the approaches to coaching discussed here involve feedback, which is usually given after an observation. Virtual coaching is a model built around feedback that occurs while the teacher is still teaching. This feedback is usually delivered through an earpiece referred to as *bug-in-ear*, or *BIE*, technology. This immediate feedback prompts teachers to reflect on their action and correct it midstream, a concept referred to by Donald Schön (1987) as *reflection-in-action*. He stated that when we "reflect in the midst of action without interrupting it . . . we can still make a difference to the situation at hand—our thinking serves to reshape what we are doing while we are doing it" (p. 26). The efficacy of this type of feedback, called real-time feedback (Canter, 2010) or cueing teaching (Marzano et al., 2011), has a strong research base, and the technology required for it is increasingly more affordable and reliable.

Real-Time Feedback

The benefits of real-time feedback are well established. In 2004, Mary Catherine Scheeler, Kathy Ruhl, and James McAfee reviewed ten studies of effective feedback to teachers and identified three general conclusions about feedback: "(a) feedback is better than no feedback, (b) immediate feedback is better than delayed feedback, and (c) feedback that is immediate, specific, positive and corrective holds the most promise for bringing about lasting change in teaching behavior" (p. 405). Furthermore, they asserted that "the only attribute that clearly demonstrates efficacy as a characteristic of effective feedback is immediacy. Thus, it seems obvious that supervisors should seek ways to provide feedback as close to the occurrence of teaching behavior as possible" (p. 404).

In a subsequent study, Scheeler, McAfee, Ruhl, and David Lee (2006) pointed out that "if feedback is deferred, learners (school aged and adult) may practice errors, especially in the acquisition phase of learning. When learners practice repeated errors, they learn to perform skills incorrectly" (p. 13). Along with others (Coulter & Grossen, 1997; O'Reilly et al., 1992; O'Reilly, Renzaglia, & Lee, 1994), Scheeler and her colleagues found that "a targeted teaching behavior was acquired faster and more efficiently when feedback was immediate" (p. 21). In sum, virtual coaching allowed coaches to:

Teach more new behaviors to teachers in less time, promoting efficiency of learning. In addition, such efficiency is likely to reduce frustration on the part of teachers who are attempting to acquire new behaviors but who otherwise must wait for feedback to confirm their performance. (Scheeler et al., 2006, p. 21)

Finally, Scheeler and her colleagues asserted that virtual coaching could positively affect student achievement: "This research demonstrates that immediate, corrective feedback when delivered via technology can result in increases in correct practice of teaching behavior, with positive results on student academic performance and minimal disruption to both teachers and students" (p. 24).

BIE Technology

Marcia Rock, Naomi Zigmond, Madeleine Gregg, and Robert Gable (2011) explained that bug-in-ear technology can be used to provide real-time feedback during virtual coaching:

Virtual coaching uses advanced online and mobile technology (termed *bug-in-ear* technology) to allow an instructional leader located remotely (down the hall or across the country) to observe a teacher's lesson while offering discreet feedback heard only by the teacher, through an earpiece the teacher wears. (p. 42)

Although this type of technology has been used for many years at the postsecondary level, it is increasingly available to teachers and coaches in K–12 education.

In 1952, Ija Korner and William Brown published an article titled "The Mechanical Third Ear." They described how they used miniature radio transmitters and hearing aids to give real-time feedback and advice to psychology students working with clients. In 1971, Philip Herold, Manuel Ramirez, and Jesse Newkirk realized that the same technology could be used to give real-time feedback to teachers while they were teaching. Along with others (Bowles & Nelson, 1976; Giebelhaus & Cruz, 1992, 1994, 1995; Kahan, 2002; Scheeler & Lee, 2002; Scheeler et al., 2006; Thomson, Holmberg, Baer, Hodges, & Moore, 1978; van der Mars, 1988), they conducted research to identify the best way to use BIE technology with teachers. Most of the research found that it was an effective method and that teachers were able to pay attention to classroom events and the voice of the coach. Rock and her colleagues (2009) found that:

BIE can be an effective instrument for delivering live feedback to trainees, including classroom teachers. Teachers-in-training overwhelmingly gave the technology favorable reviews and stated that they could easily attend simultaneously to two sets of verbal stimuli (i.e., classroom students and a university supervisor). (p. 66)

Rock and her colleagues (2009) also found that teachers who received virtual coaching used better types of praise, more research-based practices (such as verbal and nonverbal choral response, partner strategies, and cloze reading), and fewer ineffective practices (such as hand raising, round-robin, and teacher read-alouds). Additionally, students' on-task behavior increased from 73.8 percent to 92.7 percent.

Although some have raised concerns that teachers might be overwhelmed by hearing real-time feedback in their ear while teaching, participants in the Rock et al. (2009) study praised real-time feedback, labeling it as empowering (53.3 percent), helpful (73.3 percent), and positive (60.0 percent). Rock and her colleagues also stated that "teachers need three or four virtual coaching sessions before they are able to simultaneously process the voice of the coach and the voices of students and other noises in the classroom" (2011, p. 45).

Translating Research and Theory Into Practice

In this text, we use the research and theory presented in this chapter and the research and theory from books such as *The Art and Science of Teaching* (Marzano, 2007) and *Becoming a Reflective Teacher* (Marzano, 2012) to create an approach to coaching unlike that articulated in any previous model. Our approach is grounded in a very comprehensive yet detailed model of effective teaching drawn from decades of research and thousands of studies. Another foundational element of our approach is a system for assessing a teacher's initial status and tracking a teacher's progress on specific instructional strategies through a developmental continuum ranging from not being aware of a specific strategy to being so masterful at using the strategy that it can be adapted to individual student needs.

As mentioned in the introduction, throughout this book you will encounter comprehension questions to help you process the content presented as you progress through the remaining chapters. After completing each set of questions, you can check your answers with those in the appendix (page 223).

Chapter 2

A FOUNDATION FOR COACHING

When working together, a coach and teacher must establish a set of shared understandings and conditions that will drive the rest of their interaction. These shared understandings might include an agreement about what constitutes good teaching, a system to measure the teacher's progress, an evaluation of the teacher's current level of performance, and the establishment of growth goals for the teacher. Additionally, the coach might explain what he or she is planning to do to help the teacher move from where she is to where she wants to be. In this chapter, we review four practices we believe are essential for an effective coaching relationship: (1) establishing a model of effective teaching, (2) using a scale to measure teachers' progress, (3) conducting a self-audit, and (4) establishing a coaching perspective.

Establishing a Model of Effective Teaching

The first step in developing an effective coach-teacher relationship is to identify specific classroom strategies and behaviors that will be the focus of the interaction. Necessarily such specificity requires a model of what constitutes effective classroom practice. In this book, we use a model articulated in *The Art and Science of Teaching* (Marzano, 2007) and further detailed in a number of other books including *A Handbook for the Art and Science of Teaching* (Marzano & Brown, 2009), *Effective Supervision* (Marzano et al., 2011), and *Becoming a Reflective Teacher* (Marzano, 2012). That model postulates forty-one elements (that is, forty-one categories of specific classroom strategies and behaviors) that describe classroom expertise. Table 2.1 depicts the forty-one elements of the model.

Table 2.1: Forty-One Elements of *The Art and Science of Teaching* Model

Lesson Segments Involving Routine Events
Design Question: What will I do to establish and communicate learning goals, track student progress, and celebrate success?
Element 1: Providing clear learning goals and scales (rubrics)
Element 2: Tracking student progress
Element 3: Celebrating success

Continued on next page →

Lesson Segments Involving Routine Events (continued)
Design Question: What will I do to establish and maintain classroom rules and procedures?
Element 4: Establishing and maintaining classroom rules and procedures
Element 5: Organizing the physical layout of the classroom
Lesson Segments Addressing Content
Design Question: What will I do to help students effectively interact with new knowledge?
Element 6: Identifying critical information
Element 7: Organizing students to interact with new knowledge
Element 8: Previewing new content
Element 9: Chunking content into "digestible bites"
Element 10: Helping students process new information
Element 11: Helping students elaborate on new information
Element 12: Helping students record and represent knowledge
Element 13: Helping students reflect on their learning
Design Question: What will I do to help students practice and deepen their understanding of new knowledge?
Element 14: Reviewing content
Element 15: Organizing students to practice and deepen knowledge
Element 16: Using homework
Element 17: Helping students examine similarities and differences
Element 18: Helping students examine errors in reasoning
Element 19: Helping students practice skills, strategies, and processes
Element 20: Helping students revise knowledge
Design Question: What will I do to help students generate and test hypotheses about new knowledge?
Element 21: Organizing students for cognitively complex tasks
Element 22: Engaging students in cognitively complex tasks involving hypothesis generation and testing
Element 23: Providing resources and guidance
Lesson Segments Enacted on the Spot
Design Question: What will I do to engage students?
Element 24: Noticing when students are not engaged
Element 25: Using academic games
Element 26: Managing response rates
Element 27: Using physical movement
Element 28: Maintaining a lively pace
Element 29: Demonstrating intensity and enthusiasm
Element 30: Using friendly controversy
Element 31: Providing opportunities for students to talk about themselves
Element 32: Presenting unusual or intriguing information

Lesson Segments Enacted on the Spot (continued)
Design Question: What will I do to recognize and acknowledge adherence or lack of adherence to rules and procedures?
Element 33: Demonstrating "withitness"
Element 34: Applying consequences for lack of adherence to rules and procedures
Element 35: Acknowledging adherence to rules and procedures
Design Question: What will I do to establish and maintain effective relationships with students?
Element 36: Understanding students' interests and backgrounds
Element 37: Using verbal and nonverbal behaviors that indicate affection for students
Element 38: Displaying objectivity and control
Design Question: What will I do to communicate high expectations for all students?
Element 39: Demonstrating value and respect for low-expectancy students
Element 40: Asking questions of low-expectancy students
Element 41: Probing incorrect answers with low-expectancy students

As indicated in table 2.1, the forty-one elements are organized under three broad categories referred to as *lesson segments*. Within each lesson segment, the elements are further organized by specific design questions. For detailed discussions of the lesson segments and their related design questions, the reader should consult Marzano (2007; 2012; Marzano et al., 2011). Briefly though, the three lesson segments (routine events, content, and on the spot) represent different kinds of procedures that can occur in a classroom.

Lesson segments involving routine events occur on a daily or periodic basis. As the two design questions in this section indicate, elements related to establishing and communicating learning goals, tracking student progress, and celebrating success, as well as establishing and maintaining classroom rules and procedures, are all considered routine. *Lesson segments addressing content* are classroom events regarding how students approach academic content. Three design questions organize the elements in this type of lesson segment. Elements related to helping students effectively interact with new knowledge, practice and deepen their understanding of new knowledge, and generate and test hypotheses about new knowledge are all considered content lesson segments. *Lesson segments enacted on the spot* occur on an as-needed basis. On-the-spot elements are organized under four design questions. The teacher must be able to recognize when on-the-spot strategies and behaviors are called for and implement them immediately. Elements related to engaging students, recognizing and acknowledging adherence or lack of adherence to rules and procedures, establishing and maintaining effective relationships with students, and communicating high expectations for all students are considered on-the-spot lesson segments.

Figure 2.1 (page 22) provides a visual depiction of how the three segments and nine design questions interact.

Lesson Segments Enacted on the Spot

What will I do to engage students?

Lesson Segments Involving Routine Events

What will I do to establish and communicate learning goals, track student progress, and celebrate success?

What will I do to establish and maintain classroom rules and procedures?

Lesson Segments Addressing Content

What will I do to help students generate and test hypotheses about new knowledge?

What will I do to help students effectively interact with new knowledge?

What will I do to help students practice and deepen their understanding of new knowledge?

What will I do to recognize and acknowledge adherence or lack of adherence to rules and procedures?

What will I do to establish and maintain effective relationships with students?

What will I do to communicate high expectations for all students?

Figure 2.1: Visual depiction of the interaction between the lesson segments and design questions.

As shown in figure 2.1, lesson segments enacted on the spot create a context for learning. To create that context, the teacher should consider the four design questions shown in the border of figure 2.1. As stated previously, engaging students, recognizing and acknowledging adherence and lack of adherence to rules and procedures, establishing and maintaining effective relationships with students, and communicating high expectations for students require teaching moves that are used when the teacher recognizes that they are needed. For example, if a teacher notices that a student is not adhering to one of the classroom rules or procedures, he or she might make eye contact with that student and use a gesture or signal word to help him reengage. The teacher might not have planned those specific actions ahead of time but was ready to use them when the situation called for them.

The remaining lesson segments—involving routine events and addressing content—function within the context created by on-the-spot segments. As shown in figure 2.1, routine events occur before content segments because they are necessary to create an orderly, predictable environment in which students can learn most effectively. The teacher creates that predictable environment by implementing elements of the two design questions involving routine events shown in the upper portion of figure 2.1: establishing and communicating learning goals, tracking students' progress, celebrating students' success, and establishing and maintaining rules and procedures for the classroom. These differ from on-the-spot segments because the teacher plans for them ahead of time. For example, before beginning a new unit, the teacher would identify the learning goals for that unit and explain them to students. She would also set up a system for tracking students' progress and explain it to students. She might schedule specific days on which to celebrate students' progress, and enlist students' help in creating a set of classroom rules and procedures. These actions create an environment where students know what is expected of them and can gauge how well they are meeting those expectations.

Finally, within the context created by on-the-spot lesson segments and after routines are in place, the teacher addresses content. As shown by the three content-related design questions in figure 2.1, students generally interact with content in three ways: interacting with new content, practicing and deepening their understanding of content, and generating and testing hypotheses about content. As with routine events, the teacher carefully plans activities that allow students to interact with the content in three ways. For example, during a unit on light waves, the teacher might introduce new content by having students watch parts of a video and discuss the information it provided. Then the teacher might have students create drawings or other representations that express important characteristics of light waves. The teacher could then review these representations with the class to create a list of important properties of light waves. To help students practice what they have learned and deepen their knowledge in another lesson, the teacher might ask students to explain how waves are reflected, absorbed, or transmitted through objects and then provide support for their explanations. Finally, in a third lesson, the teacher might ask students to conduct experiments to verify or disprove specific claims, such as "light waves travel in straight lines" or investigate how light waves are used in real-world communication designs and models.

In summary, the model of effective teaching presented here addresses three specific types of lesson segments: routine, content, and on-the-spot. Design questions for each segment prompt the teacher to use the forty-one elements to create a context for learning where students understand what is expected of them and can measure their progress toward their goals as they interact with new content, practice and deepen their understanding, and generate and test hypotheses.

Using a Scale to Measure Teachers' Progress

Scales describing a teacher's status for each of the forty-one different elements are available online at **marzanoresearch.com/classroomstrategies** (or see Marzano, 2012). The generic form of the scale is depicted in table 2.2.

Table 2.2: Generic Form of the Scale

4 Innovating	3 Applying	2 Developing	1 Beginning	0 Not Using
The teacher integrates several strategies or behaviors associated with an element to create a macrostrategy or adapts strategies for unique student needs and situations.	The teacher uses strategies or behaviors associated with an element and monitors their effects on student outcomes.	The teacher uses strategies or behaviors associated with an element, but in a mechanistic way.	The teacher uses strategies or behaviors associated with an element incorrectly or with parts missing.	The teacher is unaware of strategies or behaviors associated with an element.

The scale shown in table 2.2 can be used to measure and discuss a teacher's progress on any one of the forty-one elements. As table 2.2 indicates, the scale values range from Not Using (0) at the low end to Innovating (4) at the high end. At the Not Using (0) level, the teacher is unaware of strategies and behaviors related to an element and consequently does not attempt to use them in the classroom. At the

Beginning (1) level, the teacher is aware of strategies and behaviors related to an element, recognizes that those strategies and behaviors are called for in the classroom, and tries to use them. However, at the Beginning (1) level, the teacher executes these strategies or behaviors incorrectly or with parts missing. At the Developing (2) level, the teacher uses strategies and behaviors related to an element mechanistically. That is, the teacher performs strategies and behaviors correctly but fails to monitor their effect on students and student outcomes. At the Applying (3) level, the teacher correctly executes strategies and behaviors related to an element while monitoring their effect on students and student outcomes. Finally, at the Innovating (4) level, the teacher integrates several strategies to create a macrostrategy for an element or adapts strategies related to an element for unique student needs or situations.

Conducting a Self-Audit

One of the first tasks in the coaching process is for the teacher (with the coach's assistance and verification) to conduct a self-audit across the forty-one elements of effective teaching. This self-audit consists of four steps: (1) completing a profile, (2) selecting growth goals, (3) verifying the teacher's selections, and (4) writing growth goals.

Completing a Profile

Even though a teacher and coach will be focusing on only a few elements, it is useful for the teacher to complete a comprehensive profile of his or her performance across all forty-one elements listed in table 2.1 (page 19). This self-rating provides an initial snapshot of a teacher's strengths and weaknesses. The teacher should score himself on each element using the five-point scale (see table 2.2, page 23). Table 2.3 shows one teacher's self-ratings. Visit **marzanoresearch.com/classroomstrategies** for a blank reproducible version of this form.

Table 2.3: Teacher's Self-Audit Ratings on the Personal Profile

Lesson Segments Involving Routine Events					
Design Question: What will I do to establish and communicate learning goals, track student progress, and celebrate success?					
Element	4 Innovating	3 Applying	2 Developing	1 Beginning	0 Not Using
1. What do I typically do to provide clear learning goals and scales (rubrics)?					
2. What do I typically do to track student progress?					
3. What do I typically do to celebrate success?					
Design Question: What will I do to establish and maintain classroom rules and procedures?					

Element	4 Innovating	3 Applying	2 Developing	1 Beginning	0 Not Using
4. What do I typically do to establish and maintain classroom rules and procedures?					
5. What do I typically do to organize the physical layout of the classroom?					

Lesson Segments Addressing Content

Design Question: What will I do to help students effectively interact with new knowledge?

Element	4 Innovating	3 Applying	2 Developing	1 Beginning	0 Not Using
6. What do I typically do to identify critical information?					
7. What do I typically do to organize students to interact with new knowledge?					
8. What do I typically do to preview new content?					
9. What do I typically do to chunk content into digestible bites?					
10. What do I typically do to help students process new information?					
11. What do I typically do to help students elaborate on new information?					
12. What do I typically do to help students record and represent knowledge?					
13. What do I typically do to help students reflect on their learning?					

Continued on next page →

Design Question: What will I do to help students practice and deepen their understanding of new knowledge?

Element	4 Innovating	3 Applying	2 Developing	1 Beginning	0 Not Using
14. What do I typically do to review content?					
15. What do I typically do to organize students to practice and deepen knowledge?					
16. What do I typically do to use homework?					
17. What do I typically do to help students examine similarities and differences?					
18. What do I typically do to help students examine errors in reasoning?					
19. What do I typically do to help students practice skills, strategies, and processes?					
20. What do I typically do to help students revise knowledge?					

Design Question: What will I do to help students generate and test hypotheses about new knowledge?

Element	4 Innovating	3 Applying	2 Developing	1 Beginning	0 Not Using
21. What do I typically do to organize students for cognitively complex tasks?					
22. What do I typically do to engage students in cognitively complex tasks involving hypothesis generation and testing?					
23. What do I typically do to provide resources and guidance?					

Lesson Segments Enacted on the Spot					

Design Question: What will I do to engage students?

Element	4 Innovating	3 Applying	2 Developing	1 Beginning	0 Not Using
24. What do I typically do to notice when students are not engaged?					
25. What do I typically do to use academic games?					
26. What do I typically do to manage response rates?					
27. What do I typically do to use physical movement?					
28. What do I typically do to maintain a lively pace?					
29. What do I typically do to demonstrate intensity and enthusiasm?					
30. What do I typically do to use friendly controversy?					
31. What do I typically do to provide opportunities for students to talk about themselves?					
32. What do I typically do to present unusual or intriguing information?					

Design Question: What will I do to recognize and acknowledge adherence or lack of adherence to rules and procedures?

Element	4 Innovating	3 Applying	2 Developing	1 Beginning	0 Not Using
33. What do I typically do to demonstrate withitness?					
34. What do I typically do to apply consequences for lack of adherence to rules and procedures?					
35. What do I typically do to acknowledge adherence to rules and procedures?					

Continued on next page →

Design Question: What will I do to establish and maintain effective relationships with students?					
Element	**4** **Innovating**	**3** **Applying**	**2** **Developing**	**1** **Beginning**	**0** **Not Using**
36. What do I typically do to understand students' interests and backgrounds?					
37. What do I typically do to use verbal and nonverbal behaviors that indicate affection for students?					
38. What do I typically do to display objectivity and control?					

Design Question: What will I do to communicate high expectations for all students?					
Element	**4** **Innovating**	**3** **Applying**	**2** **Developing**	**1** **Beginning**	**0** **Not Using**
39. What do I typically do to demonstrate value and respect for low-expectancy students?					
40. What do I typically do to ask questions of low-expectancy students?					
41. What do I typically do to probe incorrect answers with low-expectancy students?					

Selecting Growth Goals

After completing the personal profile, the teacher will be able to identify elements for which he scored himself as Beginning (1) or Not Using (0). From these elements, the teacher should select several to become growth goals. We recommend that a teacher limit himself or herself to working on one element every three months. For example, if a teacher was setting growth goals for an entire school year (typically nine months), he or she might select three elements to work on. Alternatively, if a teacher was setting a goal for the current quarter or trimester, he or she might only select one element.

Verifying the Teacher's Selections

Once a teacher has selected specific areas on which to focus, the coach should verify the teacher's selections. One way a coach does this is by observing the teacher during one or more lessons. A better appraisal might be obtained, however, if the coach and the teacher jointly examine a video recording of the teacher. When examining a video, the coach and the teacher should watch for specific strategies that the teacher is using correctly and effectively, strategies that the teacher is attempting to use but is executing incorrectly or with parts missing, and strategies that a teacher could have used but did not. Research has also shown that viewing the same recording multiple times allows teachers and coaches to notice more detail and reach more insightful conclusions than a single viewing (Brophy, 2004; Calandra, Gurvitch, & Lund, 2008; Hennessy & Deaney, 2009; Lundeberg et al., 2008; van Es, 2009).

Writing Growth Goals

After the coach verifies the teacher's selections, the teacher can write specific growth-goal statements for the elements he or she has chosen to work on. A growth-goal statement should specify what element the teacher is working on, how much growth he or she wants to make, and a time frame for achieving that growth. For example, "By the end of November, I will raise my score on demonstrating withitness from 0 to 3."

As an example of how this self-audit process might work, consider a teacher meeting with her coach for the first time during the school year. The coach begins by reviewing the model of effective teaching with the teacher and explaining what performance looks like for each of the forty-one elements at each of the scale levels. The teacher fills out her personal profile during the session. Completing the profile does not take long; most teachers can complete it in about half an hour. The coach also asks the teacher to video record herself teaching several lessons and bring the recording to their next meeting.

When the coach and teacher meet again, they review the teacher's self-ratings on the personal profile and the video data collected by the teacher. If the coach sees large discrepancies between the video and the teacher's personal profile, he discusses specific elements with the teacher to help her better understand what performance at the different levels of the scale looks like. The coach and teacher then develop growth goals for the teacher. The following vignette depicts this type of interaction between a teacher and coach.

> During their first meeting of the year, Mr. Shorn and his coach, Mike, reviewed a model of effective teaching and began filling out Mr. Shorn's self-audit form. Since then, Mr. Shorn has finished filling out the profile and has video recorded himself teaching several lessons. Today, Mr. Shorn and Mike are watching these video clips to verify his ratings on the personal profile. After watching several clips, Mr. Shorn observes that he'd really like to work on probing his low-expectancy students' answers, an on-the-spot element. He also decides to work on chunking content into digestible bites, which is a content element.
>
> "Is there an element from the lesson segments involving routine events that you'd like to work on?" asks Mike.
>
> "Well," says Mr. Shorn, "I could do a better job of celebrating my students' success. I want to make sure everybody gets celebrated, but sometimes I feel like I'm just praising people randomly, whenever I think of it."
>
> "Hmmm," says Mike. "Think about this: your profile shows that you aren't currently using strategies related to either tracking student progress or celebrating success, and we didn't see any tracking strategies when we watched your video. You may want to consider working on tracking student progress before you work on celebrating success so that you can be specific with your students about the progress they've made and the success they've experienced."

Mr. Shorn decides to work on tracking student progress as his third growth goal for the year, and he and Mike close the session by deciding which goal to work on each trimester and by writing three specific growth-goal statements:

- By the end of November, I will raise my score on tracking student progress from a 0 to a 3.

- By the end of February, I will raise my score on chunking content into digestible bites from a 0 to a 3.

- By the end of May, I will raise my score on probing incorrect answers with low-expectancy students from a 1 to a 3.

Establishing a Coaching Perspective

While it is important for a teacher to have growth goals relative to specific elements in the model, it is equally important for the coach to understand how the teacher must be supported to move from one level of the scale to the next.

Not Using (0) to Beginning (1)

For a teacher to move from the Not Using (0) level to the Beginning (1) level, he or she must learn about research, theory, and strategies associated with his or her growth-goal element and try one or more strategies related to that element. For example, consider a teacher working on element 1—providing clear learning goals and scales (rubrics). The coach reminds the teacher that the element is an important part of establishing and communicating learning goals, tracking student progress, and celebrating student success (the design question associated with element 1), which are routine events. The coach then reviews the following research and theory related to element 1 with the teacher:

- Research has shown that setting goals or objectives is associated with a 16–41 percentile gain in student achievement (Lipsey & Wilson, 1993; Walberg, 1999; Wise & Okey, 1983).

- Goal-setting strategies are most effective when used in specific ways at specific times (for example, at the beginning of a unit) (Marzano, 2007).

- It is important to accompany learning goals with a scale that defines different levels of performance (Marzano, 2006).

In addition to the research and theory behind an element, a teacher needs to be aware of classroom strategies related to the element. The coach can provide this awareness in two ways: (1) strategies listed in this book, or (2) a coach-and-teacher-developed list of strategies. Chapter 3 lists a number of strategies for each of the forty-one elements of the model. For example, the following strategies are listed for element 1—providing clear learning goals and scales (rubrics):

- Clearly articulating learning goals, being careful not to confuse them with activities or assignments

- Creating scales or rubrics for learning goals

- Student-friendly scales

- Individual student learning goals

For each strategy listed in chapter 3, we provide teacher actions required to execute the strategy (chapter 4), desired student responses to the strategy (chapter 4), and ways to adapt the strategy for advanced or struggling students (chapter 5). For fuller explanations of all of the strategies listed in this book, readers should consult the compendium section of *Becoming a Reflective Teacher* (Marzano, 2012). The compendium is a quick reference tool that describes each strategy in enough detail to allow a teacher to use it immediately in his or her classroom. For example, table 2.4 shows the strategies that the compendium lists for element 10—helping students process new information.

Table 2.4: Strategies for Helping Students Process New Information

Perspective analysis (Marzano, 1992)	The teacher asks students to consider multiple perspectives on new knowledge using perspective analysis. This strategy involves five steps, each with a corresponding question: 1. **Identify your position on a controversial topic**—What do I believe about this? 2. **Determine the reasoning behind your position**—Why do I believe that? 3. **Identify an opposing position**—What is another way of looking at this? 4. **Describe the reasoning behind the opposing position**—Why might someone else hold a different opinion? 5. **When you are finished, summarize what you have learned**—What have I learned?
Thinking hats (de Bono, 1999)	The teacher asks students to process new information by imagining themselves wearing any one of six different-colored thinking hats. Depending on the hat they wear, students look at new knowledge in a slightly different way, as follows: • **White hat** (neutral and objective perspectives)—When wearing the white hat, students examine facts and figures related to the new information without drawing conclusions or interpreting them. • **Red hat** (emotional perspectives)—When wearing the red hat, students express how they feel about the new information, but should still refrain from judging either the topic or their feelings. • **Black hat** (cautious or careful perspectives)—When wearing the black hat, students look for weaknesses or risks that stem from new information. • **Yellow hat** (optimistic perspectives)—When wearing the yellow hat, students look for positive and valuable aspects of new information. • **Green hat** (creative perspectives)—When wearing the green hat, students use the new knowledge to generate new ideas or create novel solutions to problems using the new information. • **Blue hat** (organizational perspectives)—When wearing the blue hat, students reflect on their thinking processes and decide what perspectives they would like to take (in other words, what hats they would like to put on) as they interact with new information.
Collaborative processing	The teacher asks students to meet in small groups and summarize the information just presented, ask clarifying questions about the information just presented, or make predictions about upcoming information. After allowing the students to interact in small groups, the teacher can lead the whole class in a discussion of their summaries, questions, and predictions.

Continued on next page →

Jigsaw cooperative learning	After identifying a number of specific important aspects of the content (for example, five important causes of World War I), the teacher asks students to create groups with the same number of members ("Please organize yourselves into groups of five"). Once students are in their groups, the teacher assigns each student a topic about which he or she will become an "expert." In the example, each student would be assigned one of the five causes of World War I to study.
	Once students each have their expert topic, groups disband and students with the same expert topic meet together to investigate the topic, share their findings, ask questions of each other and the teacher, and discuss their ideas. In the example, all students studying cause 1 would meet together, all students studying cause 2 would meet together, and so on.
	After each student has become an expert on their topic, the original groups re-form and students each present their expert knowledge to the other members of the group. Other group members can ask questions of the expert or the teacher as they learn the new information.
Reciprocal teaching	Small groups of students, with one student designated as the discussion leader, use this strategy to interact with new information. Before the teacher presents a chunk of new information, members of the group generate predictions about the content. After the teacher presents the chunk of content, the discussion leader asks the group questions about the information presented, and the members of the group discuss each question. After the questions have been discussed, someone from the group (not the discussion leader) summarizes the content presented so far, and the members of the group make predictions about the upcoming chunk of content, beginning the cycle again. The role of discussion leader should rotate from student to student so each student has the opportunity to generate questions about the content and practice facilitating the group's discussion.
Concept attainment	The teacher asks students to identify, compare, and contrast examples and nonexamples of a concept. Examples of a concept should clearly display the attributes of the concept, and nonexamples should clearly not have attributes of the concept. The teacher can also present a group of items to students, designating each item as an example or nonexample of a "mystery concept." Students guess the mystery concept by studying the presented examples and nonexamples.

Source: Marzano, 2012, pp. 110–111.

Table 2.4 lists and briefly describes six strategies for helping students process new information: perspective analysis, thinking hats, collaborative processing, jigsaw cooperative learning, reciprocal teaching, and concept attainment. The compendium section of *Becoming a Reflective Teacher* (Marzano, 2012) lists and describes 280 strategies like these, organized by each of the forty-one elements from the *Art and Science of Teaching* model (Marzano, 2007).

Alternatively, a teacher and coach can develop their own list of strategies associated with the teacher's growth-goal element. They begin this process by brainstorming a list of strategies they are already aware of that relate to the element. They should also research other strategies that could be used. For each strategy they develop, the coach and teacher should record specific teacher actions required to execute the strategy properly, desired student responses to the strategy, and ways to adapt the strategy for advanced or struggling students.

Regardless of whether a coach and teacher use the strategies in this book or develop their own, the coach should make sure the teacher is aware of a number of different strategies related to his or her growth-goal element. This allows the teacher to choose which strategy he or she would like to work on first. For example, the teacher described previously might select the strategy of *individual student learning goals* to work on.

Once a specific strategy has been selected, the coach should ensure that the teacher understands the teacher actions required to correctly execute the strategy so that he or she can try the strategy in the classroom. The teacher actions for each strategy in this book are listed in chapter 4. When a teacher understands the research, theory, and strategies for an element, and has selected and tried a specific strategy, he or she has moved to the Beginning (1) level.

Beginning (1) to Developing (2)

For a teacher to move from Beginning (1) to Developing (2), he or she must correctly execute strategies associated with the chosen growth-goal element. For example, the teacher focusing on element 1—providing clear learning goals and scales (rubrics)—who has selected the strategy of individual student learning goals might work on the following teacher actions associated with that strategy. The teacher:

- Identifies students' personal interests that relate to the learning goal

- Helps students articulate and write down their personal learning goals

- Tracks students' progress on individual learning goals

The coach would help the teacher identify and correct errors or omissions for each of these actions. Observations and video recordings are useful for this purpose. When a teacher executes all the teacher actions associated with a strategy correctly, he or she has reached the Developing (2) level.

Developing (2) to Applying (3)

For a teacher to move from Developing (2) to Applying (3), he or she must monitor students' responses to strategies associated with his or her growth-goal element. For example, the teacher who is focused on using individual student learning goals should watch to see if students:

- Identify personally important individual learning goals

- Can explain what they have already done and still need to do to accomplish individual learning goals

- Track their progress on individual learning goals

When a teacher is monitoring and achieving the desired student responses for a strategy, he or she has reached the Applying (3) level.

Applying (3) to Innovating (4)

Although Applying (3) is the target level of performance on the scale, a teacher can move from Applying (3) to Innovating (4) by integrating several strategies to create a macrostrategy or by adapting a strategy for unique student needs or situations.

A teacher who can correctly execute and monitor students' responses to a number of strategies for an element can create a macrostrategy. For example, a teacher at the Applying (3) level for strategies associated with element 14—reviewing content—might integrate the strategies of cloze activities, summaries, and demonstration to review a previously learned process, such as revising a written composition for clarity. The teacher first creates a summary of the steps in the process (summaries) with important bits of information left out. She then asks students to both fill in those missing pieces (cloze activities) and use the completed summary for guidance as they edit a short composition for clarity (demonstration).

A teacher can also adapt specific strategies for unique student needs or situations. English learners (ELs), special education students, students from impoverished backgrounds, and gifted education students are all populations for whom specific strategies can be adapted. For example, a teacher focusing on individual student learning goals might help an EL visually express his plan to reach his learning goal using pictures or a flowchart. A special education student might need to break her plan down into very specific and discrete steps to ensure that she can meet her learning goal. Students from impoverished backgrounds might need to hear stories about the teacher's own experiences with the content before they can set individual learning goals, and a teacher could challenge a gifted education student to incorporate comparisons into the learning goal, perhaps by comparing his or her learning with that of students at other schools or in other countries who have similar interests and goals.

The following vignette illustrates how a coach might help a teacher move through each level of the scale.

Not Using (0) to Beginning (1)

Mr. McKendree doesn't include games in his high school chemistry classes because he doesn't know of any good ones to use, so he rated himself as Not Using (0) for element 25—using academic games. When his coach, Rebecca, explained that using academic games might help his students engage more with the content, he decided to make that his growth goal for the quarter. At the beginning of their initial coaching session, Rebecca explains the principle of clozentropy and reviews research showing that humans like to fill in missing information.

"It's one of the reasons we love games and puzzles," she says. "The same principle of missing information is why academic games stimulate students' attention and help them stay engaged."

She goes on to explain how appropriate competition creates mild pressure that can keep students focused on the content. Before the end of their session together, she and Mr. McKendree develop a list of strategies related to using academic games, and Mr. McKendree decides to try Talk a Mile a Minute with his students that week. Rebecca makes sure he understands how to make a set of category cards for the game, explain the game to students, and facilitate game play in the classroom.

Beginning (1) to Developing (2)

After observing his class play the game, Rebecca gives Mr. McKendree feedback during their next session together.

"I noticed that the game cards you created were especially good. I like the way you used the element categories from the periodic table," she says.

She also points out the part of the strategy he still needs to work on.

"You need to do more to facilitate game play," says Rebecca. "Instead of staying at the front of the room while students play, walk around so that you can help if they need it."

Developing (2) to Applying (3)

After observing Mr. McKendree perform all the parts of the strategy correctly, Rebecca asks him to begin monitoring his students' responses to the game.

When they meet again, Mr. McKendree says, "I'm glad you asked me to start monitoring my students' responses. When I started listening to them more closely, I realized that some of the talkers were giving clues like 'It starts with B and rhymes with moron.' That's not what I wanted; I want them to say things like 'It's solid at room temperature, and it produces a green color when burned.'"

"Ah," says Rebecca, "I'm glad you noticed that. What can you do to get the desired response?"

After thinking for a few minutes, Mr. McKendree says, "I could make a list of do's and don'ts for talkers with rules like, 'Don't use rhyming words.' I could also have some students who use good clues come up front and demonstrate what kind of clues are best before we play next."

Rebecca agrees, and Mr. McKendree plans to make those adjustments before using the strategy again.

Applying (3) to Innovating (4)

Over the next month, Mr. McKendree tries several other strategies related to using academic games. One day, Rebecca asks him to think about specific students in his class who might still not be responding favorably to the games.

"My ELs don't like the games nearly as much as my other students," he replies. "I asked them why, and they said that people talk too fast, and they can't understand what they're saying."

"Let's adapt one of the strategies for that special population," suggests Rebecca.

For the rest of the session, she reviews research related to how ELs interact best with knowledge, and Mr. McKendree decides to incorporate more picture cues into Talk a Mile a Minute to help his ELs grasp the vocabulary in the game a bit better.

Summary

In this chapter, we reviewed the model of effective teaching from *The Art and Science of Teaching* (Marzano, 2007), which forms the basis for interactions between coaches and teachers. After reviewing the three types of lesson segments (involving routine events, addressing content, and enacted on the spot), we presented a scale that teachers and coaches can use to measure a teacher's progress. We described how a teacher can use the scale to conduct a self-audit and work with a coach to write growth goals. Finally, we explained the specific steps that a coach must take to help a teacher progress through the five levels of the scale: Not Using (0), Beginning (1), Developing (2), Applying (3), and Innovating (4).

Chapter 2: Comprehension Questions

1. Describe the model of effective teaching presented in this chapter. How do the lesson segments, design questions, and elements fit together?

2. Explain the key differences between each level of the scale presented in this chapter. What does a teacher need to do to move from Not Using (0) to Beginning (1)? Beginning (1) to Developing (2)? Developing (2) to Applying (3)? Applying (3) to Innovating (4)?

3. List teacher actions and coach actions for each of the four steps of the self-audit. What type of feedback should the coach offer during each step?

4. For each level of the scale, describe actions that a coach can take to help a teacher move to the next level and teacher responses that show they have progressed to the next level.

Chapter 3

NOT USING (0) TO BEGINNING (1)

To move from the Not Using (0) level to the Beginning (1) level, a teacher must understand the research and theory for his growth-goal element, learn about classroom strategies related to the element, select a strategy to work on, and try the strategy in his classroom. The coach begins by helping the teacher explore the research and theory associated with his growth-goal element. For example, a teacher who has selected element 9—chunking content into digestible bites—as a growth goal should be aware it is one way he can help students effectively interact with new knowledge (as denoted by the accompanying design question and the fact that it is a lesson segment addressing content). The coach reviews research by Barak Rosenshine (2002) showing that new information needs to be presented in small chunks so students can hold it in their working memories long enough to process. She also explains that research by Thomas Good and Jere Brophy (2003) and Richard Mayer (2003) found that it was important to organize chunks of information in a logical progression. Finally, the coach explains that teachers should base their decisions about how big or small chunks should be on how familiar their students are with the content.

Once a teacher understands the research and theory for an element, the coach provides him with a list of strategies for the element. The coach and teacher can work together to develop a list of strategies (as explained in chapter 2), or the coach can simply provide the strategies listed in this book. Specific strategies listed in this book for chunking content into digestible bites include the following:

- Presenting content in small chunks

- Using preassessment data to vary the size of each chunk

- Chunk processing

Once a specific strategy has been selected for growth, the coach's job is to provide an understanding of the important steps and parts of the strategy. For example, the coach explains the following steps when a teacher chooses to work on the strategy of chunk processing. The teacher:

- Groups students in threes and assigns a letter to each group member: A, B, and C

- Presents a chunk of information and asks student A to summarize the information and students B and C to add to A's summary

- Answers any questions from groups and asks each group to predict what the next chunk will be about

- Rotates the role of summarizer (A) after each chunk

Once a teacher has tried the selected strategy in his classroom, he is at the Beginning (1) level for that strategy. In this chapter, we present research and theory for each element of the model as well as a list of specific strategies associated with each element. Steps and parts of each strategy are listed in chapter 4.

Lesson Segments Involving Routine Events

As explained in chapter 2, lesson segments involving routine events are those classroom events and routines that all teachers expect students to follow every day, regardless of the content area or the age of the students. In our framework, routine elements are organized into two design questions: What will I do to establish and communicate learning goals, track student progress, and celebrate success? and What will I do to establish and maintain classroom rules and procedures?

What Will I Do to Establish and Communicate Learning Goals, Track Student Progress, and Celebrate Success?

This design question includes elements 1 through 3. Each element is supported by research and theory.

> **Element 1: Providing clear learning goals and scales (rubrics)**—Research has shown that setting goals or objectives is associated with a 16–41 percentile gain in student achievement (Lipsey & Wilson, 1993; Walberg, 1999; Wise & Okey, 1983). Goal-setting strategies are most effective when used in specific ways at specific times (for example, at the beginning of a unit) (Marzano, 2007). It is important to accompany learning goals with a scale that defines different levels of performance (Marzano, 2006).

> **Element 2: Tracking student progress**—Research has shown that feedback is associated with a 10–43 percentile gain in student achievement (Bangert-Drowns, Kulik, Kulik, & Morgan, 1991; Bloom, 1976; Haas, 2005; Haller, Child, & Walberg, 1988; Kumar, 1991; Lysakowski & Walberg, 1981, 1982; Tennenbaum & Goldring, 1989; Walberg, 1999). Feedback is more effective when accompanied by clear goals and when given frequently (Bangert-Drowns, Kulik, & Kulik, 1991; Marzano, 2007). Formative assessment (assessing students often and giving them feedback on how they are progressing toward their goals) has been shown to be very effective at increasing student achievement (Black & Wiliam, 1998).

> **Element 3: Celebrating success**—Research has shown that reinforcing students' effort is associated with a 21–48 percentile gain in student achievement (Hattie, Biggs, & Purdie, 1996; Kumar, 1991; Schunk & Cox, 1986; Stipek & Weisz, 1981). Helping students see a direct relationship between how hard they work and how much they learn is an important part of reinforcing effort (Deci, Koestner, & Ryan, 2001; Deci, Ryan, & Koestner, 2001; Marzano, 2007).

In addition to being supported by research and theory, each element has specific strategies associated with it. Table 3.1 shows the strategies for elements 1 through 3. As mentioned previously, a full description of each strategy can be found in the compendium section of *Becoming a Reflective Teacher*

(Marzano, 2012, pp. 89–96). A list of original sources and research for each strategy can be accessed online at **marzanoresearch.com/classroomstrategies**.

Table 3.1: Strategies for Elements 1–3

Element 1: Providing clear learning goals and scales (rubrics)

- Clearly articulating learning goals, being careful not to confuse them with activities or assignments
- Creating scales or rubrics for learning goals
- Student-friendly scales
- Individual student learning goals

Element 2: Tracking student progress

- Formative assessments
- Response patterns
- Individual score-level assessments
- Different types of assessments
- Formative grading
- Charting student progress
- Charting class progress

Element 3: Celebrating success

- Final status celebration
- Knowledge gain celebration
- Verbal feedback

What Will I Do to Establish and Maintain Classroom Rules and Procedures?

This design question includes elements 4 and 5. Each element is supported by research and theory.

Element 4: Establishing and maintaining classroom rules and procedures—Research shows that establishing rules and procedures results in a decrease in disruptive behavior of 28 percentile points (Marzano, 2003). Rules are general expectations (such as "keep the classroom orderly"), while procedures apply to specific behaviors ("hang up your coat and backpack when you arrive") (Emmer, Evertson, & Worsham, 2003; Evertson, Emmer, & Worsham, 2003). Rules and procedures should be established at the beginning of the year (Anderson, Evertson, & Emmer, 1980; Eisenhart, 1977; Emmer, Evertson, & Anderson, 1980; Emmer, Sanford, Clements, & Martin, 1982; Emmer, Sanford, Evertson, Clements, & Martin, 1981; Evertson & Emmer, 1982; Evertson, Emmer, Sanford, & Clements, 1983; Evertson & Weinstein, 2006; Moskowitz & Hayman, 1976; Sanford & Evertson, 1981).

Element 5: Organizing the physical layout of the classroom—Research has identified four important aspects of room organization: (1) learning centers, technology, and equipment; (2) decorations; (3) materials; and (4) student and teacher desks (Marzano, Gaddy, Foseid, Foseid, & Marzano, 2005). The physical arrangement of the classroom should be compatible with planned instructional activities (Brophy, 2006; Weinstein, 1977).

In addition to being supported by research and theory, each element has specific strategies associated with it. Table 3.2 shows the strategies for elements 4 and 5. A full description of each strategy can be found in the compendium section of *Becoming a Reflective Teacher* (Marzano, 2012, pp. 97–102). A list of original sources and research for each strategy can be accessed online at **marzano research.com/classroomstrategies**.

Table 3.2: Strategies for Elements 4 and 5

Element 4: Establishing and maintaining classroom rules and procedures

- Using a small set of rules and procedures
- Explaining rules and procedures to students
- Modifying rules and procedures with students
- Generating rules and procedures with students
- Language of responsibility and statements of school beliefs
- Posting rules around the room
- Class pledge or classroom constitution
- Posters and graphics
- Gestures and symbols
- Vignettes and role-playing
- Reviewing rules and procedures with students
- Classroom meetings
- Student self-assessment

Element 5: Organizing the physical layout of the classroom

- Learning centers
- Computers and technology equipment
- Lab equipment and supplies
- Bookshelves
- Wall space
- Displaying student work
- Classroom décor
- Classroom materials
- Teacher's desk
- Student desks
- Areas for whole-group instruction
- Areas for group work

To illustrate how a coach can facilitate a teacher's move from Not Using (0) to Beginning (1) for an element from lesson segments involving routine events, consider the following vignette. The coach in the vignette helps a teacher working on element 2—tracking student progress—review what she already knows about the element, understand the research and theory behind the element, become familiar with various strategies related to the element, and understand the steps and parts of the strategy she chooses to work on.

Fourth-grade teacher Ms. Dunigan and her coach, Ted, are meeting to work on her growth goal, tracking student progress.

"What do you already know about tracking students' progress?" Ted asks.

"Well," says Ms. Dunigan, "not very much. I've seen that chart you're getting everybody to use, and I keep track of my students' progress in my gradebook. They get report cards every semester . . ." Ms. Dunigan trails off.

Ted encourages her by saying, "That's great. I'm glad you've seen the chart that some of the other teachers have been using. Let's take a minute and talk about some of the research and theory that support tracking student progress."

Ted goes on to explain that research has shown feedback is associated with a 10–43 percentile gain in student achievement. He says that feedback is more effective when accompanied by clear goals and when given frequently. Finally, he and Ms. Dunigan talk about formative assessment.

"Wow, that's quite a bit of information," says Ms. Dunigan.

"Don't worry," Ted says. "You don't have to work on it all at once."

Ted shows Ms. Dunigan a list of strategies related to tracking student progress, and Ms. Dunigan chooses to start with formative grading—an approach in which students' scores on a topic are not averaged. Instead, students' growth in learning, along with their final status, is acknowledged at the end of the grading period.

"It makes sense to me," she says, "that I would want to be clear about the approach I'm going to use to grade my students before I work on other strategies."

Ted agrees that she's made a good choice and goes on to help Ms. Dunigan understand the various aspects of formative grading.

Lesson Segments Addressing Content

As explained in chapter 2, lesson segments addressing content are focused on students' interaction with academic content. In this framework, content elements are organized into three design questions: What will I do to help students effectively interact with new knowledge?, What will I do to help students practice and deepen their understanding of new knowledge?, and What will I do to help students generate and test hypotheses about new knowledge?

What Will I Do to Help Students Effectively Interact With New Knowledge?

This design question includes elements 6 through 13. Each element is supported by research and theory.

Element 6: Identifying critical information—Research has shown that when important information is presented visually or dramatically, students can recall 57–77 percent of it one year later (as opposed to only 53 percent for verbal presentation) (Nuthall, 1999; Nuthall & Alton-Lee, 1995). It is important to choose learning activities and presentation methods that best suit the information being presented (Marzano, 2007).

Element 7: Organizing students to interact with new knowledge—Research has shown that cooperative learning is associated with a 12–28 percentile gain in student achievement (Bowen, 2000; Haas, 2005; Hall, 1989; Johnson, Maruyama, Johnson, Nelson, & Skon, 1981; Lipsey & Wilson, 1993; Walberg, 1999) and that group sizes between two and four are associated with a 6–9 percentile gain (Lou et al., 1996). Learning in groups helps students process information because it exposes students to multiple perspectives about new knowledge (McVee, Dunsmore, & Gavelek, 2005).

Element 8: Previewing new content—Research has shown that previewing techniques such as advanced organizers and cues (direct links between previous and new content) are associated with a 3–32 percentile gain in student achievement (Bloom, 1976; Crismore, 1985; Guzzetti, Snyder, Glass, & Gamas, 1993; Hattie, 1992; Lott, 1983; Luiten, Ames, & Ackerson, 1980; Ross, 1988; Stone, 1983; Walberg, 1999; Wise & Okey, 1983). Previewing is especially important for students with low background knowledge (Mayer, 1979; West & Fensham, 1976).

Element 9: Chunking content into digestible bites—Research has shown that information must be presented in small pieces in order for students to hold it in working memory long enough to process it (Good & Brophy, 2003; Linden et al., 2003; Mayer, 2003; Rosenshine, 2002). The teacher should present chunks of information in a logical sequence, and he or she should determine the size of each chunk by how much students already know about the content (Marzano, 2007).

Element 10: Helping students process new information—Research has shown that some processing macrostrategies (such as reciprocal teaching) are associated with a 31 percentile gain in student achievement (Rosenshine & Meister, 1994). Processing macrostrategies combine several individual research-based strategies (such as summarizing, questioning, or predicting) to help students actively process information (Marzano, 2007).

Element 11: Helping students elaborate on new information—Research has shown that questioning is associated with a 10–29 percentile gain in student achievement (Guzzetti et al., 1993; Hamaker, 1986; Redfield & Rousseau, 1981; Walberg, 1999; Wise & Okey, 1983). Higher-level questions that ask students to make inferences or explain why they think something is true are more effective than lower-level questions (those that test recognition or recall) (Redfield & Rousseau, 1981).

Element 12: Helping students record and represent knowledge—Research has shown that representing information linguistically (summaries and notes) is associated with a 5–47 percentile gain in student achievement (Bangert-Drowns, Hurley, & Wilkinson, 2004; Crismore, 1985; Ganske, 1981; Hattie et al., 1996; Henk & Stahl, 1985; Marzano, Gnadt, & Jesse, 1990; Pflaum, Walberg, Karegianes, & Rasher, 1980; Raphael & Kirschner, 1985). Research has also shown that representing information nonlinguistically (models, pictures, mental images) is associated with a 7–43 percentile gain in student achievement (Guzzetti et al., 1993; Haas, 2005; Hattie et al., 1996; Lovelace, 2005; Mayer, 1989; Nesbit & Adesope, 2006; Powell, 1980; Stahl & Fairbanks, 1986). When information is both linguistic and nonlinguistic, students process information more thoroughly and deeply.

Element 13: Helping students reflect on their learning—Research has shown that asking students to identify and record what they are confused about enhances their learning.

Reflection data are also useful for diagnosing errors or gaps in students' knowledge (Butler & Winne, 1995; Cross, 1998).

In addition to being supported by research and theory, each element has specific strategies associated with it. Table 3.3 shows the strategies for elements 6 through 13. A full description of each strategy can be found in the compendium section of *Becoming a Reflective Teacher* (Marzano, 2012, pp. 103–119). A list of original sources and research for each strategy can be accessed online at **marzanoresearch.com/classroomstrategies**.

Table 3.3: Strategies for Elements 6–13

Element 6: Identifying critical information
- Identifying critical-input experiences
- Visual activities
- Narrative activities
- Tone of voice, gestures, and body position
- Pause time

Element 7: Organizing students to interact with new knowledge
- Grouping for active processing
- Group norms
- Fishbowl demonstration
- Job cards
- Predetermined "buddies" to help form ad hoc groups
- Contingency plan for ungrouped students
- Grouping students using preassessment information

Element 8: Previewing new content
- What do you think you know?
- Overt linkages
- Preview questions
- Brief teacher summary
- Skimming
- Teacher-prepared notes
- K-W-L strategy (Ogle, 1986)
- Advance organizers
- Anticipation guides
- Word splash activity
- Preassessment

Element 9: Chunking content into digestible bites
- Presenting content in small chunks
- Using preassessment data to vary the size of each chunk
- Chunk processing

Continued on next page →

Element 10: Helping students process new information
- Perspective analysis (Marzano, 1992)
- Thinking hats (de Bono, 1999)
- Collaborative processing
- Jigsaw cooperative learning
- Reciprocal teaching
- Concept attainment

Element 11: Helping students elaborate on new information
- General inferential questions
- Elaborative interrogation

Element 12: Helping students record and represent knowledge
- Informal outline
- Combination notes, pictures, and summary
- Graphic organizers
- Free-flowing web
- Academic notebooks
- Dramatic enactments
- Rhyming pegwords
- Link strategy

Element 13: Helping students reflect on their learning
- Reflective journals
- Think logs
- Exit slips
- Knowledge comparison
- Two-column notes

What Will I Do to Help Students Practice and Deepen Their Understanding of New Knowledge?

This design question includes elements 14 through 20. Each element is supported by research and theory.

Element 14: Reviewing content—Research has shown that students require about four exposures to new information before it becomes integrated into their knowledge base. These exposures should be spaced closely together (one to two days apart) (Nuthall, 1999; Rovee-Collier, 1995). One way that students integrate new information into their knowledge base is by linking it to information already there (Marzano, 2007).

Element 15: Organizing students to practice and deepen knowledge—Research has shown that cooperative learning is associated with a 12–28 percentile gain in student achievement (Bowen, 2000; Haas, 2005; Hall, 1989; Johnson et al., 1981; Lipsey & Wilson, 1993; Walberg, 1999). Students should complete practice activities individually before working with a group to describe their approach and check their work for accuracy. Students can also compare their learning with other students' and check for errors in understanding (Marzano, 2007).

Element 16: Using homework—Research has shown that homework is associated with an 8–31 percentile gain in student achievement (Bloom, 1984; Cooper, 1989; Cooper, Robinson, & Patall, 2006; Fraser, Walberg, Welch, & Hattie, 1987; Graue, Weinstein, & Walberg, 1983; Hattie, 1992; Paschal, Weinstein, & Walberg, 1984; Walberg, 1999). Homework should have a clear purpose and be structured to ensure a high rate of completion. It should not be a burden to parents or students (Marzano, 2007).

Element 17: Helping students examine similarities and differences—Research has shown that identifying similarities and differences is associated with a 12–46 percentile gain in student achievement (Alexander, White, Haensly, & Crimmins-Jeanes, 1987; Baker & Lawson, 1995; Gick & Holyoak, 1980, 1983; Halpern, Hansen, & Reifer, 1990; Lee, n.d.; McDaniel & Donnelly, 1996; Raphael & Kirschner, 1985; Ross, 1988; Stone, 1983). Comparing, classifying, finding patterns, and identifying relationships are basic activities that require students to examine similarities and differences (Marzano, 2007).

Element 18: Helping students examine errors in reasoning—Research has shown that errors are sometimes present in students' understanding of content (Brown & Burton, 1978). The best way to correct those errors is for students to reexamine the content for accuracy (Clement, Lockhead, & Mink, 1979; Tennyson & Cocchiarella, 1986). Philosophers have identified four types of errors in thinking: faulty logic, attack, weak references, and misinformation (Johnson-Laird, 1983; Johnson-Laird & Byrne, 1991; Toulmin, Rieke, & Janik, 1981).

Element 19: Helping students practice skills, strategies, and processes—Research has shown that practicing skills, strategies, or processes is associated with an 18–44 percentile gain in student achievement (Bloom, 1976; Feltz & Landers, 1983; Kumar, 1991; Ross, 1988). Effective practice is more than repetition; it involves students gradually learning and then shaping the steps of a process, and should be thoughtfully designed and guided by the teacher (Anderson, 1982, 1995; Fitts & Posner, 1967).

Element 20: Helping students revise knowledge—Research has shown that when students initially learn about an idea or concept, their knowledge about it is partial and fuzzy. To complete and sharpen their knowledge, students need to add information and correct errors in their understanding (Hofstetter, Sticht, & Hofstetter, 1999; Schwanenflugel, Stahl, & McFalls, 1997; Stahl, 1999).

In addition to being supported by research and theory, each element has specific strategies associated with it. Table 3.4 (page 46) shows the strategies for elements 14 through 20. A full description of each strategy can be found in the compendium section of *Becoming a Reflective Teacher* (Marzano, 2012, pp. 120–133). A list of original sources and research for each strategy can be accessed online at **marzanoresearch.com/classroomstrategies**.

Table 3.4: Strategies for Elements 14–20

Element 14: Reviewing content

- Cloze activities
- Summaries
- Presented problems
- Demonstration
- Brief practice test or exercise
- Questioning

Element 15: Organizing students to practice and deepen knowledge

- Perspective analysis (Marzano, 1992)
- Thinking hats (de Bono, 1999)
- Cooperative learning
- Cooperative comparisons
- Pair-check (Kagan & Kagan, 2009)
- Think-pair-share and think-pair-square (Kagan & Kagan, 2009)
- Student tournaments
- Error analysis and peer feedback
- Performances and peer critiques
- Inside-outside circle (Kagan & Kagan, 2009)

Element 16: Using homework

- Preview homework
- Homework to deepen knowledge
- Homework to practice a process or skill
- Parent-assisted homework

Element 17: Helping students examine similarities and differences

- Sentence stem comparisons
- Venn diagrams
- Double-bubble diagram
- Comparison matrix
- Classification chart
- Student-generated classification patterns
- Similes
- Metaphors
- Sentence stem analogies
- Visual analogies

Element 18: Helping students examine errors in reasoning
- Identifying errors of faulty logic
- Identifying errors of attack
- Identifying errors of weak reference
- Identifying errors of misinformation
- Practicing identifying errors in logic
- Finding errors in the media
- Examining support for claims
- Statistical limitations

Element 19: Helping students practice skills, strategies, and processes
- Close monitoring
- Frequent structured practice
- Varied practice
- Fluency practice
- Worked examples
- Practice sessions prior to testing

Element 20: Helping students revise knowledge
- Academic notebook entries
- Academic notebook review
- Peer feedback
- Assignment revision

What Will I Do to Help Students Generate and Test Hypotheses About New Knowledge?

This design question includes elements 21 through 23. Each element is supported by research and theory.

Element 21: Organizing students for cognitively complex tasks—Research has shown that cooperative learning is associated with a 12–28 percentile gain in student achievement (Bowen, 2000; Haas, 2005; Hall, 1989; Johnson et al., 1981; Lipsey & Wilson, 1993; Walberg, 1999). Students can work together to gather information for their cognitively complex tasks. Other parts of tasks can be done cooperatively or individually (Marzano, 2007).

Element 22: Engaging students in cognitively complex tasks involving hypothesis generation and testing—Research has shown that generating and testing hypotheses is associated with a 15–29 percentile gain in student achievement (El-Nemr, 1980; Hattie et al., 1996; Ross, 1988; Sweitzer & Anderson, 1983; Walberg, 1999). Projects that involve investigating or solving a problem are associated with a 29 percentile gain in students' understanding of principles and a 13 percentile gain in students' application of knowledge (Gijbels, Dochy, Van den Bossche, & Segers, 2005). Cognitively complex tasks require students to question their current knowledge and adjust it to accommodate their findings (Guzzetti et al., 1993).

Element 23: Providing resources and guidance—Research has shown that activities involving cognitive dissonance (a discrepancy between current knowledge and observations) are associated with a 29 percentile gain in student achievement (Guzzetti et al., 1993). Models of statistical inference, effective argumentation, and logical errors can be used to guide students as they use data, provide evidence, and verify their claims (Marzano, 2007).

In addition to being supported by research and theory, each element has specific strategies associated with it. Table 3.5 shows the strategies for elements 21 through 23. A full description of each strategy can be found in the compendium section of *Becoming a Reflective Teacher* (Marzano, 2012, pp. 134–141). A list of original sources and research for each strategy can be accessed online at **marzanoresearch .com/classroomstrategies**.

Table 3.5: Strategies for Elements 21–23

Element 21: Organizing students for cognitively complex tasks • Student-designed tasks • Cooperative learning • Academic notebook charts, graphs, and tables • Think logs • Journals • Peer response groups • Self-evaluations • Peer tutoring
Element 22: Engaging students in cognitively complex tasks involving hypothesis generation and testing • Experimental-inquiry tasks • Problem-solving tasks • Decision-making tasks • Investigation tasks
Element 23: Providing resources and guidance • Providing support for claims • Examining claims for errors • Scoring scales • Interviews • Circulating around the room • Expressions and gestures • Collecting assessment information • Feedback

To illustrate how a coach can facilitate a teacher's move from Not Using (0) to Beginning (1) for one of the elements from content lesson segments, consider the following vignette. The teacher in the vignette is working on element 10—helping students process new information—and his coach begins by asking what he already knows about that element. She then adds relevant research and theory and explains several strategies that the teacher could use. The teacher recognizes one of the strategies, jigsaw cooperative learning, and decides to try it. Finally, the coach explains the steps of the strategy and models it for the teacher.

> Mr. Rizzi is meeting with his coach, Kelli, to begin to work on his growth goal of helping students process new information.
>
> "What do you already know about helping students process new information?" asks Kelli.
>
> Mr. Rizzi replies, "Well, I know they need time to think about what I'm teaching them. And I know I need to keep from overloading them with too much information."
>
> "That's true," says Kelli. "One of the best ways researchers have found to encourage kids to think about their learning is called a macrostrategy. That means a strategy that incorporates things like summarizing, questioning, reflecting, clarifying, nonlinguistic representations, and predicting," she explains.
>
> "That's quite a list!" exclaims Mr. Rizzi.
>
> "Keep in mind," replies Kelli, "that a macrostrategy doesn't necessarily use every one of these elements. Some of the more popular macrostrategies are things like reciprocal teaching, jigsaw cooperative learning, concept attainment, and collaborative processing."
>
> Mr. Rizzi remembers that he participated in jigsaw cooperative learning in a professional development class and decides to start with that strategy. Kelli explains the steps of the jigsaw process and agrees to come and model it in Mr. Rizzi's classroom later that week.

Lesson Segments Enacted on the Spot

As explained in chapter 2, lesson segments enacted on the spot involve strategies that teachers must be prepared to use at a moment's notice to ensure an effective learning environment. In the framework, on-the-spot elements are organized into four design questions: What will I do to engage students?, What will I do to recognize and acknowledge adherence or lack of adherence to rules and procedures?, What will I do to establish and maintain effective relationships with students?, and What will I do to communicate high expectations for all students?

What Will I Do to Engage Students?

This design question includes elements 24 through 32. Each element is supported by research and theory.

Element 24: Noticing when students are not engaged—Research has shown that engagement is associated with a 27–31 percentile gain in student achievement (Bloom, 1976; Frederick, 1980; Lysakowski & Walberg, 1982; Walberg, 1982). Different indicators of engagement include students' on-task behavior, positive emotions toward learning, personal investment in learning, and level of attention to instructional activities (Reeve, 2006).

Element 25: Using academic games—Research has shown that games and puzzles are associated with increased attention (Jensen, 2005; Kirsch, 1999). The principle of clozentropy postulates that games and puzzles hold students' attention because of an innate human desire to fill in missing information (Broadhurst & Darnell, 1965; Darnell, 1970, 1972; Ebbinghaus, 1987; Taylor, 1953; Weiner, 1967). Another theory states that humans pay attention to games and puzzles because we seek to decrease the discrepancy between what we predict will happen and what actually happens (Weiner, 1967).

Element 26: Managing response rates—Research has shown that mild pressure has a positive influence on students' learning (Becker, 1988; Skinner, Fletcher, & Hennington, 1996). Mild pressure prompts students to focus their attention on the source of the pressure. Increasing the rate at which students respond during questioning is one way to apply mild pressure in the classroom (Good & Brophy, 2003).

Element 27: Using physical movement—Research has shown that increased physical activity is associated with higher energy levels (Dwyer, Blizzard, & Dean, 1996; Dwyer, Sallis, Blizzard, Lazarus, & Dean, 2001). Higher energy, in turn, allows students to pay more attention to what is happening in class. Additionally, physical movement increases blood flow to the brain, which facilitates thinking and learning (Jensen, 2005).

Element 28: Maintaining a lively pace—Research has shown that the instructional pace affects students' ability to pay attention to classroom activities (Emmer & Gerwels, 2006). To maintain a lively pace, a teacher must transition smoothly and quickly from one instructional activity to the next. Interruptions, lulls in activity, and slow transitions waste time and make it hard for students to stay engaged (Arlin, 1979; Smith, 1985).

Element 29: Demonstrating intensity and enthusiasm—Research has shown that a teacher's intensity and enthusiasm are positively associated with students' energy, engagement, and achievement (Armento, 1978; Bettencourt, Gillett, Gall, & Hull, 1983; Coats & Smidchens, 1966; Land, 1980; Mastin, 1963; McConnell, 1977; Rosenshine, 1970; Williams & Ware, 1976, 1977; Wyckoff, 1973). Intensity involves directly stating the importance of content to students. Enthusiasm involves viewing a topic as interesting, meaningful, and important and communicating those views to students while studying the topic (Good & Brophy, 2003).

Element 30: Using friendly controversy—Research has shown that mild controversy and mild competition have a positive influence on students' learning (Cahill, Prins, Weber, & McGaugh, 1994; Jensen, 2005). Mild controversy involves asking students to express their opinions on an issue and then resolve discrepancies between individuals' perspectives (Good & Brophy, 2003). Mild competition involves competing in the spirit of fun, without embarrassment or consequences for losing (Epstein & Harackiewicz, 1992; Moriarity, Douglas, Punch, & Hattie, 1995; Reeve & Deci, 1996).

Element 31: Providing opportunities for students to talk about themselves—Research has shown that students pay more attention to information that is personally meaningful to them (Csikszentmihalyi, 1990; McCaslin et al., 2006; McCombs, 2001; Roeser, Peck, & Nasir, 2006). If students perceive that information is relevant to their personal goals and self-images, they will take greater interest in it (Marzano, 2007; McCombs, 2001).

Element 32: Presenting unusual or intriguing information—Research has shown that missing or unknown information captures students' attention (Jensen, 2005; Kirsch, 1999). Unusual information that is unrelated to the content can be used to capture students' attention at the beginning of a lesson (Marzano, 2007). Unusual information related to the content can increase students' engagement during a lesson (Jonas, 2004).

In addition to being supported by research and theory, each element has specific strategies associated with it. Table 3.6 shows the strategies for elements 24 through 32. A full description of each strategy can be found in the compendium section of *Becoming a Reflective Teacher* (Marzano, 2012, pp. 142–157). A list of original sources and research for each strategy can be accessed online at **marzanoresearch .com/classroomstrategies**.

Table 3.6: Strategies for Elements 24–32

Element 24: Noticing when students are not engaged
- Scanning the room
- Monitoring levels of attention
- Measuring engagement

Element 25: Using academic games
- What Is the Question?
- Name That Category
- Talk a Mile a Minute
- Classroom Feud
- Which One Doesn't Belong?
- Inconsequential competition
- Turning questions into games
- Vocabulary review games

Element 26: Managing response rates
- Random names
- Hand signals
- Response cards
- Response chaining
- Paired response
- Choral response
- Wait time
- Elaborative interrogation
- Multiple types of questions

Element 27: Using physical movement
- Stand up and stretch
- Give one, get one
- Vote with your feet
- Corners activities
- Stand and be counted
- Body representations
- Drama-related activities

Continued on next page →

Element 28: Maintaining a lively pace

- Instructional segments
- Pace modulation
- The parking lot
- Motivational hook/launching activity

Element 29: Demonstrating intensity and enthusiasm

- Direct statements about the importance of content
- Explicit connections
- Nonlinguistic representations
- Personal stories
- Verbal and nonverbal signals
- Humor
- Quotations
- Movie and film clips

Element 30: Using friendly controversy

- Friendly controversy
- Class vote
- Seminars
- Expert opinions
- Opposite point of view
- Diagramming perspectives
- Lincoln-Douglas debate
- Town hall meeting (Hess, 2009)
- Legal model (Hess, 2009)

Element 31: Providing opportunities for students to talk about themselves

- Interest surveys
- Student learning profiles
- Life connections
- Informal linkages during class discussion

Element 32: Presenting unusual or intriguing information

- Teacher-presented information
- Webquests
- One-minute headlines
- Believe it or not
- History files
- Guest speakers and firsthand consultants

What Will I Do to Recognize and Acknowledge Adherence or Lack of Adherence to Rules and Procedures?

This design question includes elements 33 through 35. Each element is supported by research and theory.

Element 33: Demonstrating withitness—Research has shown that teacher withitness (being aware of what is going on in the classroom at all times) is associated with a 42 percentile decrease in classroom disruptions (Brophy, 1996; Kounin, 1983; Marzano, 2003). Appropriate teacher reactions to positive or negative behavior are associated with a 34 percentile decrease in classroom disruptions (Marzano, 2003).

Element 34: Applying consequences for lack of adherence to rules and procedures—Research has shown that applying consequences for lack of adherence to rules and procedures is associated with a 28–33 percentile decrease in classroom disruptions (Stage & Quiroz, 1997). Direct cost and home contingency consequences are both associated with a 21 percentile decrease in classroom disruptions (Marzano, 2003).

Element 35: Acknowledging adherence to rules and procedures—Research has shown that recognizing adherence to rules and procedures is associated with a 31–33 percentile decrease in classroom disruptions (Stage & Quiroz, 1997). Tangible recognition and group contingency are associated with 29 and 34 percentile decreases in classroom disruptions, respectively (Marzano, 2003).

In addition to being supported by research and theory, each element has specific strategies associated with it. Table 3.7 shows the strategies for elements 33 through 35. A full description of each strategy can be found in the compendium section of *Becoming a Reflective Teacher* (Marzano, 2012, pp. 158–164). A list of original sources and research for each strategy can be accessed online at **marzanoresearch.com/classroomstrategies**.

Table 3.7: Strategies for Elements 33–35

Element 33: Demonstrating withitness
- Being proactive
- Occupying the whole room physically and visually
- Noticing potential problems
- Series of graduated actions

Element 34: Applying consequences for lack of adherence to rules and procedures
- Verbal cues
- Pregnant pause
- Nonverbal cues
- Time-out
- Overcorrection
- Interdependent group contingency
- Home contingency
- Planning for high-intensity situations
- Overall disciplinary plan

Continued on next page →

> **Element 35: Acknowledging adherence to rules and procedures**
> - Verbal affirmations
> - Nonverbal affirmations
> - Tangible recognition
> - Token economies
> - Daily recognition forms
> - Color-coded behavior
> - Certificates
> - Phone calls, emails, and notes

What Will I Do to Establish and Maintain Effective Relationships With Students?

This design question includes elements 36 through 38. Each element is supported by research and theory.

Element 36: Understanding students' interests and backgrounds—Research has shown that positive teacher-student relationships are associated with a 31 percentile decrease in classroom disruptions (Marzano, 2003). When teachers get to know students and seek to understand their interests and backgrounds, it creates an atmosphere of cooperation, rather than an "I-them" mentality (Plax & Kearney, 1990).

Element 37: Using verbal and nonverbal behaviors that indicate affection for students—Research has shown that teacher behaviors such as gestures, smiles, and encouraging remarks are associated with percentile gains of 23 to 32 points for student achievement and other outcomes (Harris & Rosenthal, 1985). Teachers who smile, joke, and show enthusiasm positively affect student engagement and enthusiasm (Anderman & Wolters, 2006; Bettencourt et al., 1983; Gettinger & Kohler, 2006; Moskowitz & Hayman, 1976; Perry, Turner, & Meyer, 2006; Rosenshine & Furst, 1973).

Element 38: Displaying objectivity and control—Research has shown that teachers who objectively viewed their students as young learners (as opposed to friends or enemies) produced greater achievement gains than teachers who are overly warm or overly cold toward students (Brophy & Evertson, 1976; Nelson, Martella, & Galand, 1998; Soar & Soar, 1979). Teachers should maintain a balance of dominance (leadership) and cooperation in the classroom (Brekelmans, Wubbels, & Creton, 1990; Wubbels, Brekelmans, den Brok, & van Tartwijk, 2006; Wubbels, Brekelmans, van Tartwijk, & Admiral, 1999; Wubbels & Levy, 1993).

In addition to being supported by research and theory, each element has specific strategies associated with it. Table 3.8 shows the strategies for elements 36 through 38. A full description of each strategy can be found in the compendium section of *Becoming a Reflective Teacher* (Marzano, 2012, pp. 165–173). A list of original sources and research for each strategy can be accessed online at **marzanoresearch .com/classroomstrategies**.

Table 3.8: Strategies for Elements 36–38

Element 36: Understanding students' interests and backgrounds

- Student background surveys
- Opinion questionnaires
- Individual teacher-student conferences
- Parent-teacher conferences
- School newspaper, newsletter, or bulletin
- Informal class interviews
- Investigating student culture
- Autobiographical metaphors and analogies
- Six-word autobiographies
- Independent investigations
- Quotes
- Commenting on student achievements or areas of importance
- Lineups
- Individual student learning goals

Element 37: Using verbal and nonverbal behaviors that indicate affection for students

- Greeting students at the classroom door
- Informal conferences
- Attending after-school functions
- Greeting students by name outside of school
- Giving students special responsibilities or leadership roles in the classroom
- Scheduled interaction
- Photo bulletin board
- Physical behaviors
- Humor

Element 38: Displaying objectivity and control

- Self-reflection
- Self-monitoring
- Identifying emotional triggers
- Self-care
- Assertiveness
- Maintaining a cool exterior
- Active listening and speaking
- Communication styles
- Unique student needs

What Will I Do to Communicate High Expectations for All Students?

This design question includes elements 39 through 41. Each element is supported by research and theory.

Element 39: Demonstrating value and respect for low-expectancy students—Research has shown that teachers' interactions with high-expectancy students (those from whom they expect high achievement) are more positive than their interactions with low-expectancy students (those from whom they expect low achievement) (Chaiken, Sigler, & Derlega, 1974; Cooper, 1979; Kester & Letchworth, 1972; Page, 1971). When interacting with low-expectancy students, teachers usually praise them less (Babad, Inbar, & Rosenthal, 1982; Brophy & Good, 1970; Cooper & Baron, 1977; Firestone & Brody, 1975; Good, Cooper, & Blakey, 1980; Good, Sikes, & Brophy, 1973; Martinek & Johnson, 1979; Page, 1971; Rejeski, Darracott, & Hutslar, 1979), seat them farther away (Rist, 1970), are less friendly to them (Babad et al., 1982; Chaikin et al., 1974; Kester & Letchworth, 1972; Meichenbaum, Bowers, & Ross, 1969; Page, 1971; Smith & Luginbuhl, 1976), smile at them less, and make eye contact with them less often than they do with high-expectancy students (Chaikin et al., 1974).

Element 40: Asking questions of low-expectancy students—Research has shown that, compared to high-expectancy students, low-expectancy students are less frequently called on to answer questions (Mendoza, Good, & Brophy, 1972; Rubovits & Maehr, 1971), allowed less time to answer questions (Allington, 1980; Taylor, 1979), and more frequently "given" answers to questions (Brophy & Good, 1970; Jeter & Davis, 1973). If a low-expectancy student cannot answer a question, teachers usually call on a different student instead of helping the low-expectancy student answer (Brophy & Good, 1970; Jeter & Davis, 1973).

Element 41: Probing incorrect answers with low-expectancy students—Research has shown that teachers are more willing to probe an incorrect answer with high-expectancy students than with low-expectancy students (Brophy, 1983; Cooper, 1979). Teachers also give low-expectancy students less feedback about their answers (Brophy & Good, 1970; Cooper, 1979; Cornbleth, Davis, & Button, 1972; Good et al., 1973; Jeter & Davis, 1973; Willis, 1970) and spend less time trying to uncover the logic and structure of low-expectancy students' answers to questions (Brophy & Good, 1970; Jeter & Davis, 1973).

In addition to being supported by research and theory, each element has specific strategies associated with it. Table 3.9 shows the strategies for elements 39 through 41. A full description of each strategy can be found in the compendium section of *Becoming a Reflective Teacher* (Marzano, 2012, pp. 174–178). A list of original sources and research for each strategy can be accessed online at **marzanoresearch .com/classroomstrategies**.

Table 3.9: Strategies for Elements 39–41

Element 39: Demonstrating value and respect for low-expectancy students
- Identifying expectation levels for all students
- Identifying differential treatment of low-expectancy students
- Nonverbal and verbal indicators of respect and value

Element 40: Asking questions of low-expectancy students

- Question levels
- Response opportunities
- Follow-up questioning
- Evidence and support for student answers
- Encouragement
- Wait time
- Tracking responses
- Avoiding inappropriate reactions

Element 41: Probing incorrect answers with low-expectancy students

- Using an appropriate response process
- Letting students "off the hook" temporarily
- Answer revision
- Think-pair-share (Lyman, 2006)

To illustrate how a coach can facilitate a teacher's move from Not Using (0) to Beginning (1) for one of the elements from lesson segments enacted on the spot, consider the following vignette. To help a teacher working on element 37—using verbal and nonverbal behaviors that indicate affection for students—the coach first listens to the teacher's concerns about her classroom and affirms that the teacher has chosen a good goal. The coach then explains research and theory related to the teacher's growth-goal element and clarifies important concepts and terms. Finally, she gives the teacher concrete strategies that can be used to make progress on the growth goal and shares specific knowledge related to the strategy the teacher selects.

Ms. Foerde and her coach, Louise, are meeting about her growth goal, displaying objectivity and control. As a physical education teacher, Ms. Foerde has found that when she feels cranky or upset, her students tend to misbehave more.

"If I'm having a bad day," she says, "we're all having a bad day."

"Then I think this is a great goal for you," replies Louise. "Especially since research shows that teachers who maintain emotional objectivity in the classroom have a positive effect on student engagement and achievement."

Louise explains that teacher-student relationships are founded on an appropriate balance of dominance and cooperation.

"Don't let the word *dominance* scare you," she cautions, "it just means providing a clear purpose and strong guidance. It means being a leader. An important part of dominance is maintaining emotional objectivity—that is, not letting the ups and downs of the classroom affect your behavior."

Louise further explains that cooperation involves building a sense of community in the classroom.

"There are a number of different strategies that you can use to maintain objectivity and control," Louise says.

She and Ms. Foerde review a list of strategies, and Ms. Foerde says, "Well, maintaining a cool exterior seems like a logical place to start."

Louise agrees and proceeds to explain different ways to appear calm in the face of conflict or stress, even if Ms. Foerde doesn't feel completely calm inside.

Summary

In this chapter, we described how a coach can help a teacher move from the Not Using (0) level of the scale to the Beginning (1) level of the scale. That move involves learning about research, theory, and strategies associated with his or her growth-goal element; selecting a strategy to work on; and learning about the steps and parts of that strategy. We also provided research and theory for each of the forty-one elements of *The Art and Science of Teaching* (Marzano, 2007) model and strategies for each of those elements.

Chapter 3: Comprehension Questions

1. What must a teacher do to grow from the Not Using (0) level to the Beginning (1) level? As described in chapter 2 and in this chapter, what can a coach do to support that growth?

2. Choose one of the forty-one elements, and find the following information for it:

    *   Which lesson segment and design question are associated with the element?

    *   What research and theory are associated with the element?

    *   What strategies are associated with the element?

Role-Play

With a partner, role-play a situation (like those in the vignettes) where a teacher and coach are meeting to begin work on a growth goal. If you are playing the teacher, choose a growth-goal element. If you are playing the coach, guide the teacher from Not Using (0) to Beginning (1) for his or her chosen growth-goal element.

After role-playing once, switch roles and repeat the process. The "teacher" should select a different growth-goal element than the one used the first time.

Chapter 4

BEGINNING (1) TO DEVELOPING (2) AND DEVELOPING (2) TO APPLYING (3)

As we saw in chapter 3, a teacher at the Beginning (1) level understands why a particular strategy is important and is actively trying the strategy out in his or her classroom. To move from the Beginning (1) level to the Developing (2) level, a teacher must execute all the steps of the strategy without errors or omissions. To move from the Developing (2) to the Applying (3) level for a strategy, a teacher must monitor students' responses to the strategy by watching to see if the strategy is producing the desired effect on students.

As an example of these moves, consider the teacher from chapter 3 who selected element 9—chunking content into digestible bites—as a growth-goal area and who decided to start by using a specific strategy for chunk processing in his classroom. As described in chapter 3, that strategy involves four steps. The teacher:

- Groups students in threes and assigns a letter to each group member: A, B, and C

- Presents a chunk of information and asks student A to summarize the information and students B and C to add to A's summary

- Answers any questions from groups and asks each group to predict what the next chunk will be about

- Rotates the role of summarizer (A) after each chunk

The coach might initially observe that while the teacher executes the first two steps of the strategy correctly, he is executing the third step incorrectly and is leaving out the fourth step. By recognizing and correcting these errors and omissions, the coach can help the teacher move to the Developing (2) level.

To progress from the Developing (2) to the Applying (3) level, the coach would help the teacher monitor how the strategies that he uses in the classroom affect students. For example, the teacher working on chunk processing could look for the following student responses that indicate he is using the strategy effectively. Students:

- Follow the procedure for chunk processing

- Accurately summarize new information

- Ask pertinent questions about new information

- When asked, can describe their predictions about new information

The coach might help the teacher notice that his students are not accurately summarizing new information—one of the desired outcomes for students. In response to this, the coach might suggest that the teacher give more explicit directions about how to summarize information or that he clarify the main ideas and key details of new information before asking students to summarize it. As the teacher gains confidence monitoring his students' responses, he should be able to make these adjustments with increasing independence. Once the teacher is monitoring students' responses and adjusting his actions to achieve the desired student responses, the teacher is at the Applying (3) level.

Coaching Is Not Necessarily a Linear Process

As presented in chapters 2 and 3, the steps that a coach follows to help a teacher move from Not Using (0) to Beginning (1) are fairly linear: the coach and teacher conduct a self-audit to select a growth-goal element, the coach reviews research and theory about that element, the coach and teacher examine a list of strategies for the element, the teacher selects a strategy to work on, the coach explains the steps and parts of that strategy, and the teacher tries the strategy in her classroom.

For the teacher, the moves from Beginning (1) to Developing (2) and from Developing (2) to Applying (3) also progress in a fairly linear fashion. As shown in the previous example, the coach observes the teacher using a strategy and gives him feedback about parts of the strategy he is executing incorrectly or omitting. Once the teacher has fixed those problems, he is at the Developing (2) level. The coach then prompts the teacher to monitor his students' responses to the strategy and make adjustments in his use of the strategy in order to achieve the desired student responses. The teacher has then reached the Applying (3) level.

For the coach, however, the process for helping a teacher move from Beginning (1) to Applying (3) must be more eclectic. A coach must begin to monitor students' responses to a strategy while the teacher is still at the Developing (2) level. In fact, one of the ways a coach can identify errors or omissions in a teacher's use of a strategy is by examining its effect on students. To illustrate, the coach in the previous example might think that the teacher is correctly executing the chunk processing strategy until the coach begins to ask students to describe their predictions about new information. Upon discovering that students cannot describe their predictions, the coach might reexamine the teacher's execution of the third part of the strategy and realize that he is not giving them enough time or direction to make meaningful predictions. The coach would then alert the teacher that he needs to correct his execution of that part of the strategy.

To help a teacher become more aware of his or her students' responses, a coach might observe students and give the teacher feedback or video record the class while the teacher is using the strategy and watch the video with the teacher. The coach might also use bug-in-ear technology to help a teacher monitor students' responses to a strategy (see chapter 6, page 219). In this way, the coach can guide the teacher toward the Applying (3) level.

In summary, there is a causal interplay between teacher actions and student responses. A coach may think that the teacher is executing all the steps of a strategy correctly until he or she examines students' responses. If the desired responses are not being elicited, the coach reexamines the teacher's actions and helps the teacher make adjustments to achieve the preferred outcome. In this chapter, we present the necessary *teacher actions* for each strategy within each element. These are the actions a teacher must execute correctly to reach the Developing (2) level. We also list the *desired student responses*, which indicate whether a strategy is having the desired effect.

These are the indicators that the teacher's use of a particular strategy is producing the anticipated results. When a teacher independently monitors students' responses and makes adaptations as necessary, the teacher is functioning at the Applying (3) level. Again, coaches should consider both teacher actions and student responses simultaneously when helping teachers move from Beginning (1) to Developing (2) and from Developing (2) to Applying (3). The following vignette depicts this progression.

> Mrs. Dungee has reached the Developing (2) level for the strategy of chunk processing and is ready to start monitoring her students' responses. Her coach, Ryan, meets with her to explain what she needs to do.
>
> He begins by saying, "Do you remember two weeks ago when I told you that you needed to give your students more time and direction to make meaningful predictions?"
>
> "Yes," replies Mrs. Dungee.
>
> "How do you think I knew you needed to do that?" asks Ryan.
>
> "I don't know," says Mrs. Dungee. "It seemed like a pretty specialized adjustment, and it wasn't on the list of steps you gave me for the strategy."
>
> "That's true," Ryan responds. "I started asking your students to describe their predictions to me, which is one of the desired student responses for chunk processing. I discovered they couldn't do it. That prompted me to ask you to adjust your use of that part of the strategy."
>
> "Oh," says Mrs. Dungee. "So you knew I was making a mistake because my students weren't responding like they should."
>
> "Exactly," says Ryan.
>
> He goes on to explain that monitoring and adjusting for herself is what characterizes the move from Developing (2) to Applying (3), and Mrs. Dungee makes plans to begin monitoring her students' responses as she uses the chunk processing strategy.

Lesson Segments Involving Routine Events

Elements of lesson segments involving routine events are organized into two design questions: What will I do to establish and communicate learning goals, track student progress, and celebrate success? and What will I do to establish and maintain classroom rules and procedures?

What Will I Do to Establish and Communicate Learning Goals, Track Student Progress, and Celebrate Success?

This design question includes elements 1 through 3. Here we present teacher actions and desired student responses for each of the strategies for these elements.

Element 1: Providing clear learning goals and scales (rubrics)

Clearly articulating learning goals, being careful not to confuse them with activities or assignments

Teacher Actions:

- Designs activities and assignments that directly relate to the learning goals
- Clearly communicates the learning goal for each activity or assignment to students

Desired Student Responses:

- Know what learning goal each activity or assignment is addressing
- Can describe what proficient performance looks like for each learning goal

Creating scales or rubrics for learning goals

Teacher Actions:

- Writes target, simpler, and more complex learning goals
- Uses a simplified or complex scale

Desired Student Responses:

- Can explain what each score on the scale means
- Can describe what performance on the learning goal looks like at each level of the scale

Student-friendly scales

Teacher Actions:

- Explains the scale to students
- Helps students write content statements for different levels of the scale in their own words

Desired Student Responses:

- Ask questions to clarify understanding of the learning goal
- Accurately describe performance at different levels of the scale

Individual student learning goals

Teacher Actions:

- Identifies students' personal interests that relate to the class's learning goal
- Helps students articulate and write down their individual learning goals
- Tracks students' progress on individual learning goals

Desired Student Responses:

- Identify personally important individual learning goals

- Can explain what they have already done and still need to do to accomplish individual learning goals

- Track their progress on individual learning goals

Element 2: Tracking student progress

Formative assessments

Teacher Actions:

- Writes assessment tasks for two different levels of content using appropriate scales

- Decides which scale to grade an assessment with (simplified or complex)

Desired Student Responses:

- Know what kinds of test items normally correspond to different levels of content

- Generate their own assessments to demonstrate proficiency at higher levels of the scale

Response patterns

Teacher Actions:

- Classifies items as correct, incorrect, or partially correct for various levels of difficulty on the scale

- Analyzes students' patterns of responses to assign a score

- Addresses aberrant response patterns

Desired Student Response:

- Can explain why they were assigned specific scores on an assessment

Individual score-level assessments

Teacher Actions:

- Creates assessments that measure one level of a scale

- Helps students use individual score-level assessments to demonstrate their proficiency

Desired Student Responses:

- Can explain the purpose of individual score-level assessments

- Use individual score-level assessments to progress at their own pace through the levels of a scale

Different types of assessments

Teacher Actions:

- Administers and scores pencil-and-paper tests
- Conducts and scores demonstrations, performances, or oral reports
- Conducts and scores unobtrusive assessments
- Encourages students to create student-generated assessments

Desired Student Responses:

- Can describe different types of assessments used by the teacher
- Create student-generated assessments to demonstrate their knowledge levels for specific learning goals

Formative grading

Teacher Actions:

- Uses multiple approaches to assigning summative scores to students
- Explains the various approaches for assigning summative scores to students and parents

Desired Student Responses:

- Know their current status for each learning goal
- Can explain why they were assigned a specific summative score for each learning goal

Charting student progress

Teacher Actions:

- Determines students' initial and final statuses on a learning goal
- Reminds students to update their progress charts

Desired Student Responses:

- Keep their progress charts updated
- Use data from progress charts to set short term goals (for the next assessment or assignment)

Charting class progress

Teacher Actions:

- Selects data points for whole-class tracking
- Adjusts instruction based on whole-class progress

Desired Student Response:

- Can explain the class's progress on specific learning goals

Element 3: Celebrating success

Final status celebration

Teacher Actions:

- Uses appropriate celebrations (round of applause, peer compliments, poster display, parent communication)
- Emphasizes effort and growth during celebrations

Desired Student Responses:

- Exhibit pride in their accomplishments
- Can explain how they achieved their final status for a learning goal
- Take steps to improve their final status if they did not meet their goal

Knowledge gain celebration

Teacher Actions:

- Creates knowledge gain charts for students
- Helps students calculate their knowledge gains

Desired Student Responses:

- Exhibit pride in their knowledge gain
- Can explain the difference between final status and knowledge gain

Verbal feedback

Teacher Actions:

- Uses words and phrases that emphasize effort and growth
- Explains specific actions that made a student successful
- Explains specific aspects of tasks that students can improve on

Desired Student Response:

- Say things like "I succeeded because I worked hard at this" or "I love a challenge"

As indicated, the strategies and their selected teacher actions for this design question focus on providing students with a clear understanding of the learning goals being addressed, their status on those learning goals, and their progress on those learning goals. Desired student responses include being aware of learning goals and the relationship between classroom activities and those goals, knowing their status on learning goals, and understanding what they did to accomplish the goals.

What Will I Do to Establish and Maintain Classroom Rules and Procedures?

This design question includes elements 4 and 5. Here we present teacher actions and desired student responses for each of the strategies for these elements.

Element 4: Establishing and maintaining classroom rules and procedures

Using a small set of rules and procedures

Teacher Actions:

- Creates five to eight rules and procedures per class
- Creates procedures to make rules more explicit

Desired Student Response:

- Can explain the classroom rules and procedures

Explaining rules and procedures to students

Teacher Actions:

- Discusses the need for rules and procedures with students
- Presents and explains a set of teacher-designed rules

Desired Student Responses:

- Can explain why rules and procedures are necessary
- Can explain the rationale for teacher-designed rules

Modifying rules and procedures with students

Teacher Actions:

- Invites students to modify existing rules and procedures
- Facilitates students' voting to gain consensus on suggested changes
- Incorporates students' suggestions into existing rules

Desired Student Responses:

- Suggest changes to existing rules and procedures
- Can explain why existing rules and procedures need to be modified

Generating rules and procedures with students

Teacher Actions:

- Discusses the need for rules and procedures with students

- Facilitates students' small-group work to create lists of rules
- Compiles students' lists into final class rules

Desired Student Responses:

- Can explain why rules and procedures are necessary
- Create rules that support a safe and orderly classroom

Language of responsibility and statements of school beliefs

Teacher Actions:

- Discusses concepts like freedom, equality, responsibility, and rights with students
- Helps students create written statements about their rights and responsibilities at school

Desired Student Responses:

- Can explain concepts like freedom, equality, responsibility, threats, opinions, and rights
- Can explain their rights and responsibilities at school

Posting rules around the room

Teacher Actions:

- Posts rules near relevant locations in the classroom
- Reminds students to refer to posted classroom rules

Desired Student Responses:

- Follow posted rules
- Refer to posted rules when working in the classroom

Class pledge or classroom constitution

Teacher Actions:

- Helps students write a class pledge or classroom constitution based on classroom rules and procedures
- Ensures that pledges and constitutions describe what the ideal classroom looks like and sounds like

Desired Student Responses:

- Can explain what the ideal classroom looks like and sounds like
- Create a class pledge or classroom constitution that supports a safe and orderly classroom

Posters and graphics

Teacher Actions:

- Helps students identify rules, procedures, and character traits that are important to proper classroom functioning

- Helps students create posters and graphics that emphasize their identified rules, procedures, or character traits

Desired Student Responses:

- Can explain which rules, procedures, and character traits are important to proper classroom functioning

- Create posters and graphics that emphasize important rules, procedures, or character traits

Gestures and symbols

Teacher Actions:

- Works with students to identify basic classroom messages (quietness, attention)

- Establishes gestures or symbols to communicate basic classroom messages

Desired Student Responses:

- Can explain the gestures and symbols used to communicate basic classroom messages (quietness, attention)

- Respond quickly and appropriately to teacher gestures and symbols

Vignettes and role-playing

Teacher Actions:

- Helps students identify what appropriate behavior looks and sounds like

- Helps students write vignettes or role plays that illustrate appropriate behavior

Desired Student Responses:

- Can explain what appropriate behavior looks and sounds like

- Create vignettes and role plays that depict appropriate behavior

Reviewing rules and procedures with students

Teacher Actions:

- Identifies rules or procedures that students are systematically violating or ignoring

- Works with students to create procedures for, suspend, or drop rules

Desired Student Responses:

- Show remorse about ignoring or violating rules or procedures
- Can explain why a rule or procedure should be modified, suspended, or dropped

Classroom meetings

Teacher Actions:

- Designates time to discuss classroom issues
- Creates guidelines for classroom meetings

Desired Student Responses:

- Can explain the purpose of classroom meetings
- Follow guidelines for classroom meetings
- Participate appropriately during classroom meetings

Student self-assessment

Teacher Actions:

- Creates a scale that students can use to evaluate their adherence to classroom rules and procedures
- Asks students to assess their level of adherence to classroom rules and procedures

Desired Student Responses:

- Can explain what different levels of adherence to classroom rules and procedures look like using a teacher-designed scale
- Can explain their level of adherence to classroom rules and procedures

Element 5: Organizing the physical layout of the classroom

Learning centers

Teacher Actions:

- Places centers away from major traffic patterns
- Places centers where he or she can monitor them at all times
- Places centers where students can easily access required materials and resources

Desired Student Responses:

- Work effectively and efficiently at learning centers
- Easily access required materials and resources at learning centers

Computers and technology equipment

Teacher Actions:

- Places technology equipment away from major traffic patterns
- Places technology equipment where it is easy to use
- Places computers where he or she can monitor them at all times

Desired Student Responses:

- Use technology equipment effectively and efficiently
- Follow school and classroom guidelines while using technology equipment

Lab equipment and supplies

Teacher Actions:

- Places lab equipment and supplies in safe areas
- Places lab equipment and supplies where students can easily access them

Desired Student Responses:

- Access lab equipment and supplies easily
- Follow classroom guidelines for using lab equipment and supplies

Bookshelves

Teacher Actions:

- Places bookshelves where students can easily access them
- Places bookshelves close to areas requiring their resources

Desired Student Responses:

- Access resources on bookshelves easily
- Know where to find specific resources in the classroom

Wall space

Teacher Actions:

- Posts items that highlight learning goals, timelines, or announcements
- Posts student work on the walls
- Posts learning resources on the walls

Desired Student Responses:

- Refer to information posted on the walls

- Know where their own work is posted

Displaying student work

Teacher Actions:

- Creates a system for displaying current and past student work
- Uses guidelines to select exemplary work for display

Desired Student Responses:

- Can explain why specific items of their work are posted
- Can explain why posted items are exemplary

Classroom décor

Teacher Actions:

- Considers what students will see as they enter and exit the room
- Considers what students will see from different work areas in the room
- Eliminates distracting classroom décor

Desired Student Responses:

- Describe the classroom as a great place to learn
- Feel alert and positive upon entering the room
- Focus on the learning at hand while in the room

Classroom materials

Teacher Actions:

- Organizes materials so students can quickly find what they need
- Locates materials close to student work spaces
- Orders new materials when needed

Desired Student Responses:

- Find needed materials quickly and easily
- Alert the teacher when supplies are running low

Teacher's desk

Teacher Actions:

- Places the teacher's desk to accommodate whole-group instruction
- Places the teacher's desk to facilitate eye contact and monitoring students

Desired Student Responses:

- Can easily see and hear the teacher while in the classroom

- Can easily see and hear any media used in the classroom

Student desks

Teacher Actions:

- Considers how many students will be in the class

- Places student desks to accommodate pairings and groupings

- Creates walkways to each student's desk

Desired Student Responses:

- Move to and from desks safely and easily

- Easily work with other students while at their desks

- Can receive individual assistance from the teacher while seated at their desks

Areas for whole-group instruction

Teacher Actions:

- Creates areas to store whole-group instructional materials

- Ensures that all students can see the blackboard/whiteboard, teacher, and projection screen

- Ensures that all students can hear the teacher easily

Desired Student Responses:

- Can easily see the teacher, blackboard/whiteboard, and projection screen

- Can easily hear the teacher and any media used during instruction

Areas for group work

Teacher Actions:

- Ensures easy access to collaborative materials (chart paper, markers)

- Arranges seating to facilitate discussion

Desired Student Responses:

- Can easily access collaborative materials (chart paper, markers)

- Focus on group mates during discussions

As indicated, the strategies and their related teacher actions for this design question focus on creating and communicating classroom rules and procedures and creating a classroom environment conducive to learning. Desired student responses include understanding why they are expected to behave in certain ways in the classroom, adhering to classroom rules and procedures, and learning effectively and efficiently in the classroom.

To illustrate how a coach can facilitate a teacher's move from Beginning (1) to Developing (2) and from Developing (2) to Applying (3) for one of the elements from lesson segments involving routine events, consider the following vignette. Here, the teacher is working on *areas for whole-group instruction*, a strategy associated with element 5—organizing the physical layout of the classroom. The coach helps the teacher move from Beginning (1) to Developing (2) by providing feedback about errors and omissions in her use of the strategy. Notice specifically that the coach identifies the teacher's error by examining students' responses. The coach also gives the teacher specific positive feedback about her use of the strategy. Once the teacher is confident at the Developing (2) level for the strategy, the coach helps her move to Applying (3) by prompting the teacher to begin monitoring her students' responses. The teacher examines her students' responses and discovers an adjustment that needs to be made in her execution of the strategy, which the coach helps her implement.

> With the help of her coach, Eva, Mrs. Haggerty has decided to make organizing the physical layout of her classroom a growth goal for this year. She started by focusing on her whole-group instruction area, and Eva came to observe her teaching a lesson. After the observation, Eva asked several students if they could always see the board, the teacher, and the projection screen.
>
> Later, when they meet together, Eva gives Mrs. Haggerty feedback about what she heard.
>
> "Not all of your students can see the projection screen," she says. "You need to adjust your projector so the images are displayed higher on the screen." She then praises Mrs. Haggerty's storage system for her whole-group instruction materials, saying, "You had everything you needed at your fingertips!"
>
> Once Mrs. Haggerty and Eva feel confident that she is at the Developing (2) level for the strategy, Eva asks Mrs. Haggerty to begin monitoring her students' responses. She points out that she modeled this when she asked students if they could see the screen.
>
> At their next session, Mrs. Haggerty says, "I asked my students if they could hear, and some said they couldn't, but I'm not sure how to fix it."
>
> Eva asks, "Do you ever talk while your back is turned to the class?"
>
> After thinking for a few moments, Mrs. Haggerty says, "You know, I think I might. When I use my laptop to run a slide show or show online content, I have to turn away from the class to use the keyboard. I keep talking though, and I bet it's hard for my students to hear me."
>
> Eva helps her figure out a new configuration for her laptop that doesn't require her to turn away, and she reminds Mrs. Haggerty to continue monitoring her students' responses to the new configuration to see if the adjustments helped.

Lesson Segments Addressing Content

Elements of lesson segments addressing content are organized into three design questions: What will I do to help students effectively interact with new knowledge?, What will I do to help students practice and deepen their understanding of new knowledge?, and What will I do to help students generate and test hypotheses about new knowledge?

What Will I Do to Help Students Effectively Interact With New Knowledge?

This design question includes elements 6 through 13. Here we present teacher actions and desired student responses for each of the strategies for these elements.

Element 6: Identifying critical information

Identifying critical-input experiences

Teacher Actions:

- Identifies critical content

- Designs learning experiences focused on critical content (two to three experiences per learning goal)

Desired Student Responses:

- Can explain which content is most important to achieving the learning goal

- Can explain which learning goal is being addressed by a critical-input experience

Visual activities

Teacher Actions:

- Identifies critical information

- Uses storyboards, graphic organizers, and pictures to highlight critical information

Desired Student Response:

- Can explain critical information as cued by storyboards, graphic organizers, or pictures

Narrative activities

Teacher Actions:

- Identifies critical information

- Tells stories about critical information

Desired Student Response:

- Can explain critical information as cued by teacher stories

Tone of voice, gestures, and body position

Teacher Actions:

- Identifies critical information

- Raises or lowers voice, makes eye contact with students, uses gestures, smiles, or moves around the room when presenting critical information

Desired Student Responses:

- Can identify when the teacher is presenting critical information
- Can describe specific behaviors the teacher uses when presenting critical information

Pause time

Teacher Actions:

- Identifies key points of critical information
- Pauses after key points while presenting critical information
- Prompts students to think during pauses about what was just said

Desired Student Responses:

- Can explain why the teacher pauses while presenting critical information
- Think during pauses about the information just presented

Element 7: Organizing students to interact with new knowledge

Grouping for active processing

Teacher Actions:

- Asks students to process new information in groups
- Creates operating rules for student processing groups

Desired Student Responses:

- Process new information with other students
- Can explain how their understanding of new information changed after interacting with peers

Group norms

Teacher Actions:

- Presents examples of norms that ensure participation and respect
- Asks students to create norms for their processing groups

Desired Student Responses:

- Create processing group norms that ensure equal participation from all group members
- Create processing group norms that ensure respect for all group members

Fishbowl demonstration

Teacher Actions:

- Prepares a small group of students to demonstrate effective group work

- Asks students to observe the group's demonstration

- Discusses effective group behaviors that students saw during the demonstration

Desired Student Responses:

- Demonstrate effective group behaviors (if in demonstration group)

- Can explain specific things that group members did to facilitate the group's work (paraphrasing, clarifying, active listening)

Job cards

Teacher Actions:

- Creates cards that describe student roles in groups

- Assigns roles to students working in groups

Desired Student Responses:

- Can describe the expectations for various roles in groups

- Fulfill the expectations for their roles in a group

Predetermined "buddies" to help form ad hoc groups

Teacher Actions:

- Creates a "buddy" chart with a graphic and blanks for student names

- Asks students to find a partner for each blank

- Uses charts to create ad hoc groups

Desired Student Responses:

- Fill in other students' names on their charts appropriately

- Use their buddy charts to form ad hoc groups

Contingency plan for ungrouped students

Teacher Actions:

- Designates a meeting spot for students who don't have a partner or group

- Helps ungrouped students pair off or join existing groups

Desired Student Responses:

- Quickly signal the teacher if they do not have a partner

- Pair up with other ungrouped students and begin to work

Grouping students using preassessment information

Teacher Actions:

- Administers a preassessment
- Identifies students with high and low prior knowledge
- Groups students heterogeneously or homogenously

Desired Student Responses:

- Can explain the purpose of preassessments
- Can explain the content for which they have high and low prior knowledge

Element 8: Previewing new content

What do you think you know?

Teacher Actions:

- Asks students to write down what they already know about a topic
- Asks students to pair up and discuss what they wrote
- Asks students to identify the most important knowledge and ideas they wrote down

Desired Student Responses:

- Share what they already know about a topic
- Can explain what they learned by sharing their prior knowledge
- Can explain the connections they made between their prior knowledge and new knowledge

Overt linkages

Teacher Actions:

- Identifies connections between previous and new content
- Explains connections between previous and new content to students

Desired Student Response:

- Can explain how new content is connected to previously learned content

Preview questions

Teacher Actions:

- Asks questions that make students curious about new content
- Asks questions that connect new content to students' prior knowledge

Desired Student Responses:

- Share answers to preview questions as they learn about a topic
- Link answers to questions to their prior knowledge

Brief teacher summary

Teacher Actions:

- Summarizes content that is about to be presented for students (written or oral)
- Highlights key ideas and patterns in upcoming content for students

Desired Student Responses:

- Can explain the main ideas of upcoming content
- Can describe patterns in upcoming content

Skimming

Teacher Actions:

- Teaches students to look at section headings and subheadings when skimming text about new information
- Asks students to summarize passages after skimming them

Desired Student Responses:

- Use section headings and subheadings to skim text
- Can summarize the main ideas of text passages after skimming them

Teacher-prepared notes

Teacher Actions:

- Outlines new information about to be presented
- Discusses the outline with students before presenting new information
- Prompts students to ask questions about the outline

Desired Student Responses:

- Can list the main ideas and important details of information about to be presented
- Follow along with the teacher-prepared notes as content is presented
- Ask questions about teacher-prepared notes

K-W-L strategy (Ogle, 1986)

Teacher Actions:

- Asks students before a lesson what they already know about a topic and records responses under K

- Asks students before a lesson what they want to know about a topic and records responses under W

- Asks students after a lesson what they learned about a topic and records responses under L

- Identifies and resolves misconceptions or confusions recorded under K

Desired Student Responses:

- Identify what they already know and want to know about a topic before a lesson

- Identify what they have learned and resolve misconceptions or confusions after a lesson

Advance organizers

Teacher Actions:

- Creates a visual representation showing the structure and organization of new information for students

- Visually represents how new information connects to information previously learned in class

- Prompts students to ask questions about the advance organizer, identifies information they already know, or finds information that is connected to their interests

Desired Student Responses:

- Can explain the structure and organization of new information

- Can explain how new information connects to previously learned information

- Ask questions about advance organizers

- Identify information that they already know or that is connected to their interests in advance organizers

Anticipation guides

Teacher Actions:

- Creates a series of statements about upcoming information

- Presents the statements to students

- Discusses students' opinions about the statements

Desired Student Responses:

- State their opinions about statements involving new content

- Can explain other students' opinions about statements involving new content

Word splash activity

Teacher Actions:

- Identifies words and short phrases associated with new content

- Presents the words and phrases to students

- Asks students to sort the words and phrases into categories and share their classification rules with the class

Desired Student Responses:

- Sort words and phrases associated with new content into categories

- Can explain the rules they used to classify words and phrases

Preassessment

Teacher Actions:

- Creates a preassessment featuring upcoming content

- Administers the preassessment to students

- Uses preassessment results to identify areas where students have more or less prior knowledge

Desired Student Responses:

- Can explain the purpose of a preassessment

- Identify parts of new content for which they have more or less prior knowledge

Element 9: Chunking content into digestible bites

Presenting content in small chunks

Teacher Actions:

- Chunks content into small, digestible bites

- Presents each chunk of content to students

- Follows each chunk of content with an opportunity for students to process it

Desired Student Responses:

- Can explain why the teacher chunks content into small bites

- Process each chunk of new information after it is presented

Using preassessment data to vary the size of each chunk

Teacher Actions:

- Administers a preassessment featuring upcoming content to students

- Presents content that students scored well on in larger chunks

- Presents content that students scored poorly on in smaller chunks

Desired Student Responses:

- Can explain why the teacher presents larger or smaller chunks of content

- Alert the teacher if the size of a particular chunk is too large (overwhelming) or too small (boring)

Chunk processing

Teacher Actions:

- Groups students in threes and assigns a letter to each group member: A, B, and C

- Presents a chunk of information and asks student A to summarize the information and students B and C to add to A's summary

- Answers any questions from groups and asks each group to predict what the next chunk will be about

- Rotates the role of summarizer (A) after each chunk

Desired Student Responses:

- Follow the procedure for chunk processing

- Accurately summarize new information

- Ask pertinent questions about new information

- When asked, can describe their predictions about new information

Element 10: Helping students process new information

Perspective analysis (Marzano, 1992)

Teacher Actions:

- Asks students questions that prompt them to consider multiple perspectives on new information

- Asks students to state their position, the reasoning behind their position, an opposing position, the reasoning behind the opposing position, and a summary of what they learned about a topic

Desired Student Responses:

- Answer questions in ways that show they are considering new information from multiple perspectives

- Can state their position, the reasoning behind their position, an opposing position, and the reasoning behind the opposing position for a topic

- Can summarize what they learned through perspective analysis

Thinking hats (de Bono, 1999)

Teacher Actions:

- Asks students to consider new information from six different perspectives: neutral/objective, emotional, cautious, optimistic, creative, and organizational

- Discusses students' conclusions about new information from each perspective

Desired Student Responses:

- Can explain the six "thinking hat" perspectives: neutral/objective, emotional, cautious, optimistic, creative, and organizational

- Discuss new information from each of the thinking hat perspectives

Collaborative processing

Teacher Actions:

- Asks students to summarize, ask clarifying questions, and make predictions about new information in small groups

- Discusses students' summaries, questions, and predictions

Desired Student Responses:

- Accurately summarize new information

- Ask questions that clarify their understanding of new information

- Evaluate their predictions about new information

Jigsaw cooperative learning

Teacher Actions:

- Identifies specific important aspects of the content

- Groups students with the same number of members as there are important aspects of the content

- Assigns each student in a group one important aspect of the content and asks students with the same aspects to meet together to study them

- Asks students to reconvene in their original groups to share what they learned about their topic

Desired Student Responses:

- Follow the process for jigsaw cooperative learning

- Collect important information about their expert topics

- Teach their original group members what they learned about the expert topic

- Can explain how the jigsaw process helped their understanding

Reciprocal teaching

Teacher Actions:

- Organizes students in small groups and designates one student as the discussion leader

- Asks students to predict (in their groups) what the upcoming chunk of information will be about

- Presents new information and asks students to discuss questions about the content (asked by the discussion leader), summarize the content, and make predictions about the next chunk of content

Desired Student Responses:

- Follow the process for reciprocal teaching

- Make reasonable predictions about new content

- Ask clarifying questions about new content (when discussion leader)

- Accurately summarize new content

Concept attainment

Teacher Actions:

- Asks students to identify examples and nonexamples of a concept

- Asks students to compare and contrast examples and nonexamples of a concept

- Asks students to guess a mystery concept by examining examples and nonexamples of it

Desired Student Responses:

- Identify examples and nonexamples of a concept

- Compare and contrast examples and nonexamples of a concept

- Identify and describe a mystery concept by examining examples and nonexamples of it

Element 11: Helping students elaborate on new information

General inferential questions

Teacher Actions:

- Asks students questions that require them to use their background knowledge to come up with an answer

- Asks students questions that require them to generate inferences about new information to come up with an answer

Desired Student Responses:

- Use their background knowledge to answer questions without obvious answers

- Generate inferences to answer questions without obvious answers

Elaborative interrogation

Teacher Actions:

- Asks students questions that help them provide evidence to support their answers
- Asks students questions that help them create and defend generalizations about new information

Desired Student Responses:

- Provide evidence to support their answers
- Create and defend generalizations about new information

Element 12: Helping students record and represent knowledge

Informal outline

Teacher Actions:

- Helps students identify big ideas and details about a topic
- Helps students arrange big ideas and details about a topic in an informal outline format

Desired Student Responses:

- Identify big ideas and details about a topic
- Arrange big ideas and details about a topic in an informal outline format

Combination notes, pictures, and summary

Teacher Actions:

- Helps students identify information about content to include in notes
- Helps students create nonlinguistic representations for information in their notes
- Helps students summarize the content in their notes

Desired Student Responses:

- Identify important information about content to include in their notes
- Use nonlinguistic representations in their notes
- Summarize the content in their notes

Graphic organizers

Teacher Actions:

- Explains different kinds of graphic organizers and their purposes to students
- Helps students use graphic organizers to express information

Desired Student Responses:

- Can explain the relationships shown by different graphic organizers
- Use graphic organizers to accurately represent information

Free-flowing web

Teacher Actions:

- Helps students identify the relationships between big ideas and details for a topic
- Helps students show relationships between big ideas and details for a topic in a free-flowing web

Desired Student Responses:

- Identify relationships between big ideas and details for a topic
- Use free-flowing webs to show relationships between big ideas and details for a topic

Academic notebooks

Teacher Actions:

- Creates a system to keep track of students' academic notebooks
- Helps students organize their notes to create a permanent record of their learning

Desired Student Responses:

- Bring their academic notebooks to class or use the teacher's organizational system to keep track of their notebooks
- Organize notes by date to keep track of learning
- Accurately record information in their academic notebooks

Dramatic enactments

Teacher Actions:

- Asks students to act out scenes, processes, or events being studied
- Asks students to use their bodies to express concepts being studied

Desired Student Responses:

- Act out scenes, processes, or events being studied
- Use their bodies to accurately express concepts being studied

Rhyming pegwords

Teacher Actions:

- Creates a collection of facts that need to be memorized

- Helps students attach information to each pegword

Desired Student Responses:

- Identify facts that are important enough to be memorized
- Associate information with different pegwords
- Successfully recall information using pegwords

Link strategy

Teacher Actions:

- Creates a collection of important ideas that need to be memorized
- Helps students create and link together symbols or substitutes for important ideas

Desired Student Responses:

- Identify important ideas that need to be memorized
- Create symbols and substitutes for important ideas
- Link symbols and substitutes together into a narrative or easily remembered sequence
- Successfully recall information using the link strategy

Element 13: Helping students reflect on their learning

Reflective journals

Teacher Actions:

- Designates a portion of students' academic notebooks to be used for reflection
- Asks questions that prompt students to reflect on their learning during a lesson
- Asks students to identify what they could have done to improve their learning during a lesson

Desired Student Responses:

- Can explain what they learned during a lesson
- Identify information they learned well and didn't learn well during a lesson
- Can explain what they could have done to improve learning during a lesson

Think logs

Teacher Actions:

- Asks students to identify specific cognitive skills they used during a lesson
- Asks students to identify specific cognitive skills they could use to improve their learning during future lessons

Desired Student Responses:

- Can explain the cognitive skills they used during a lesson

- Identify cognitive skills they could have used to improve learning during a lesson

Exit slips

Teacher Actions:

- Asks students to respond to reflective questions before leaving the room after a lesson

- Evaluates students' responses to identify misconceptions and areas of confusion

Desired Student Responses:

- Complete exit slips and turn them in to the teacher

- Write down misconceptions or areas of confusion on exit slips

Knowledge comparison

Teacher Actions:

- Helps students compare their current level of knowledge about a topic to previous levels

- Helps students show their knowledge growth using a chart, graph, or diagram

- Helps students identify what they did to increase their knowledge about a topic

Desired Student Responses:

- Can explain their current and previous levels of knowledge about a topic

- Can explain what they did to increase their knowledge about a topic

Two-column notes

Teacher Actions:

- Helps students identify important information about a topic to record in their notes

- Prompts students to record their reactions, questions, and extended ideas about information in their notes

Desired Student Responses:

- Record important information about a topic in their notes

- Record reactions, questions, and extended ideas about information in their notes

As indicated, the strategies and their related teacher actions for this design question focus on helping students process, understand, elaborate, and represent new information. Desired student responses include collaborative processing, effective representation, and understanding and elaborating on new information.

What Will I Do to Help Students Practice and Deepen Their Understanding of New Knowledge?

This design question includes elements 14 through 20. Here we present teacher actions and desired student responses for each of the strategies for these elements.

Element 14: Reviewing content

Cloze activities

Teacher Actions:

- Deletes specific pieces of information from previously learned content

- Presents the previously learned content (with pieces missing) to students and asks them to fill in the missing pieces

Desired Student Responses:

- Accurately fill in pieces of missing information in previously learned content

- Can explain why the information they filled in makes sense

Summaries

Teacher Actions:

- Creates a summary of previously learned information

- Asks students to create summaries of previously learned information

- Discusses teacher and student summaries of previously learned information

Desired Student Responses:

- Create accurate, concise summaries of previously learned information

- Can explain why they included or excluded information in their summaries

Presented problems

Teacher Actions:

- Creates problems that require students to use previously learned information to solve them

- Prompts students to think about previously learned information while working on presented problems

Desired Student Responses:

- Correctly solve presented problems

- Can explain what previously learned information they used while solving presented problems

Demonstration

Teacher Actions:

- Identifies skills or procedures whose performance requires students to use previously-learned information

- Prompts students to think about previously-learned information while demonstrating skills or procedures

Desired Student Responses:

- Correctly perform skills or procedures requiring the use of previously learned information

- Can explain what previously learned information they used to perform a skill or procedure

Brief practice test or exercise

Teacher Actions:

- Creates a test or exercise that requires students to remember and apply previously-learned information

- Prompts students to think about previously-learned information while working on the test or exercise

Desired Student Responses:

- Correctly complete tasks requiring recall and application of previously learned information

- Can explain what previously learned information they used to complete a task

Questioning

Teacher Actions:

- Asks students questions that require them to recall, recognize, and apply previously learned information

- Asks students questions that require them to make inferences or decisions based on previously learned information

Desired Student Responses:

- Correctly answer questions requiring recall or recognition and application of previously learned information

- Make inferences or decisions based on previously learned information

Element 15: Organizing students to practice and deepen knowledge

Perspective analysis (Marzano, 1992)

Teacher Actions:

- Asks students questions that prompt them to consider multiple perspectives on knowledge

- Asks students to state their position, the reasoning behind their position, an opposing position, the reasoning behind the opposing position, and a summary of what they learned about an issue

Desired Student Responses:

- Answer questions in ways that show they are considering knowledge from multiple perspectives

- Can state their position, the reasoning behind their position, an opposing position, and the reasoning behind the opposing position for an issue

- Can summarize what they learned through perspective analysis

Thinking hats (de Bono, 1999)

Teacher Actions:

- Asks students to consider knowledge from six different perspectives: neutral/objective, emotional, cautious, optimistic, creative, and organizational

- Discusses students' conclusions about knowledge from each perspective

Desired Student Responses:

- Can explain the six thinking hat perspectives: neutral/objective, emotional, cautious, optimistic, creative, and organizational

- Consider their knowledge from each of the thinking hat perspectives

Cooperative learning

Teacher Actions:

- Asks students to complete practice activities or answer questions independently

- Asks students to compare their solutions and answers with their peers' in small groups

Desired Student Responses:

- Follow the process for cooperative learning

- Complete practice activities or answer questions independently before discussing them with peers

- Can explain how comparing solutions or answers with peers' deepened their knowledge

Cooperative comparisons

Teacher Actions:

- Asks small groups of students to compare their current knowledge level with previous knowledge levels

- Asks small groups of students to classify different techniques for improving their knowledge levels

- Asks small groups of students to identify how they could coach others with a strategy or process

Desired Student Responses:

- Identify multiple techniques used to improve their knowledge levels

- Identify techniques that peers used to improve their knowledge that they would like to try

- Coach others to improve knowledge or skill with a strategy or process

Pair-check (Kagan & Kagan, 2009)

Teacher Actions:

- Groups pairs of students together to make groups of four

- Asks one student in a pair to work on an exercise while the other student coaches him or her and offers feedback

- Asks partners to switch roles for each problem

- Asks pairs to compare their answers with the other pair in their group of four

Desired Student Responses:

- Offer helpful feedback and coaching while their partner is working on an exercise

- Can explain what they learned by comparing answers with other students

Think-pair-share and think-pair-square (Kagan & Kagan, 2009)

Teacher Actions:

- Asks students to complete a problem individually

- Asks students to share their work with a partner and revise if necessary

- For think-pair-square, asks pairs to check their solution with another pair

- Asks pairs to share their solutions with the class

Desired Student Responses:

- Complete problems individually before comparing work with their partner

- Revise answers, if necessary, after conferring with a partner

- Can explain how their learning was improved by conferring with peers

Student tournaments

Teacher Actions:

- Organizes students into teams

- Asks teams to compete in various academic games

- Tracks each team's points over a period of time (like a unit) and gives a small reward or recognition to the top teams

- Remixes teams after each unit

Desired Student Responses:

- Are more engaged when participating in student tournaments

- Are on teams with a wide variety of other students over the course of a year (due to mixing teams)

- Can explain how tournaments enhanced their learning

Error analysis and peer feedback

Teacher Actions:

- Groups students in pairs and gives each pair a list of criteria to evaluate a task or process

- Asks one partner to watch the other complete a task or process and evaluate their performance

Desired Student Responses:

- Evaluate peers' completion of a task or process according to a list of criteria

- Give helpful feedback to peers after observing them completing a task or process

- Can explain what they learned from the activity

Performances and peer critiques

Teacher Actions:

- Groups students to complete culminating performances

- Asks other students to offer praise, ask questions, and give suggestions for ways the group can improve its performance

Desired Student Responses:

- Work with peers to present culminating performances

- Offer praise, ask questions, and give suggestions for improvement after observing a group's culminating performance

Inside-outside circle (Kagan & Kagan, 2009)

Teacher Actions:

- Divides students into two equal groups and arranges them in two concentric circles with inside students facing out and outside students facing in

- Asks students to discuss an issue, problem, or question with the person facing them

- Asks students in the inside circle to move one position to the left and discuss the issue, problem, or question with their new partner

Desired Student Responses:

- Follow the appropriate process for inside-outside circle

- Discuss issues, problems, or questions respectfully with their partners

- Can explain how hearing different students' perspectives on issues, problems, or questions improved their own understanding of the topic

Element 16: Using homework

Preview homework

Teacher Actions:

- Asks students to read text or review media about an upcoming concept or idea

- Asks students to list their questions, observations, and connections for the content

- Discusses students' questions, observations, and connections in class

Desired Student Responses:

- List questions, observations, and connections that arose while they were reading text or reviewing media about a concept or idea

- Can explain the purpose of preview homework and how it relates to the class's learning goals

Homework to deepen knowledge

Teacher Actions:

- Ensures that students thoroughly understand specific content

- Asks students to compare or classify aspects of the content

- Asks students to create analogies or metaphors involving aspects of the content

Desired Student Responses:

- Compare or classify aspects of content they have already learned

- Create analogies or metaphors involving content they have already learned

- Can explain the purpose of homework to deepen knowledge and how it relates to the class's learning goals

Homework to practice a process or skill

Teacher Actions:

- Ensures that students can independently perform a process or skill

- Asks students to practice a process or skill to increase their fluency, speed, and accuracy

Desired Student Responses:

- Perform a process or skill independently to increase fluency, speed, and accuracy

- Can explain why it is important to develop fluency, speed, and accuracy with the skill or process assigned as practice homework

- Can explain the purpose of homework to practice a process or skill and how it relates to the class's learning goals

Parent-assisted homework

Teacher Actions:

- Ensures that parents/guardians have a clear understanding of their role regarding homework

- Asks parents/guardians to ask their students reflective questions about content

- Asks parents/guardians to listen to their students give an oral summary of content

- Asks parents/guardians to time their students performing a skill or process

Desired Student Responses:

- Can explain their parents'/guardians' role regarding homework

- Answer their parents'/guardians' questions about homework

- Give oral summaries of content to their parents/guardians

- Perform skills or processes while their parents/guardians time them

Element 17: Helping students examine similarities and differences

Sentence stem comparisons

Teacher Actions:

- Creates sentence stems that require students to compare and contrast aspects of the content

- Asks students to complete sentence stem comparisons

- Discusses students' responses to sentence stem comparisons

Desired Student Responses:

- Compare and contrast aspects of the content to complete sentence stems

- Can explain the thinking and reasoning behind their sentence stem comparisons

Venn diagrams

Teacher Actions:

- Explains Venn diagrams to students

- Asks students to use Venn diagrams to compare or contrast two or three things

- Discusses students' Venn diagrams in class

Desired Student Responses:

- Use Venn diagrams to compare or contrast two or three things

- Can explain the thinking and reasoning behind their Venn diagrams

Double-bubble diagram

Teacher Actions:

- Explains double-bubble diagrams to students
- Asks students to use double-bubble diagrams to compare the attributes of different elements of the content
- Asks students to show relationships between different elements of the content by drawing lines between the bubbles on their diagrams

Desired Student Responses:

- Use double-bubble diagrams to compare attributes of different elements of the content
- Show relationships between different elements of the content by drawing lines between the bubbles on the diagrams
- Can explain the thinking and reasoning behind their double-bubble diagrams

Comparison matrix

Teacher Actions:

- Asks students to identify elements of the content to compare and write them at the top of each matrix column
- Asks students to identify attributes of each content element that they want to compare and write one in each matrix row
- Asks students to identify similarities and differences for each content element and attribute
- Asks students to summarize what they learned while completing the comparison matrix

Desired Student Responses:

- Identify elements of the content to compare and fill them in each matrix column
- Identify attributes of each element of the content they wish to compare and fill them in each matrix row
- Identify similarities and differences for each content element and attribute
- Summarize what they learned while completing a comparison matrix

Classification chart

Teacher Actions:

- Creates a chart with several categories across the top
- Asks students to fill in examples that fit in each category
- Asks students to compare their charts in pairs or groups and revise them as necessary

Desired Student Responses:

- Fill in examples for various teacher-generated categories
- Confer with peers and revise their charts as necessary
- Can explain what they learned as a result of the activity

Student-generated classification patterns

Teacher Actions:

- Asks students to find representative examples of various concepts
- Asks students to sort their examples into categories
- Asks students to present their examples and categories to the class

Desired Student Responses:

- Find representative examples of a concept
- Sort examples of a concept into categories
- Can explain the thinking and reasoning behind their examples and categories

Similes

Teacher Actions:

- Asks students to state comparisons using like or as
- Asks students to explain their similes

Desired Student Responses:

- State comparisons using like or as
- Can explain the thinking and reasoning behind their similes

Metaphors

Teacher Actions:

- Asks students to state comparisons as direct relationships
- Asks students to extend their metaphors to include multiple comparisons
- Asks students to explain their metaphors

Desired Student Responses:

- State comparisons as direct relationships
- Create metaphors that express multiple comparisons
- Can explain the thinking and reasoning behind their metaphors

Sentence stem analogies

Teacher Actions:

- Asks students to complete sentence stems such as: Item 1 is to ——————— as item 2 is to ———————.

- Asks students to complete sentence stems such as: Item 1 is to item 2 as ——————— is to ———————.

Desired Student Responses:

- Complete sentence stems that compare relationships

- Can explain the thinking and reasoning behind their sentence stem analogies

Visual analogies

Teacher Actions:

- Helps students express their analogies using a visual organizer

- Helps students label the types of relationships expressed by their analogies

Desired Student Responses:

- Express analogies visually

- Identify and label the type of relationship expressed by an analogy

- Can explain the thinking and reasoning behind their visual analogies

Element 18: Helping students examine errors in reasoning

Identifying errors of faulty logic

Teacher Actions:

- Explains errors of faulty logic to students with examples

- Asks students to recognize examples of errors of faulty logic

- Asks students to create examples of errors of faulty logic

Desired Student Responses:

- Can explain different kinds of errors of faulty logic

- Recognize examples of errors of faulty logic

- Create examples of errors of faulty logic

Identifying errors of attack

Teacher Actions:

- Explains errors of attack to students with examples

- Asks students to recognize examples of errors of attack
- Asks students to create examples of errors of attack

Desired Student Responses:

- Can explain different kinds of errors of attack
- Recognize examples of errors of attack
- Create examples of errors of attack

Identifying errors of weak reference

Teacher Actions:

- Explains errors of weak reference to students with examples
- Asks students to recognize examples of errors of weak reference
- Asks students to create examples of errors of weak reference

Desired Student Responses:

- Can explain different kinds of errors of weak reference
- Recognize examples of errors of weak reference
- Create examples of errors of weak reference

Identifying errors of misinformation

Teacher Actions:

- Explains errors of misinformation to students with examples
- Asks students to recognize examples of errors of misinformation
- Asks students to create examples of errors of misinformation

Desired Student Responses:

- Can explain different kinds of errors of misinformation
- Recognize examples of errors of misinformation
- Create examples of errors of misinformation

Practicing identifying errors in logic

Teacher Actions:

- Asks students to complete exercises that require them to recognize errors in reasoning
- Asks students to explain why an item represents a specific error in reasoning

Desired Student Responses:

- Correctly complete exercises that require recognizing errors in reasoning
- Can explain why an item represents a specific error in reasoning

Finding errors in the media

Teacher Actions:

- Asks students to find errors in teacher-selected media
- Asks students to bring media containing errors in reasoning to class

Desired Student Responses:

- Find errors in teacher-selected media
- Bring media containing errors in reasoning to class

Examining support for claims

Teacher Actions:

- Explains grounds, backing, and qualifiers to students
- Asks students to examine support provided for claims to find grounds, backing, and qualifiers
- Asks students to determine if claims are valid or invalid

Desired Student Responses:

- Can explain what grounds, backing, and qualifiers are
- Can determine if a claim is valid or invalid by examining the support provided for it
- Can explain why a claim is valid or invalid

Statistical limitations

Teacher Actions:

- Explains statistical limitations to students
- Asks students to examine claims for errors involving statistical limitations

Desired Student Responses:

- Can explain different kinds of errors involving statistical limitations
- Recognize examples of errors involving statistical limitations
- Can explain how an error involving statistical limitations invalidates a claim

Element 19: Helping students practice skills, strategies, and processes

Close monitoring

Teacher Actions:

- Creates a highly structured environment for students to practice new skills
- Monitors students' actions very closely to correct early errors or misunderstandings
- Prompts students to monitor their own performance of a skill

Desired Student Responses:

- Quickly correct errors or misunderstandings about a process or skill
- Can describe their level of performance and improvement with a skill

Frequent structured practice

Teacher Actions:

- Provides a clear demonstration of the skill or process to be learned
- Gives students frequent opportunities to practice a skill or process with a high rate of success
- Ensures that students experience success with a skill or process multiple times

Desired Student Responses:

- Can explain the steps required to correctly perform a process or skill
- Experience success repeatedly and often during frequent structured practice

Varied practice

Teacher Actions:

- Creates challenging situations for students to practice a skill or process
- Ensures that students experience success after overcoming challenges and obstacles
- Prompts students to monitor their progress with a skill or process

Desired Student Responses:

- Persevere with a process or skill when confronted with challenges
- Experience success on a regular basis during varied practice
- Can describe their levels of performance and improvement with a skill or process

Fluency practice

Teacher Actions:

- Ensures that students are comfortable with a skill or process and have experienced success in a wide range of situations

- Asks students to focus on performing a skill with increasing speed and accuracy
- Helps students track their progress and improvement with a skill or process

Desired Student Responses:

- Feel comfortable with a skill or process
- Experience success with a skill or process in a wide range of situations
- Perform a skill or process with increasing speed and accuracy
- Can describe their levels of performance and improvement with a skill or process

Worked examples

Teacher Actions:

- Creates examples showing each step involved in solving a problem
- Discusses worked examples with students

Desired Student Responses:

- Can explain each step involved in solving a problem
- Identify discrepancies between their performance of a skill or process and what is shown in the worked example

Practice sessions prior to testing

Teacher Actions:

- Creates a practice schedule to ensure that each student practices a skill or process before being tested or retested
- Monitors students to ensure that they practice skills and processes prior to testing or retesting

Desired Student Responses:

- Practice skills or processes multiple times before testing or retesting
- Can explain how their practice sessions have improved their performance of a skill or process
- Improve their performance on tests

Element 20: Helping students revise knowledge

Academic notebook entries

Teacher Actions:

- Asks students to make entries in their academic notebooks after critical-input experiences, group work, processing activities, or review activities
- Asks students to reexamine their academic notebooks to identify and correct inaccuracies and incomplete information

Desired Student Responses:

- Make entries in their academic notebooks after critical-input experiences, group work, processing activities, or review activities

- Identify and correct inaccuracies and incomplete information in their academic notebooks

Academic notebook review

Teacher Actions:

- Asks students to identify important ideas, concepts, and vocabulary in their academic notebooks

- Asks students to create study guides from their academic notebooks

- Prompts students to ask questions about the information in their academic notebooks

Desired Student Responses:

- Identify important ideas, concepts, and vocabulary in their academic notebooks

- Create study guides from their academic notebooks

- Ask questions about the information in their academic notebooks

Peer feedback

Teacher Actions:

- Creates a set of questions or guidelines to guide students' review of their peers' academic notebooks

- Asks students to evaluate their peers' academic notebooks according to teacher criteria or guidelines

Desired Student Responses:

- Evaluate peers' academic notebooks according to a set of teacher-generated questions or guidelines

- Provide helpful feedback to peers about improvements that could be made to their academic notebooks

- Use peer feedback to revise their understanding of content

Assignment revision

Teacher Actions:

- Records students' grades for an assignment in a gradebook but not on the assignment

- Records comments about assignments on students' assignments

- Returns assignments with comments to students and invites them to revise and resubmit the assignment for a better grade

- Adjusts students' scores based on the quality of their revised assignments

Desired Student Responses:

- Resubmit revised assignments to improve their grade

- Revise assignments in ways that address teacher comments and suggestions

As indicated, the strategies and their related teacher actions for this design question focus on helping students remember, practice, and examine new information on a deeper level. Desired student responses include being able to demonstrate their knowledge of a process or skill, correct errors in information, and compare or classify new information.

What Will I Do to Help Students Generate and Test Hypotheses About New Knowledge?

This design question includes elements 21 through 23. Here we present teacher actions and desired student responses for each of the strategies for these elements.

Element 21: Organizing students for cognitively complex tasks

Student-designed tasks

Teacher Actions:

- Asks students questions that prompt them to create their own cognitively complex tasks

- Helps students select the appropriate type of cognitively complex task

- Helps students plan their own cognitively complex tasks

Desired Student Responses:

- Design their own cognitively complex tasks

- Can explain why they selected a particular type of cognitively complex task

- Can explain how they plan to conduct their cognitively complex tasks

Cooperative learning

Teacher Actions:

- Designs ways to keep individual students and groups accountable during cognitively complex tasks

- Coaches students to improve their interpersonal and group-work skills during cognitively complex tasks

- Specifies clear roles and responsibilities for group members during cognitively complex tasks

- Uses a variety of grouping structures, criteria, and sizes during cognitively complex tasks

Desired Student Responses:

- Can produce artifacts and documents to verify progress on their cognitively complex tasks

- Can describe how their interpersonal and group-work skills have improved during their cognitively complex tasks
- Can explain the roles and responsibilities of each group member for a cognitively complex task

Academic notebook charts, graphs, and tables

Teacher Actions:

- Asks students to track their progress on class learning goals during cognitively complex tasks
- Asks students to track their progress on personal learning goals during cognitively complex tasks

Desired Student Responses:

- Can describe their progress on class learning goals over the course of a cognitively complex task
- Can describe their progress on personal learning goals over the course of a cognitively complex task

Think logs

Teacher Actions:

- Asks students to identify specific cognitive skills they used during cognitively complex tasks
- Asks students to identify specific cognitive skills they could use to improve their performance on cognitively complex tasks

Desired Student Responses:

- Can explain the cognitive skills they used during a cognitively complex task
- Identify cognitive skills they could have used to improve learning during a cognitively complex task

Journals

Teacher Actions:

- Asks questions that help students reflect on what they learned during their cognitively complex task
- Asks students to identify what they could have done to learn more during their cognitively complex task

Desired Student Responses:

- Can explain what they learned during a cognitively complex task
- Identify information they learned well and didn't learn well during a cognitively complex task
- Can explain what they could have done to improve learning during a cognitively complex task

Peer response groups

Teacher Actions:

- Creates scoring scales or checklists to evaluate students' performance on their cognitively complex tasks

- Asks students to give their peers feedback about their performance on cognitively complex tasks using scoring scales or checklists

Desired Student Responses:

- Use teacher-generated scoring scales and checklists to evaluate their progress on cognitively complex tasks

- Give peers helpful feedback about their cognitively complex tasks based on teacher-generated scoring scales and checklists

- Incorporate feedback from peers into their cognitively complex tasks

Self-evaluations

Teacher Actions:

- Asks students to evaluate their own performance on cognitively complex tasks

- Asks students to suggest the score or grade they think they deserve on their cognitively complex task

Desired Student Responses:

- Evaluate their own performance on cognitively complex tasks

- Suggest reasonable scores or grades for themselves on cognitively complex tasks

Peer tutoring

Teacher Actions:

- Identifies advanced students who are interested in helping other students with their cognitively complex tasks

- Creates guidelines for peer tutoring to ensure that both students involved increase their learning (one by explaining what he or she already knows, one by hearing their peer's explanation of an idea or concept)

Desired Student Responses:

- Volunteer suggestions or positive feedback to peers during cognitively complex tasks

- Follow guidelines for peer tutoring

- Can explain what they learned from a peer tutoring experience

Element 22: Engaging students in cognitively complex tasks involving hypothesis generation and testing

Experimental-inquiry tasks

Teacher Actions:

- Asks students to make predictions, test them, and evaluate the results of their experimental-inquiry tasks
- Asks students to reflect on the process they used for their experimental-inquiry tasks

Desired Student Responses:

- Make predictions, test them, and evaluate the results of their experimental-inquiry tasks
- Can explain what they learned from their experimental-inquiry tasks
- Can explain what they could have done to learn more from their experimental-inquiry tasks

Problem-solving tasks

Teacher Actions:

- Asks students to set goals, identify obstacles or constraints to achieving their goals, find solutions, and predict the effectiveness of different solutions for problem-solving tasks
- Asks students to reflect on the process they used for their problem-solving tasks

Desired Student Responses:

- Set goals, identify obstacles or constraints to achieving the goals, find solutions, and predict the effectiveness of different solutions for their problem-solving tasks
- Can explain what they learned from their problem-solving tasks
- Can explain what they could have done to learn more from their problem-solving tasks

Decision-making tasks

Teacher Actions:

- Asks students to identify alternatives and judgment criteria, apply criteria to alternatives, and select appropriate alternatives during decision-making tasks
- Teaches students how to use a decision-making matrix
- Asks students to reflect on the process they used for their decision-making tasks

Desired Student Responses:

- Identify alternatives and judgment criteria, apply criteria to alternatives, and select appropriate alternatives during decision-making tasks
- Can explain what they learned from their decision-making tasks
- Can explain what they could have done to learn more from their decision-making tasks

Investigation tasks

Teacher Actions:

- Asks students to identify interesting concepts or events, research current knowledge about them, identify confusions or contradictions about them, and develop a resolution for the contradictions or confusions during investigation tasks

- Asks students to reflect on the process they used for their investigation tasks

Desired Student Responses:

- Identify interesting concepts or events, research current knowledge about them, identify confusions or contradictions about them, and develop a resolution for the contradictions or confusions during investigation tasks

- Can explain what they learned from their investigation tasks

- Can explain what they could have done to learn more from their investigation tasks

Element 23: Providing resources and guidance

Providing support for claims

Teacher Actions:

- Explains grounds, backing, and qualifiers to students

- Asks students to provide grounds, backing, and qualifiers for their claims

- Asks students to explain why their claims are valid

Desired Student Responses:

- Provide grounds, backing, and qualifiers for their claims

- Can explain why their claims are valid

Examining claims for errors

Teacher Actions:

- Explains common errors that occur in claims to students

- Helps students find and resolve errors in their claims and conclusions

Desired Student Responses:

- Can explain and give examples of common errors that occur in claims

- Recognize and correct errors in their claims

Scoring scales

Teacher Actions:

- Creates a scale to monitor students' progress toward the class learning goal during cognitively complex tasks

- Helps students track their progress on the learning goal during cognitively complex tasks

Desired Student Response:

- Can describe the progress they have made toward the class learning goal during the cognitively complex task using a teacher-generated scale

Interviews

Teacher Actions:

- Asks students questions about their progress on cognitively complex tasks

- Creates and uses a checklist or scoring scale to guide interviews and help students plan next steps

Desired Student Responses:

- Can describe what they have done and still need to do for their cognitively complex tasks

- Identify and resolve potential problems related to their cognitively complex tasks

- Revise plans for their cognitively complex tasks when necessary

Circulating around the room

Teacher Actions:

- Walks around the room while students work on cognitively complex tasks

- Offers assistance or resources to students who seem to be having trouble

Desired Student Responses:

- Describe the teacher as "available" to help with cognitively complex tasks

- Receive assistance from the teacher quickly and easily

Expressions and gestures

Teacher Actions:

- Uses nonverbal gestures and expressions (smile, eye level, eye contact, nodding) while providing guidance to students

- Asks questions to gain a clear idea of what students need help with

Desired Student Responses:

- Describe the teacher as "happy to help" with cognitively complex tasks

- Can explain how the teacher's assistance helped them make progress on cognitively complex tasks

Collecting assessment information

Teacher Actions:

- Uses assessment information to anticipate student needs for their cognitively complex tasks

- Obtains and offers appropriate resources to students

Desired Student Response:

- Describe the teacher as someone who anticipates their needs during cognitively complex tasks

Feedback

Teacher Action:

- Tells students when they answer questions correctly, perform tasks well, or give their best effort during cognitively complex tasks

Desired Student Responses:

- Describe the teacher as someone who recognizes and appreciates students who do their best

- Can describe times when they have answered questions correctly, performed tasks well, or given their best effort during cognitively complex tasks

As indicated, the strategies and their related teacher actions for this design question focus on helping students challenge their current thoughts and beliefs about knowledge by generating and testing hypotheses about that knowledge. Desired student responses include working collaboratively on tasks involving investigation, problem solving, decision making, or experimentation and effectively using teacher-provided resources and guidance.

To illustrate how a coach can facilitate a teacher's move from Beginning (1) to Developing (2) and from Developing (2) to Applying (3) for one of the elements from lesson segments addressing content, consider the following vignette. The teacher is working on *homework to deepen knowledge*, a strategy associated with element 16—using homework. The coach helps the teacher move from Beginning (1) to Developing (2) by alerting him to a part of the strategy that he is omitting. Notice that the coach accompanies this message with positive feedback about parts of the strategy the teacher is using effectively. Once the teacher has added the missing part and feels confident that he is at the Developing (2) level for the strategy, the coach helps him move to the Applying (3) level by prompting him to monitor his students' responses to the strategy. When the teacher does this, he realizes that he needs to adjust his use of the strategy to include more explanation of the tasks involved.

Mr. McMartin's coach, Nora, is meeting with him to see how his first try at using homework to deepen knowledge went.

"So, how did it go?" she asks.

"Pretty good," replies Mr. McMartin, who teaches high school art. "We're studying personal expression in art, and we've been studying a number of different pieces of controversial art. I asked each student to take home a small reproduction of a controversial piece of art and describe it. We'd discussed all the pieces in class, so they already knew a lot about the piece they were describing."

"Great," says Nora, "I like that you gave them a visual representation of the piece of art they were describing. And good job discussing the art in class before assigning it as homework. But I think you may be leaving out an important part of this strategy."

Nora goes on to explain that in order for homework to deepen students' knowledge, they need to perform activities with the content that involve complex thinking, like comparing, classifying, finding patterns, or analyzing relationships.

Mr. McMartin uses the homework strategy again, but this time he asks students to compare two different pieces of controversial art. When both he and Nora think that he is at the Developing (2) level for the strategy, Nora explains that he needs to monitor his students' responses to the homework. They meet again after a week has passed.

Nora asks, "Have you been monitoring your students' responses?"

Mr. McMartin replies, "Yes, and I've realized something. The other day I asked them to create analogies about different artists for homework. But during our discussion the next day, I realized that a lot of them didn't know what an analogy was. So I explained it to them and asked them to revise their assignments that night."

Nora affirms that Mr. McMartin has made a good adjustment to the strategy to achieve the desired student responses and explains that monitoring students' responses and adjusting instruction to achieve the desired student responses is characteristic of an Applying (3) teacher.

Lesson Segments Enacted on the Spot

Elements of lesson segments enacted on the spot are organized into four design questions: What will I do to engage students?, What will I do to recognize and acknowledge adherence or lack of adherence to rules and procedures?, What will I do to establish and maintain effective relationships with students?, and What will I do to communicate high expectations for all students?

What Will I Do to Engage Students?

This design question includes elements 24 through 32. Here we present teacher actions and desired student responses for each of the strategies for these elements.

Element 24: Noticing when students are not engaged

Scanning the room

Teacher Actions:

- Looks for students who show signs of low attention and engagement
- Uses specific interventions (questioning, proximity, physical movement) to reengage disengaged or unfocused students

Desired Student Responses:

- Describe the teacher as someone who notices when they are not engaged
- Reengage in response to teacher interventions

Monitoring levels of attention

Teacher Actions:

- Identifies students or groups of students with low levels of attention and engagement
- Engages the class in activities to help unfocused or disengaged students reengage

Desired Student Responses:

- Describe the teacher as someone who notices when they are not paying attention
- Focus their attention on class activities in response to teacher interventions

Measuring engagement

Teacher Actions:

- Creates a system that allows students to signal their level of engagement
- Periodically prompts students to signal their level of engagement

Desired Student Response:

- Signal the teacher when they are disengaged, distracted, or bored

Element 25: Using academic games

What Is the Question?

Teacher Actions:

- Creates a matrix with content-based categories and point values
- Creates clues for each matrix cell (harder clues = higher point values)

- Explains the game What Is the Question? to students
- Facilitates students' game play of What Is the Question?

Desired Student Responses:

- Follow the rules and procedures for What Is the Question?
- Answer clues correctly during What Is the Question?
- Exhibit increased engagement during What Is the Question?
- Treat other students respectfully during What Is the Question?

Name That Category

Teacher Actions:

- Creates a pyramid-shaped game board with categories and point values
- Explains the game Name That Category to students
- Facilitates students' game play of Name That Category

Desired Student Responses:

- Follow the rules and procedures for Name That Category
- List multiple words for each category when acting as the clue giver
- Correctly identify categories when acting as the guesser
- Exhibit increased engagement during Name That Category
- Treat other students respectfully during Name That Category

Talk a Mile a Minute

Teacher Actions:

- Creates a set of cards with categories and lists of items for each category
- Explains the game Talk a Mile a Minute to students
- Facilitates students' game play of Talk a Mile a Minute

Desired Student Responses:

- Follow the rules and procedures for Talk a Mile a Minute
- Accurately describe terms when acting as the talker
- Correctly identify terms when acting as a guesser
- Exhibit increased engagement during Talk a Mile a Minute
- Treat other students respectfully during Talk a Mile a Minute

Classroom Feud

Teacher Actions:

- Creates at least one question for each student in the class

- Explains the game Classroom Feud to students

- Facilitates students' game play of Classroom Feud

Desired Student Responses:

- Follow the rules and procedures for Classroom Feud

- Answer questions correctly during Classroom Feud

- Exhibit increased engagement during Classroom Feud

- Treat other students respectfully during Classroom Feud

Which One Doesn't Belong?

Teacher Actions:

- Creates word groups with three similar terms and one different term

- Explains the game Which One Doesn't Belong? to students

- Plays Which One Doesn't Belong? informally within presentations

Desired Student Responses:

- Follow the rules and procedures for Which One Doesn't Belong?

- Correctly identify items that do not belong in a group

- Exhibit increased engagement during Which One Doesn't Belong?

- Treat other students respectfully during Which One Doesn't Belong?

Inconsequential competition

Teacher Actions:

- Clearly delineates students' roles on their teams

- Changes team/group membership systematically so students get a chance to be on a team with most of the students in the class

- Considers giving tangible rewards to top teams

Desired Student Responses:

- Can explain what their roles are on their team

- Have been on a team at one time or another with most of the students in the class

- Can explain why the teacher gives tangible rewards to the top teams

Turning questions into games

Teacher Actions:

- Organizes students into equal-sized groups before asking a series of questions

- Provides teams with response cards

- Keeps track of teams' points and acknowledges high-scoring teams

Desired Student Responses:

- Correctly respond to teacher questions

- Exhibit increased engagement during impromptu games

- Treat other students respectfully during impromptu games

Vocabulary review games

Teacher Actions:

- Explains the purpose of playing games with vocabulary terms and concepts to students

- Asks students to play games with vocabulary terms and concepts

Desired Student Responses:

- Correctly respond to vocabulary questions

- Can explain why the teacher asks the class to play games involving vocabulary terms and concepts

- Follow the rules and procedures for vocabulary review games

Element 26: Managing response rates

Random names

Teacher Actions:

- Writes each student's name on a slip of paper or tongue depressor

- After asking a question, selects a student name at random

- Puts the selected name back in the jar or hat before the next question

Desired Student Responses:

- Are always ready to answer a question

- Attempt to answer questions even if they aren't sure of the answer

Hand signals

Teacher Actions:

- Explains hand signals to students (thumbs-up or down, flat palm, one to four fingers)

- Creates questions that students can respond to with hand signals
- Prompts students to respond to a question with hand signals

Desired Student Responses:

- Can explain what different hand signals mean
- Use hand signals to respond to teacher questions

Response cards

Teacher Actions:

- Procures response card materials (small chalk- or whiteboards, paper, note cards)
- Creates a system to pass out and collect response card materials
- Creates questions that students can respond to using response cards

Desired Student Responses:

- Take out and put away response card materials quickly and quietly
- Use response cards to respond to teacher questions

Response chaining

Teacher Actions:

- Asks students to explain why their peers' answers to questions were correct, incorrect, or partially correct
- Asks students to paraphrase their peers' answers to questions

Desired Student Responses:

- Can explain why peers' answers were correct, incorrect, or partially correct
- Paraphrase peers' answers before elaborating on them

Paired response

Teacher Actions:

- Asks students to talk in pairs about their answers to a question
- Calls on a pair to share one or both of their answers

Desired Student Responses:

- Answer questions individually before talking to a peer
- Revise their answers to questions, if necessary, after conferring with a peer

Choral response

Teacher Actions:

- Creates clear, concise statements of target information
- Asks students to say target information statements together as a group

Desired Student Responses:

- Participate in choral response
- Can explain the purpose of choral response
- Remember target information after the teacher uses choral response

Wait time

Teacher Actions:

- Pauses for at least three seconds after asking a question
- Prompts students to wait at least three seconds if a student pauses while answering a question and between student answers
- Prompts students to think about their answers during wait time

Desired Student Responses:

- Wait at least three seconds if a peer pauses while answering a question
- Wait at least three seconds between peers' answers
- Think about their answers during wait time

Elaborative interrogation

Teacher Actions:

- Asks students how they know their answer to a question is true
- Asks students to provide evidence to support their answers to questions

Desired Student Responses:

- Can explain why their answer to a question is accurate
- Can provide evidence to support their answers to questions
- Revise answers, as necessary, in response to elaborative interrogation

Multiple types of questions

Teacher Actions:

- Asks retrieval questions to prompt students to recognize or recall information

- Asks analytical questions to prompt students to determine how parts of information relate to the whole

- Asks predictive questions to help students form conjectures and hypotheses about information

- Asks interpretive questions to prompt students to generate and defend inferences

- Asks evaluative questions to prompt students to make judgments and evaluate alternatives

Desired Student Responses:

- Recognize or recall information in response to retrieval questions

- Determine how parts of information relate to the whole in response to analytical questions

- Form conjectures and hypotheses in response to predictive questions

- Generate and defend inferences in response to interpretive questions

- Make judgments and evaluate alternatives in response to evaluative questions

Element 27: Using physical movement

Stand up and stretch

Teacher Actions:

- Asks students to stand up and stretch on a regular basis

- Asks students to stand and stretch to change focus or reengage

Desired Student Responses:

- Stretch in a safe and orderly fashion when prompted by the teacher

- Stretch unobtrusively in their seats when their energy is low

- Increase their level of energy

Give one, get one

Teacher Actions:

- Asks students to locate specific information in their academic notebooks

- Asks students to stand up and share the information with a partner

- Asks students to record one piece of information from their partner's notebook in their own notebook

Desired Student Responses:

- Find specific information in their academic notebooks

- Share information from their notebooks with peers

- Record new information that they learned from a peer in their academic notebooks

Vote with your feet

Teacher Actions:

- Posts signs in various areas of the room that express different answers to a question or opinions on an issue

- Asks students to move to the area with the sign that expresses their answer or opinion

- Asks students to discuss with their peers why they think their answer or opinion is accurate

Desired Student Responses:

- Move in a safe and orderly fashion to the appropriate area of the room

- Can explain why they think their answer or opinion is accurate

Corners activities

Teacher Actions:

- Assigns a content-related question to each corner of the room

- Assigns a recorder to stay in each corner of the room and record students' comments from that corner

- Asks students to rotate through the corners and discuss the question at each location with other students there

Desired Student Responses:

- Move in a safe and orderly fashion to the appropriate corner of the room

- Accurately summarize students' comments when acting as recorder

- Discuss each question respectfully and actively with peers

Stand and be counted

Teacher Actions:

- Creates a scoring scale for students to self-assess their understanding of key ideas and concepts from a lesson

- Asks students to stand at different times based on how they scored themselves

Desired Student Responses:

- Can explain their level of understanding of key ideas and concepts from a lesson using a teacher-generated scale

- Stand up in a safe and orderly fashion when appropriate

Body representations

Teacher Actions:

- Asks students to act out important content or critical aspects of a topic with their bodies

- Asks students to explain how their body representations express the target concept

Desired Student Responses:

- Express important aspects of concepts when creating body representations

- Can explain how their body representations express the target concept

Drama-related activities

Teacher Actions:

- Identifies events or information being studied that lend themselves to dramatic representation (historical situations, current events, literary events)

- Asks students to act out events being studied

Desired Student Responses:

- Accurately portray historical situations, current events, or literary events

- Act in a safe and orderly fashion

Element 28: Maintaining a lively pace

Instructional segments

Teacher Actions:

- Explains the purpose of each different kind of instructional segment to students (that is, administrative tasks, presentation of new content, practicing and deepening understanding of key knowledge and skills, getting organized into groups, seat work, and transitions)

- Ensures that students understand what type of segment is occurring at all times

- Uses effective transitions to move from one segment to another

Desired Student Responses:

- Can describe different kinds of instructional segments

- Can say what kind of instructional segment is occurring at any time

- Transition from one segment to another quickly and efficiently

Pace modulation

Teacher Actions:

- Slows down the lesson in response to student indications that they are overwhelmed

- Speeds up the lesson in response to student indications that they are bored

Desired Student Responses:

- Let the teacher know if they are overwhelmed or bored

- Show increased engagement in response to increases or decreases in pace

The parking lot

Teacher Actions:

- Designates an area of the board as the parking lot

- Writes unresolved issues or questions in the parking lot

- Revisits parking lot issues or questions with students to find resolutions

Desired Student Responses:

- Think about or research issues or questions in the parking lot

- Find resolutions to issues or questions in the parking lot

Motivational hook/launching activity

Teacher Actions:

- Presents students with anecdotes, video or audio clips, and headlines that relate to the current content

- Tells students unusual facts or personal stories that relate to the current content

Desired Student Response:

- Exhibit increased engagement in response to anecdotes, video or audio clips, headlines, unusual facts, or personal stories related to the content

Element 29: Demonstrating intensity and enthusiasm

Direct statements about the importance of content

Teacher Actions:

- Explains to students why the content is important

- Gives students examples of how the content is used in life

Desired Student Responses:

- Can explain why the content is important to learn

- Can explain how the content relates to their lives

Explicit connections

Teacher Actions:

- Identifies connections between the content and students' interests or current events

- Explains connections between the content and students' interests or current events to students

Desired Student Responses:

- Can explain how the content is connected to their interests or to current events

- Describe the content as exciting, useful, or relevant

Nonlinguistic representations

Teacher Actions:

- Creates visual representations that illustrate connections and patterns in the content
- Presents visual representations featuring the content to students with enthusiasm and intensity

Desired Student Responses:

- Can explain visual representations of the content
- Describe the content as interesting and fascinating

Personal stories

Teacher Actions:

- Identifies content that provided important personal insights or was difficult to understand at first
- Tells students stories about his or her personal interaction with the content
- Invites students to tell stories about their personal interaction with the content

Desired Student Responses:

- Tell personal stories about the content
- Can explain how the content relates to their lives

Verbal and nonverbal signals

Teacher Actions:

- Modifies his or her volume and tone of voice, verbal emphases, and rate of speech while presenting information
- Smiles, gestures, makes eye contact with students, and pauses to build anticipation while presenting information

Desired Student Responses:

- Describe the teacher as someone who really cares about the content
- Describe the teacher as someone who gets excited about the content

Humor

Teacher Actions:

- Presents funny headlines or silly quotes related to the content to students
- Uses self-directed humor or refers to a class symbol for humor while presenting information

Desired Student Responses:

- Laugh or smile in response to the teacher's use of humor

- Exhibit increased engagement in response to headlines or silly quotes related to the content

- Describe the teacher as appropriate in his or her use of humor

- Refer to class jokes or symbols for humor while talking about the content

Quotations

Teacher Actions:

- Selects quotations that relate to the content being presented

- Incorporates content-related quotations into presentations of information

Desired Student Responses:

- Exhibit increased engagement in response to quotations related to the content

- Bring quotations to class that are related to the content

Movie and film clips

Teacher Actions:

- Selects movie and film clips that relate to the content being presented

- Incorporates content-related movie and film clips into presentations of information

Desired Student Responses:

- Can explain how a movie or film clip made the content more interesting and engaging

- Refer to movie or film clips shown by the teacher when describing the content

Element 30: Using friendly controversy

Friendly controversy

Teacher Actions:

- Creates guidelines for friendly controversy activities to prevent negativity

- Asks students to express their opinions about topics and issues

- Asks students to defend their opinions about topics and issues

Desired Student Responses:

- Follow guidelines for friendly controversy activities

- Express and defend their opinions about topics during friendly controversy activities

- Stay positive and respectful during friendly controversy activities

Class vote

Teacher Actions:

- Asks students to vote about a topic or issue

- Asks students to discuss the merits of various perspectives about a topic or issue

- Incorporates movement by having students move to a specific area of the room based on how they voted

Desired Student Responses:

- Can explain why they voted for or against a topic or issue

- Can describe alternative perspectives from their own about a topic or issue

Seminars

Teacher Actions:

- Asks students to review a text, video, or other resource that presents an opinion or perspective about a topic or issue

- Organizes students in groups of three to five

- Designates roles in each group

- Asks each group to discuss the opinions or perspectives presented in the text, video, or other resource

Desired Student Responses:

- Can explain the expectations for their roles in a seminar group

- Fulfill the expectations for their roles in a seminar group

- Respectfully discuss the opinions and perspectives presented in a text, video, or other resource

Expert opinions

Teacher Actions:

- Asks students to research experts' opinions about a topic or issue

- Discusses the merits and validity of various perspectives about a topic or issue

Desired Student Responses:

- Accurately summarize an expert's opinion about a topic or issue

- Can explain the strengths and weaknesses of an expert's opinion

Opposite point of view

Teacher Actions:

- Asks students to express their opinions about a topic or issue

- Asks students to identify and defend the opposite opinion from their own on a topic or issue

Desired Student Responses:

- Express their opinions about topics and issues

- Can defend the opposite opinion from their own on a topic or issue

Diagramming perspectives

Teacher Actions:

- Asks students to diagram two or three perspectives on a Venn diagram

- Discusses areas of congruence and disagreement

Desired Student Responses:

- Diagram two or three perspectives on a Venn diagram

- Can describe areas of congruence or disagreement between perspectives

Lincoln-Douglas debate

Teacher Actions:

- Explains the parts of a Lincoln-Douglas debate to students (opening argument, cross-examination, rebuttal)

- Separates students into two teams and asks one team to argue for a policy or issue and the other to argue against the policy or issue

- Debriefs with students after the debate

Desired Student Responses:

- Can describe the different parts of a Lincoln-Douglas debate

- Follow the rules and procedures for a Lincoln-Douglas debate

- Prepare arguments for or against an issue

- Participate fully and respectfully in Lincoln-Douglas debates

Town hall meeting (Hess, 2009)

Teacher Actions:

- Identifies various perspectives on an issue and the roles of people who might hold them

- Assigns specific roles for students to assume during the town hall meeting

- Mediates a discussion where students stay in character for their assigned role

- Debriefs with students after the town hall meeting

Desired Student Responses:

- Defend the perspective of their assigned role during a town hall meeting

- Stay in character for their roles

- Can explain how their personal perspective differs from their role in a town hall meeting

Legal model (Hess, 2009)

Teacher Actions:

- Selects a Supreme Court decision that relates to the content

- Asks students to review the opinions and arguments in the case and create an outline of the key ideas of each justice about the case

- Leads a discussion about the case and asks questions to help students focus on different aspects of the case

- Helps students articulate their personal opinions and arguments about the case

- Debriefs with students after the legal model discussion

Desired Student Responses:

- Create tickets that summarize the key ideas of each justice in a Supreme Court case

- Articulate their personal opinions and arguments about a case

- Can explain how the legal model helped them look at an issue or topic from different perspectives

Element 31: Providing opportunities for students to talk about themselves

Interest surveys

Teacher Actions:

- Creates survey questions that elicit students' interests and goals

- Encourages students to answer survey questions thoroughly and completely

- Evaluates survey responses to identify students' interests and goals

Desired Student Responses:

- Respond to survey questions honestly and in detail

- Describe the teacher as someone who is interested in them

Student learning profiles

Teacher Actions:

- Creates learning profile questions that elicit students' learning styles and preferences

- Encourages students to think about how they learn best while completing learning profiles

- Evaluates learning profile responses to identify students' learning styles and preferences

Desired Student Responses:

- Respond to profile questions honestly and in detail

- Can explain how they prefer to learn and how they learn best

Life connections

Teacher Actions:

- Schedules breaks during instruction for students to make connections between the content and their experiences and interests

- Asks students to share and explain connections between the content and their lives

- Takes notes about students' connections to the content

Desired Student Responses:

- Can explain how the content is connected to their experiences and interests

- Describe the content as relevant and interesting

Informal linkages during class discussion

Teacher Actions:

- Compiles a list of students' interests

- Identifies content that relates to students' interests

- Highlights connections and refers to students' interests while presenting information

Desired Student Responses:

- Describe the teacher as someone who knows what they are interested in

- Elaborate on their interests and connect them to the content when prompted by the teacher

Element 32: Presenting unusual or intriguing information

Teacher-presented information

Teacher Actions:

- Identifies unusual or intriguing facts or information related to the content

- Presents content-related unusual or intriguing facts during lessons to increase students' engagement with the content

- Identifies unusual or intriguing facts or information unrelated to the content

- Presents non-content-related unusual or intriguing facts at the beginning of class to capture students' attention

Desired Student Responses:

- Exhibit increased attention and engagement in response to unusual or intriguing facts or information

- Refer to unusual facts or information when talking about the content

Webquests

Teacher Actions:

- Creates guidelines to help students explore the Internet productively

- Asks students to find interesting content-related facts and information on the Internet

Desired Student Responses:

- Find interesting content-related facts and information on the Internet

- Follow guidelines for exploring the Internet

One-minute headlines

Teacher Actions:

- Asks students to bring unusual factual information about a topic to class

- Asks different students to briefly share their unusual information

Desired Student Responses:

- Bring unusual factual information about a topic to class

- Share their unusual information succinctly

Believe it or not

Teacher Actions:

- Asks students to bring little-known or unusual information about the content to class

- Compiles students' contributions from year to year

- Refers to facts found by previous students while presenting content

Desired Student Responses:

- Bring little-known or unusual information about the content to class

- Describe the teacher as someone who loves to learn about the content

History files

Teacher Actions:

- Identifies different historical perspectives about the content being studied
- Asks students to research and report on different historical perspectives on content
- Asks students to compare different historical perspectives about content

Desired Student Responses:

- Report about a historical perspective of the content
- Compare different historical perspectives of the content
- Can describe different historical perspectives of the content

Guest speakers and firsthand consultants

Teacher Actions:

- Invites people who use the content in their lives and professions to share their experiences with students
- Helps students prepare questions to ask guest speakers and firsthand consultants

Desired Student Responses:

- Can describe how the content is used in the real world
- Ask relevant questions of guest speakers and firsthand consultants

As indicated, the strategies and their related teacher actions for this design question focus on engaging students in the classroom using games, questioning, physical movement, pacing, and controversy. Desired student responses include exhibiting increased engagement in response to teacher behaviors and describing the teacher as someone who is excited about the content.

What Will I Do to Recognize and Acknowledge Adherence or Lack of Adherence to Rules and Procedures?

This design question includes elements 33 through 35. Here we present teacher actions and desired student responses for each of the strategies for these elements.

Element 33: Demonstrating withitness

Being proactive

Teacher Actions:

- Reviews specific students who might have trouble behaving appropriately in class
- Is aware of incidents from outside of class that could affect student behavior in class

- Talks to potentially disruptive students before class
- Arranges cues to signal misbehavior to potentially disruptive students

Desired Student Responses:

- Respond to teacher cues by correcting inappropriate behavior
- Tell the teacher if they are having a hard day

Occupying the whole room physically and visually

Teacher Actions:

- Visually scans the classroom while teaching to look for potential problems
- Makes eye contact with each student on a regular basis
- Spends time in each quadrant of the room on a regular basis

Desired Student Response:

- Cease disruptive behavior in response to teacher eye contact or proximity

Noticing potential problems

Teacher Actions:

- Looks for signals of potential problems (whispering, smiling/giggling, unusual noises)
- Investigates signals of potential problems to determine if there is a real problem

Desired Student Responses:

- Describe the teacher as aware of their behavior
- Encourage peers who are causing a problem to stop their behavior

Series of graduated actions

Teacher Actions:

- Makes eye contact with misbehaving students
- Moves in the direction of misbehaving students
- Uses nonverbal cues to let misbehaving students know their conduct is inappropriate
- Talks to misbehaving students, inviting them to rejoin the class
- Offers misbehaving students a choice between consequences and appropriate behavior

Desired Student Responses:

- Cease disruptive behavior in response to teacher eye contact, proximity, cues, or confrontation
- Reengage in class activities in response to teacher requests

Element 34: Applying consequences for lack of adherence to rules and procedures

Verbal cues

Teacher Actions:

- Says a misbehaving student's name to call attention to his or her misbehavior
- Tells a misbehaving student what rule or procedure he or she is violating
- Asks a misbehaving student questions that prompt him or her to stop the inappropriate behavior

Desired Student Responses:

- Cease inappropriate behavior in response to the teacher saying their name, reminding them of a rule or procedure, or asking them to stop
- Can explain the impact of their behavior on learning

Pregnant pause

Teacher Actions:

- Stops teaching in response to disruptive behavior
- Directs the attention in the room toward the misbehaving student
- Confronts the misbehaving student in front of the class if necessary

Desired Student Response:

- Cease inappropriate behavior in response to a pregnant pause or direct teacher confrontation

Nonverbal cues

Teacher Actions:

- Makes eye contact with misbehaving students
- Moves close to misbehaving students
- Uses gestures to signal that a student's behavior is inappropriate

Desired Student Response:

- Cease inappropriate behavior in response to teacher eye contact, proximity, or gestures

Time-out

Teacher Actions:

- Designates in-class and outside-class time-out locations
- Ensures that outside-class time-out locations are supervised
- Asks misbehaving students to take an in-class time-out

- Asks students to go to outside-class time-out if they continue to misbehave in in-class time-out

- Asks students in outside-class time-out to create a plan to change their behavior when they return to class

Desired Student Responses:

- Cease inappropriate behavior in response to teacher warnings

- Go to the time-out location when asked to

- Behave appropriately while in time-out

- Create a plan to change their behavior when returning to class

Overcorrection

Teacher Actions:

- Identifies ways that students who have behaved destructively can improve a situation beyond its original state

- Explains to a student why he or she is expected to overcompensate for destructive behavior

- Monitors students' work on overcorrection tasks to prevent further destructive behavior

Desired Student Responses:

- Improve situations in which they have behaved destructively beyond their original state

- Can explain what they did wrong and why they are expected to compensate for misbehavior

Interdependent group contingency

Teacher Actions:

- Explains the behavioral standard that the whole class must meet to earn positive consequences

- Selects an appropriate way to track whole-class behavior (marble jar, tally marks, countdown)

Desired Student Responses:

- Can explain why the whole class received or did not receive positive consequences

- Treat other students respectfully regardless of whether or not positive consequences were earned

Home contingency

Teacher Actions:

- Identifies students who need extra support to behave appropriately in class

- Contacts the student's parents/guardians to explain the problematic behavior and arrange a meeting

- Helps the student identify positive and negative consequences for his or her school and home behavior

- Implements positive and negative consequences for the student

- Communicates with parents/guardians about the student's daily behavior

Desired Student Responses:

- Improve their behavior in response to the teacher's communication with parents/guardians

- Can explain the expected behaviors for class and home and the consequences for not adhering to those behaviors

Planning for high-intensity situations

Teacher Actions:

- Determines the level of crisis that an out-of-control student represents

- Steps back from a situation involving an out-of-control student and calms down

- Actively listens to an out-of-control student and paraphrases what he or she is saying

- Repeats a simple verbal request to the out-of-control student

Desired Student Responses:

- Calm down in response to the teacher's actions

- Comply with teacher requests in high-intensity situations

Overall disciplinary plan

Teacher Actions:

- Creates guidelines for developing relationships with students

- Identifies specific actions to use to demonstrate withitness

- Articulates positive and negative consequences for behavior

- Creates a plan to deal with high-intensity situations

Desired Student Response:

- Describe the teacher as in control of the classroom, interested in them, fair, and calm

Element 35: Acknowledging adherence to rules and procedures

Verbal affirmations

Teacher Actions:

- Says "thank you," "good job," or "very good" to students when they follow rules and procedures

- Explains what students did that constituted following rules and procedures
- Contrasts a student's current positive behavior with past inappropriate behavior

Desired Student Responses:

- Describe the teacher as someone who recognizes and appreciates good behavior
- Can explain how their behavior contributed to the proper functioning of the classroom

Nonverbal affirmations

Teacher Actions:

- Gives students a smile, wink, nod, or other positive gesture to recognize their adherence to a rule or procedure
- Gives students a pat on the shoulder or back to recognize their adherence to a rule or procedure

Desired Student Responses:

- Adhere to the rules more often in response to the teacher's affirmations
- Describe the teacher as someone who appreciates good behavior

Tangible recognition

Teacher Actions:

- Identifies privileges, activities, or items that are appropriate rewards for positive behavior
- Explains to students that tangible recognition is not meant to be a bribe or coercive device

Desired Student Responses:

- Can explain the purpose of tangible recognition
- Adhere to the rules more often in response to tangible recognition

Token economies

Teacher Actions:

- Gives students tokens to recognize positive behavior
- Creates a system that allows students to exchange their tokens for privileges, activities, or items

Desired Student Responses:

- Can explain the purpose of token economies
- Adhere to the rules more often when token economies are in place

Daily recognition forms

Teacher Actions:

- Identifies expectations for daily classroom behavior and assigns point values to each expectation

- Creates a tracking sheet for daily classroom behavior points

- Adjusts students' point totals based on their classroom behavior

- Records students' totals at the end of each class period

- Designates privileges, activities, or items that students with certain point totals can earn

Desired Student Responses:

- Set point goals for their daily behavior

- Adhere to the rules more often when daily recognition forms are used

Color-coded behavior

Teacher Actions:

- Creates red, yellow, and green cards or a poster with red, yellow, and green levels for each student

- Starts each student on green at the beginning of every day

- Adjusts students' colors in accordance with their behavior

- Reinstates students who correct inappropriate behavior to yellow or green

Desired Student Responses:

- Can explain why their color was adjusted

- Adjust their behavior to have a better color reinstated

Certificates

Teacher Actions:

- Creates certificates that can be personalized with a student's name and a description of his or her positive behavior

- Creates preprinted certificates for specific desired positive behaviors

- Gives certificates to students who display desired positive behaviors

Desired Student Responses:

- Can explain what they did to earn a certificate

- Describe the teacher as someone who recognizes and appreciates good behavior

Phone calls, emails, and notes

Teacher Actions:

- Calls students' parents/guardians or sends notes to recognize students' positive behavior

- Specifies what students did that constituted positive behavior and how it contributed to the class's learning

Desired Student Responses:

- Can explain what they did that prompted the teacher to communicate with parents/guardians

- Can explain how their behavior contributed to the proper functioning of the classroom

As indicated, the strategies and their related teacher actions for this design question focus on being aware of what is going on in the classroom and applying appropriate positive or negative consequences for students' behavior. Desired student responses include understanding that the teacher is aware of their conduct and adjusting their behavior favorably in response to positive or negative consequences.

What Will I Do to Establish and Maintain Effective Relationships With Students?

This design question includes elements 36 through 38. Here we present teacher actions and desired student responses for each of the strategies for these elements.

Element 36: Understanding students' interests and backgrounds

Student background surveys

Teacher Actions:

- Creates survey questions that elicit information about students' backgrounds, interests, and goals

- Encourages students to answer survey questions thoroughly and completely

- Evaluates survey responses to identify students' backgrounds, interests, and goals

Desired Student Responses:

- Respond to survey questions honestly and in detail

- Describe the teacher as someone who is interested in them

Opinion questionnaires

Teacher Actions:

- Creates questions that prompt students to share their perspectives on classroom topics

- Discusses students' opinions about classroom topics

- Incorporates students' opinions into classroom activities

Desired Student Responses:

- Respond to questions honestly and in detail

- Can explain the reasons for their opinions

Individual teacher-student conferences

Teacher Actions:

- Schedules individual teacher-student conferences

- Summarizes what he or she already knows about a student prior to his or her conference

- Prepares questions that probe more deeply into a student's interests, perspectives, and experiences

Desired Student Responses:

- Respond to teacher questions honestly and in detail

- Describe the teacher as someone who is interested in them

Parent-teacher conferences

Teacher Actions:

- Summarizes what is already known about a student prior to meeting with his or her parents

- Prepares questions that elicit critical details about students' recent life experiences in their families (births, deaths, marriages, divorces, job changes, vacations, relocations)

Desired Student Responses:

- Tell the teacher about important events in their lives

- Describe the relationship between their parents/guardians and teacher as good

School newspaper, newsletter, or bulletin

Teacher Actions:

- Identifies school publications that contain information about students' involvement in athletic events, clubs, performances, or community activities

- Schedules time to read selected school publications each week

- Notes students' achievements and upcoming events

Desired Student Responses:

- Describe the teacher as someone who knows about their activities

- Tell the teacher about activities they are involved in

Informal class interviews

Teacher Actions:

- Prepares questions that prompt students to describe what is happening in their lives

- Prepares questions that prompt students to describe what students are talking about that teachers should be aware of

Desired Student Responses:

- Share information about important student events and topics with the teacher

- Describe the teacher as someone who understands students

Investigating student culture

Teacher Actions:

- Becomes familiar with popular recording artists and their works

- Notices popular places where students like to gather

- Takes note of local events that are significant to students

- Is aware of rivalries between different groups of students

- Notices popular terms and phrases students use

Desired Student Responses:

- Share information about student culture with the teacher

- Describe the teacher as someone who understands students

Autobiographical metaphors and analogies

Teacher Actions:

- Asks students to compare their lives to the content being studied

- Asks students to express comparisons between their lives and the content as metaphors

- Asks students to identify relationships between academic content and their lives

- Asks students to express relationships between their lives and the content as analogies

Desired Student Responses:

- Create metaphors that express comparisons between the content and their lives

- Create analogies that express relationships between the content and their lives

Six-word autobiographies

Teacher Actions:

- Creates or identifies examples of effective six-word autobiographies and shares them with students

- Asks students to create an autobiography in six words

- Asks students to create posters for their six-word autobiographies

- Discusses students' six-word autobiographies with the class

Desired Student Responses:

- Can explain why they chose specific words or phrases for their autobiographies

- Create posters for their autobiographies that communicate multiple messages about themselves (conveyed through literal meaning, visual design [font, color, formatting], and inferred or implied meanings)

Independent investigations

Teacher Actions:

- Helps students identify a topic that interests them

- Asks students to investigate their topic of interest and report back to the class

- Discusses students' findings with the class

Desired Student Responses:

- Identify topics that interest them for investigation

- Present their research to the class in an interesting way

- Ask questions about other students' independent investigations

Quotes

Teacher Actions:

- Finds examples of quotes that express different personality traits or interests and shares them with students

- Asks students to find quotes that describe their personalities and interests

- Discusses student-presented quotes with the class

Desired Student Responses:

- Share quotes that are personally relevant

- Can explain why they think specific quotes represent their personalities or interests

Commenting on student achievements or areas of importance

Teacher Actions:

- Notices individual students' accomplishments in school, outside of school, and in their families

- Makes comments to students about their accomplishments

- Notices events that are important to individual students in school, outside of school, and in their families

- Makes comments to students about important events in their lives

Desired Student Responses:

- Share information about achievements and interests with the teacher

- Describe the teacher as someone who knows how they are doing

Lineups

Teacher Actions:

- Creates questions that elicit students' likes, dislikes, and preferences

- Asks students to line up or sit in groups according to their likes, dislikes, and preferences

Desired Student Responses:

- Treat other students respectfully during lineups

- Describe the teacher as someone who wants to know them better

Individual student learning goals

Teacher Actions:

- Identifies students' personal interests that relate to the class's learning goal

- Helps students articulate and write down their individual learning goals

- Tracks students' progress on individual learning goals

Desired Student Responses:

- Identify personally important individual learning goals

- Can explain what they have already done and still need to do to accomplish individual learning goals

- Track their progress on individual learning goals

Element 37: Using verbal and nonverbal behaviors that indicate affection for students

Greeting students at the classroom door

Teacher Actions:

- Learns all students' names
- Stands at the door as students enter
- Greets each student with his or her name
- Asks students how they are doing or makes a positive comment about their achievements

Desired Student Responses:

- Describe the teacher as someone who is glad to see them
- Smile or express pleasure in response to the teacher's greeting

Informal conferences

Teacher Actions:

- Schedules time to talk informally with students (between classes, before or after school, in the lunchroom)
- Gives compliments to students, mentions their successes, or passes on positive comments from other teachers about students
- Asks students for their opinions about classroom topics

Desired Student Responses:

- Describe the teacher as someone who cares about their opinions
- Respond to teacher questions honestly and in detail

Attending after-school functions

Teacher Actions:

- Identifies students who may feel alienated or disengaged in class
- Identifies after-school activities that alienated or disengaged students are involved in
- Tells students that he or she will be attending their event
- Connects with the student at the event

Desired Student Responses:

- Invite the teacher to after-school functions
- Are pleased to see the teacher at their after-school functions
- Are more engaged in class after the teacher attends their after-school functions

Greeting students by name outside of school

Teacher Actions:

- Learns all students' names

- Greets students when he or she sees them outside of school (grocery store, movie theater, shopping mall)

Desired Student Responses:

- Respond to the teacher when greeted outside of school

- Describe the teacher as someone who likes seeing them

Giving students special responsibilities or leadership roles in the classroom

Teacher Actions:

- Identifies the level of responsibility a student can handle

- Identifies roles or classroom responsibilities that can be delegated to students

- Asks students to assume roles or classroom responsibilities they can be successful with

- Monitors students' levels of performance and satisfaction with their roles and responsibilities

Desired Student Responses:

- Describe the teacher as someone who trusts them

- Fulfill their roles or responsibilities successfully

Scheduled interaction

Teacher Actions:

- Selects a few students each day with whom to interact intentionally

- Creates a schedule to ensure intentional interaction with each student over a specific period of time

- Seeks out and talks to selected students in the lunchroom, between classes, or before or after school

Desired Student Responses:

- Describe the teacher as someone who likes to talk to them

- Can remember a recent interaction with the teacher outside normal class time

Photo bulletin board

Teacher Actions:

- Creates a bulletin board with a photo of each student

- Asks students to post information about themselves by their picture (thoughts, goals, interests)

- Changes photos and information periodically

Desired Student Responses:

- Post information about themselves by their pictures

- Read other students' comments

Physical behaviors

Teacher Actions:

- Smiles and makes eye contact with students while talking or listening to them

- Gives students hugs, high fives, or pats on the back

- Puts a hand on a student's shoulder or stands close enough to communicate interest (without invading his or her personal space) while talking or listening to him or her

Desired Student Responses:

- Maintain eye contact while talking to the teacher

- Feel comfortable while talking to the teacher

- Describe the teacher as someone who cares about them

Humor

Teacher Actions:

- Jokes or banters playfully with students

- Uses self-directed humor or historical or popular sayings when talking to students or teaching

- Incorporates cartoons, jokes, puns, and plays on words into instruction

Desired Student Responses:

- Laugh or smile in response to the teacher's use of humor

- Describe the teacher as appropriate in his or her use of humor

- Maintain a respectful attitude toward the teacher, themselves, and other students when engaging in playful banter or jokes

Element 38: Displaying objectivity and control

Self-reflection

Teacher Actions:

- Reflects daily on how consistently positive and negative consequences were enforced in the classroom

- Makes plans to resolve inconsistency in enforcing consequences in the classroom
- Progressively increases expectations for students to regulate their own behavior

Desired Student Responses:

- Describe the teacher as fair
- Regulate their own behavior more frequently

Self-monitoring

Teacher Actions:

- Mentally reviews all students before class to identify those who might cause problems
- Identifies specific negative thoughts and feelings toward potentially problematic students
- Identifies past events that may have caused negative feelings toward specific students
- Reframes negative beliefs about students by identifying reasons for students' past behavior that do not imply disrespect or aggression toward the teacher

Desired Student Responses:

- Describe the teacher as someone who respects all students
- Describe the teacher as someone who doesn't hold grudges

Identifying emotional triggers

Teacher Actions:

- Identifies events or times in his or her personal life that may make it difficult to maintain emotional objectivity
- Takes specific steps to counteract emotional triggers and support emotional objectivity

Desired Student Responses:

- Describe the teacher as in control of his or her emotions
- Describe the teacher as someone who doesn't let "bad days" affect him or her

Self-care

Teacher Actions:

- Spends time in places (like a comfortable chair in a quiet room) and engaged in activities (like deep breathing exercises) that are calming and relaxing
- Watches or reads humorous movies and books to maintain a healthy sense of humor about negative events
- Rewards himself or herself after particularly difficult days or events

Desired Student Responses:

- Describe the teacher as someone who likes teaching

- Describe the teacher as a happy person

Assertiveness

Teacher Actions:

- Identifies his or her legitimate rights

- Uses communication strategies that make it difficult for others to ignore or circumvent his or her legitimate rights

Desired Student Responses:

- Can describe the teacher's and their own legitimate rights

- Respect the rights of the teacher and other students in the classroom

Maintaining a cool exterior

Teacher Actions:

- Uses tone of voice and facial expressions that communicate respect but not emotion

- Uses body language that expresses interest but not aggression

- Listens to legitimate explanations but does not argue with students or allow them to blame others for their actions

- Describes students' behavior, not their perceived motives

Desired Student Responses:

- Describe the teacher as calm and collected

- Calm down in response to the teacher's calm exterior

- Can explain their behavior without arguing, denying, or blaming others for that behavior

Active listening and speaking

Teacher Actions:

- Listens to students without agreeing or disagreeing

- Maintains a neutral facial expression and body language while listening to students

- Paraphrases what students have said when they stop speaking and prompts them to say more

- Makes corrections to paraphrases based on students' feedback

Desired Student Responses:

- Describe the teacher as someone who listens to and understands students

- Feel at ease talking to the teacher

- Provide corrections in response to teacher summaries

Communication styles

Teacher Actions:

- Uses an assertive communication style with students
- Teaches students how to communicate assertively
- Helps students respond to others who may not communicate assertively

Desired Student Responses:

- Communicate assertively with the teacher and other students
- Describe the teacher as a good communicator

Unique student needs

Teacher Actions:

- Responds appropriately to students with various unique needs
- Helps students with unique needs recognize and moderate their behavior to be more successful in the classroom
- Helps students successfully interact with others who may have unique needs

Desired Student Responses:

- Describe the teacher as someone who understands that students may have different needs
- Interact more successfully with the teacher and other students over time

As indicated, the strategies and their related teacher actions for this design question focus on understanding students' backgrounds and initiating and maintaining positive relationships with them. Desired student responses include feeling safe and welcome in the classroom and describing the teacher as someone who likes them and is interested in them and their interests.

What Will I Do to Communicate High Expectations for All Students?

This design question includes elements 39 through 41. Here we present teacher actions and desired student responses for each of the strategies for these elements.

Element 39: Demonstrating value and respect for low-expectancy students

Identifying expectation levels for all students

Teacher Actions:

- Anticipates how each student would score on a comprehensive assessment covering the more difficult content addressed in class
- Writes down his or her expectation level for each student: high, medium, or low

Desired Student Responses:

- Describe the teacher as someone who expects all students to achieve at high levels
- Treat other students with respect

Identifying differential treatment of low-expectancy students

Teacher Actions:

- Tracks his or her behavior toward each student in the class for several days
- Identifies differences in affective tone or quality of interaction toward specific students
- Examines whether he or she has generalized low expectations for students based on their ethnicity, appearance, speech patterns, or socioeconomic status
- Counteracts differential treatment of students by suppressing biased patterns of thought and using a consistent affective tone and quality of interaction toward all students

Desired Student Responses:

- Describe the teacher as someone who treats all students as if they are able to achieve at high levels
- Treat other students with respect

Nonverbal and verbal indicators of respect and value

Teacher Actions:

- Smiles and makes eye contact when listening and talking to low-expectancy students
- Uses body language and physical contact that communicate value and respect for low-expectancy students
- Jokes and banters playfully with low-expectancy students

Desired Student Responses:

- Increase their personal expectations in response to the teacher's behavior
- Describe the teacher as someone who believes that all students can achieve at high levels

Element 40: Asking questions of low-expectancy students

Question levels

Teacher Actions:

- Creates complex questions that require students to analyze information, evaluate conclusions, or make inferences
- Asks low-expectancy students to answer complex questions frequently
- Gives low-expectancy students encouragement and helps them answer complex questions

Desired Student Responses:

- Analyze information, evaluate conclusions, or make inferences in response to teacher questions

- Try to answer complex questions, even if they are unsure of the answers

- Can explain their answers to questions

Response opportunities

Teacher Actions:

- Asks low-expectancy students to answer questions with the same frequency used for high-expectancy students

- Uses strategies for managing response rates

Desired Student Responses:

- Answer questions regularly, regardless of personal expectations

- Mentally prepare answers to all teacher questions

- Describe the teacher as someone who expects everyone to participate

Follow-up questioning

Teacher Actions:

- Restates a question if a student is having trouble answering

- Asks students to collaborate if a student is having trouble answering a question

- Gives a student hints or cues if he or she is having trouble answering a question

- Lets a student opt out temporarily if he or she is having trouble answering a question

Desired Student Responses:

- Answer questions correctly in response to restatement of the question, collaboration, or teacher hints and cues

- Answer questions correctly at a later time if they opt out temporarily

Evidence and support for student answers

Teacher Actions:

- Asks all students to give evidence and support for their answers

- Asks all students to provide grounds and backing for their claims

- Asks all students to explain inferences they made to answer a question

Desired Student Responses:

- Give evidence and support for answers regardless of their personal expectations

- Provide grounds and backing for claims regardless of their personal expectations
- Explain inferences regardless of their personal expectations

Encouragement

Teacher Actions:

- Attributes ideas and comments to the student who offered them
- Thanks students when they ask or answer questions (even if incorrectly)
- Acknowledges any correct portions of student responses
- Explains how incorrect responses can be altered to make them correct
- Identifies the question that an incorrect response answered

Desired Student Responses:

- Describe the teacher as someone who appreciates students' answers
- Can explain what part of their answers were correct and incorrect
- Revise answers to be fully correct

Wait time

Teacher Actions:

- Pauses for at least three seconds after asking a question
- Prompts students to wait at least three seconds if a student pauses while answering a question and between student answers
- Prompts students to think about their answers during wait time

Desired Student Responses:

- Wait at least three seconds if a peer pauses while answering a question
- Wait at least three seconds between peers' answers
- Think about their answers during wait time

Tracking responses

Teacher Actions:

- Calls on students randomly (rather than on students who raise their hands)
- Tracks which students have already answered or been asked questions
- Focuses on specific students to ensure they are asked to respond to questions

Desired Student Responses:

- Answer teacher questions regularly

- Mentally prepare answers for all teacher questions

- Describe the teacher as someone who makes sure that everyone answers questions

Avoiding inappropriate reactions

Teacher Actions:

- Never tells a student they should have known the answer to a question

- Never ignores a student's response to a question

- Never makes subjective comments about students' incorrect answers

- Never allows other students to make negative comments about answers to questions

Desired Student Responses:

- Act respectfully toward peers who answer questions incorrectly

- Attempt to answer questions even if they are unsure of the answer

- Describe the teacher as someone who will help students find the right answer

Element 41: Probing incorrect answers with low-expectancy students

Using an appropriate response process

Teacher Actions:

- Thanks each student for his or her response

- Identifies correct and incorrect portions of students' responses

- Emphasizes correct portions of answers and identifies the question that an incorrect portion would have answered

- Helps students answer questions correctly

Desired Student Responses:

- Describe the teacher as someone who appreciates students' responses

- Can explain which parts of their answers were correct and incorrect

- Describe the teacher as someone who will help students answer questions

Letting students "off the hook" temporarily

Teacher Actions:

- Lets students pass temporarily if they become embarrassed or flustered while answering a question

- Follows up at a later time with students who passed

- Uses different questions or rephrases the original question during follow-up

Desired Student Responses:

- Correctly respond at a later time to questions that they temporarily opted out of

- Correctly answer alternative or rephrased questions

- Describe the teacher as someone who won't embarrass students

Answer revision

Teacher Actions:

- Asks a student probing questions to help him or her realize the answer given is not defensible

- Helps a student revise his or her answer to be defensible

Desired Student Responses:

- Recognize when their answers are not defensible

- Revise indefensible answers to include valid evidence and support

Think-pair-share (Lyman, 2006)

Teacher Actions:

- Asks students to answer a question individually

- Asks students to share their answers with a partner and revise them if necessary

- Asks students to share their answer or their partner's answer with the class

Desired Student Responses:

- Answer questions individually before conferring with a partner

- Revise answers, if necessary, after conferring with a partner

As indicated, the strategies and their related teacher actions for this design question focus on treating low-expectancy students in the same way that high-expectancy students are treated. Desired student responses include low-expectancy students achieving at higher levels and responding to questions with more confidence and accuracy.

To illustrate how a coach can facilitate a teacher's move from Beginning (1) to Developing (2) and from Developing (2) to Applying (3) for one of the elements from lesson segments enacted on the spot, consider the following vignette. The teacher is working on *series of graduated actions*, a strategy associated with element 33—demonstrating withitness. The coach helps the teacher move from Beginning (1) to Developing (2) by assisting her in identifying a part of the strategy she is omitting. He positively reinforces the parts of the strategy that she *is* performing correctly, and observes a lesson to verify that she is at the Developing (2) level for the strategy. At that point, the coach helps the teacher move to the Applying (3) level by prompting her to begin monitoring her students' responses to the strategy. Finally, he helps her identify adjustments she needs to make in response to what she observes her students doing.

Mrs. Warner has been using a series of graduated actions to address behavior problems in her classroom for about a week. She video recorded a few lessons, and she and her coach, Fernando, are reviewing them together. As they watch, Fernando notices that she is omitting part of the strategy. He gives Mrs. Warner a list of the teacher actions associated with the strategy and asks her to figure out which one she is omitting.

After watching a few minutes of video, she says, "I'm not moving to where they are."

"That's right," affirms Fernando, "and that's probably one reason why the strategy isn't working very well. I see you making eye contact, and I see you using nonverbal cues, but they're not as effective since you're doing those things from the front of the room."

Mrs. Warner corrects that part of the strategy, and Fernando observes her class to verify that she is at the Developing (2) level for the strategy. Then he prompts her to begin monitoring her students' responses. After another week, they meet to review video together again.

Mrs. Warner says, "My students have stopped misbehaving, but I don't feel like they're reengaging in the class's activity after they stop being disruptive."

"What could you do differently to help them reengage?" asks Fernando.

"Well, I've been so focused on getting them to not misbehave that I haven't really been inviting them to rejoin the class's activity. I'd like to do a better job of that and see if it makes a difference," she says.

Mrs. Warner makes the adjustment in her use of the strategy and reports at their next session that more of her students are rejoining the class after they stop misbehaving.

Summary

This chapter provided a detailed explanation of how a coach can help a teacher move from the Beginning (1) level to the Developing (2) level and from the Developing (2) level to the Applying (3) level. To move from Beginning (1) to Developing (2), the coach must help the teacher correct mistakes and identify parts of strategies that he or she may be omitting. To move from Developing (2) to Applying (3), the coach must help the teacher monitor a strategy's effect on students and adjust instruction to achieve desired student responses and outcomes. There are several ways that a coach can help a teacher learn to do such monitoring, including observation, video recordings, and bug-in-ear technology. Finally, this chapter presented teacher actions and desired student responses for specific strategies associated with each of the forty-one elements of *The Art and Science of Teaching* (Marzano, 2007) model.

Chapter 4: Comprehension Questions

1. What must a teacher do to grow from the Beginning (1) level to the Developing (2) level? As described in chapter 2 and in this chapter, what can a coach do to support that growth?

2. What must a teacher do to grow from the Developing (2) level to the Applying (3) level? As described in chapter 2 and in this chapter, what can a coach do to support that growth?

Role-Play

With a partner, role-play a situation (like those in the vignettes) where a teacher and coach are meeting to work on a specific strategy. If you are playing the teacher, choose a strategy. If you are playing the coach, guide the teacher from the Beginning (1) level to the Developing (2) level and from the Developing (2) level to the Applying (3) level for the strategy.

After role-playing once, switch roles and repeat the process. The "teacher" should select a different strategy than the one used the first time.

Chapter 5

APPLYING (3) TO INNOVATING (4)

As described in chapter 4, a teacher at the Applying (3) level is effectively using a strategy and monitoring the effect of the strategy on students. The Applying (3) level is the minimum goal that teachers should aim to achieve when working on their growth-goal areas. However, a coach can guide a teacher beyond the Applying (3) level to the Innovating (4) level by helping him or her integrate several strategies to create a macrostrategy or adapt strategies for unique student needs and situations.

Integrate Several Strategies to Create a Macrostrategy

A macrostrategy is a set of instructional strategies used together for a specific purpose. For example, reciprocal teaching (Palincsar & Brown, 1984) is a macrostrategy that combines summarizing, questioning, clarifying, and predicting for the purpose of helping students process content. The strategies used in a macrostrategy typically have research supporting their use individually and in combination. As an example, Barak Rosenshine, Carla Meister, and Saul Chapman (1996) found relatively large effects for questioning by itself and for macrostrategies that include questioning, such as reciprocal teaching.

To create a macrostrategy, a teacher must have reached the Applying (3) level for several different strategies related to an element. For example, if a teacher was working on element 27—using physical movement—he or she might first work on the following five strategies: stand up and stretch, vote with your feet, corners activities, stand and be counted, and body representations. Once a teacher is fluent with several individual strategies, he or she can combine them to create a macrostrategy. For example, the teacher working on physical movement might create a macrostrategy that involves students standing up, moving to different corners of the classroom based on how they vote on a particular issue, working with other students in their corner to investigate a specific aspect of the issue, creating body representations for important ideas related to the issue, and finally sharing their findings and representations with the class. The teacher could finish the macrostrategy by asking students to stand and be counted in response to a series of questions about how their thinking changed during the activity. The following vignette illustrates how this might manifest in one teacher's classroom.

> Mr. Gussy's fourth graders are learning about different geographical regions in their state, and he has created a macrostrategy for his growth goal of using physical movement. He has designated each corner of his classroom as a different geographical region. First, he asks his students to stand up, stretch, and go to the corner of the classroom with the region they think is most important to the state's citizens and businesses. In each corner, students learn more about their

> particular region and prepare to defend why they think that region is most important. After each corner shares its findings with the class, Mr. Gussy asks students to return to their desks. He finishes by asking them a series of questions about how their thinking changed during the activity. Students stand up if their answer to a question is yes and stay seated if their answer is no.

When a teacher integrates strategies to create a macrostrategy and uses that macrostrategy successfully in the classroom (while monitoring its effect on students), he or she is at the Innovating (4) level.

Adapt a Strategy for Unique Student Needs or Situations

To move to the Innovating (4) level, a teacher can also adapt a strategy associated with an element for unique student needs or situations. For example, English learners, special education students, students from impoverished backgrounds, and gifted education students are all special populations of students who may have unique needs.

Many have researched the special adaptations that most benefit specific subgroups of students. Jane Hill and Kathleen Flynn (2006) explained that focusing on vocabulary development is an excellent way to support English learners. They report on research that found that "an enriched vocabulary program can close the gap in vocabulary knowledge and reading comprehension between ELLs and English-dominant students" (p. 27). Eric Jensen (2009) stated that students of poverty need more guidance to make connections between information and suggested that teachers support them by providing the background knowledge they lack and by making explicit connections between information. Carol Ann Tomlinson and Marcia Imbeau (2010) listed several ways to challenge advanced learners and support struggling students. Their suggestions are summarized in table 5.1.

Table 5.1: Differentiation Strategies for Advanced Learners and Struggling Students

Advanced Learners	Struggling Students
Complex applications of content: Students apply their current knowledge to unfamiliar, abstract, or multifaceted problems.	**Learning contracts, menus, centers, and computer programs:** Students use structures that allow them to work on individualized and varied work.
Advanced and extended resources: Students use books, websites, or experts to investigate a topic more deeply.	**Regular individual and small-group instruction:** Students work individually or in small groups with the teacher to receive targeted instruction and support.
Focus on interest: Students investigate topics that are personally meaningful to them.	**Alternative homework assignments:** Students complete homework that is tailored to help them progress past their specific learning gaps.
Making connections: Students make connections between their knowledge in different content areas.	**Scaffolded assignments:** Students' assignments include step-by-step directions, examples, hints, content rewritten in straightforward language, or recorded directions and materials.
Moving on: Students move at a faster pace in a specific content area.	**Double-dipping:** Students work on content more than once a day.

Source: Adapted from Tomlinson & Imbeau, 2010.

Along with the strategies specified previously, those on the right side of table 5.1 can be used to adapt strategies for EL students, special education students, and students from impoverished backgrounds. Those on the left side of table 5.1 can be used to adapt strategies for gifted education or advanced students. In other words, teachers can adapt strategies for special populations in two different ways: either by providing extra support and scaffolding (for ELs, special education students, students from impoverished backgrounds, and other students who may struggle) or by providing extensions (for gifted education or advanced students). In this chapter, we present two adaptations for each strategy associated with the forty-one elements of the model of effective teaching: one that provides extra support and scaffolding and one that provides extensions.

Lesson Segments Involving Routine Events

Elements of lesson segments involving routine events are organized into two design questions: What will I do to establish and communicate learning goals, track student progress, and celebrate success? and What will I do to establish and maintain classroom rules and procedures?

What Will I Do to Establish and Communicate Learning Goals, Track Student Progress, and Celebrate Success?

Elements 1 through 3 are associated with this design question. Here we present adaptations for the strategies for these elements.

Element 1: Providing clear learning goals and scales (rubrics)

Clearly articulating learning goals, being careful not to confuse them with activities or assignments

Extra Support/Scaffolding: Identify key words or concepts in the learning goal, and use pictures and other visuals to explain them in greater detail.

Extension: Ask students to categorize learning goals (for example, those that address information and those that address skills) and predict what they will learn while working on different learning goals.

Creating scales or rubrics for learning goals

Extra Support/Scaffolding: Use pictures or diagrams to explain what performance at each level of the scale looks and sounds like.

Extension: Ask students to identify alternative statements that could be used for the more complex content in a particular scale.

Student-friendly scales

Extra Support/Scaffolding: Help students to draw pictures or describe in their own words what each level of the scale looks and sounds like.

Extension: Ask students to compare different groups' interpretations of the scale, identify similarities and differences, and explain which translation they think is best.

Individual student learning goals

Extra Support/Scaffolding: Conduct individual interviews with students who are having trouble identifying their interests or connecting their interests to the learning goal.

Extension: Ask students to give a presentation to the class at the end of a unit explaining what they learned by studying their individual learning goal.

Element 2: Tracking student progress

Formative assessments

Extra Support/Scaffolding: Use pictures or diagrams to make assessment task instructions or questions clearer.

Extension: Ask students to write assessment tasks for each level of a scale or rubric.

Response patterns

Extra Support/Scaffolding: Give students feedback about what they could have done to make partially correct or incorrect answers fully correct.

Extension: Ask students to suggest the grade they think they should receive for an assessment, and have them explain why it is an appropriate grade.

Individual score-level assessments

Extra Support/Scaffolding: Create a study guide that describes in detail, with visuals and practice activities, what students need to know or be able to do to pass an individual score-level assessment.

Extension: Ask students to create their own individual score-level assessments, accompanied by an explanation of how the assessment demonstrates a specific level of performance.

Different types of assessments

Extra Support/Scaffolding: Provide students with clear examples of how different types of assessments can be used to demonstrate competence on specific types of content.

Extension: Ask students to compare different kinds of assessment activities (pencil-and-paper, demonstration or performance, oral report) and to explain why a specific assessment activity is best for their student-generated assessment.

Formative grading

Extra Support/Scaffolding: Use a storyboard or flowchart (with pictures) to explain to students what is required to demonstrate competence within the teacher's chosen grading approach.

Extension: In addition to teacher communications, ask students to summarize the teacher's grading approach for their parents/guardians.

Charting student progress

Extra Support/Scaffolding: Have students set a series of goals for particular scores (for example, attain a score of 1.5 by October 5, a score of 2.0 by October 19, a score of 2.5 by November 2, and a score of 3.0 by November 16).

Extension: Have students compare their growth on different learning goals to identify behaviors on their part that led to faster growth.

Charting class progress

Extra Support/Scaffolding: Describe specific elements of a measurement topic on which the whole class is doing well and specific elements on which the whole class needs more work.

Extension: Ask students who perform specific elements of a measurement topic well to give feedback and advice to students who need help with the same measurement topic.

Element 3: Celebrating success

Final status celebration

Extra Support/Scaffolding: Describe specific things individual students did to accomplish their goals.

Extension: Ask students to describe specific things they did to accomplish their goals.

Knowledge gain celebration

Extra Support/Scaffolding: Describe specific things individual students did to achieve their knowledge gain.

Extension: Ask students to describe specific things they did to achieve their knowledge gain.

Verbal feedback

Extra Support/Scaffolding: Create visuals (posters, flowcharts, diagrams) illustrating learning strategies that students in the class found effective.

Extension: Ask students to create visuals (posters, flowcharts, diagrams) illustrating learning strategies they found effective.

As indicated, the extra support/scaffolding techniques that might be used for this design question include using pictures to represent learning goals and scales and tracking progress at a very fine-grained level of detail. Extension activities include asking students to analyze their own learning and effort, generate different ways to state or depict goals, or create new ways to assess their progress.

What Will I Do to Establish and Maintain Classroom Rules and Procedures?

Elements 4 and 5 are associated with this design question. Here we present adaptations for the strategies for these elements.

Element 4: Establishing and maintaining classroom rules and procedures

Using a small set of rules and procedures

Extra Support/Scaffolding: Create rules that use simple, easily understood vocabulary; if more complex terms are necessary, accompany them with pictures.

Extension: Present a large number of potential classroom rules to students, and ask them to use a decision-making matrix to narrow the list to five to eight.

Explaining rules and procedures to students

Extra Support/Scaffolding: Use pictures, drama, or diagrams while explaining rules and procedures.

Extension: Ask students to classify rules and procedures and explain why they grouped them as they did.

Modifying rules and procedures with students

Extra Support/Scaffolding: Focus rule modification sessions on one rule at a time, and specifically explain (or have students explain) why the rule needs to be modified.

Extension: Ask students to use a problem-solving process when rules need to be changed (define the problem, identify obstacles or constraints, find solutions, predict outcomes, try solutions).

Generating rules and procedures with students

Extra Support/Scaffolding: Show movie or television clips demonstrating situations in which rules and procedures would have helped.

Extension: Ask students to identify similarities and differences among student-generated rules in order to condense a large group of rules into a smaller group.

Language of responsibility and statements of school beliefs

Extra Support/Scaffolding: Tell stories that illustrate concepts like freedom, equality, responsibility, threats, opinions, and rights.

Extension: Ask students to write fiction or nonfiction stories about situations involving concepts like freedom, equality, responsibility, threats, opinions, and rights.

Posting rules around the room

Extra Support/Scaffolding: Create posters that include pictures for each rule.

Extension: Ask students to create pictures that clarify and summarize each rule.

Class pledge or classroom constitution

Extra Support/Scaffolding: Accompany a classroom constitution with pictures or diagrams that explain its concepts and ideas.

Extension: Ask students to create pictures or diagrams that illustrate the concepts and ideas of the classroom constitution.

Posters and graphics

Extra Support/Scaffolding: Tell personal stories about specific rules and procedures or specific character traits before asking students to illustrate them.

Extension: Ask students to accompany their posters and graphics with personal stories about specific rules and procedures or specific character traits.

Gestures and symbols

Extra Support/Scaffolding: Create a poster to hang in the room that summarizes (using words and pictures) each gesture or symbol used in the classroom.

Extension: Ask students to create posters that summarize (using words and pictures) each gesture or symbol used in the classroom.

Vignettes and role-playing

Extra Support/Scaffolding: Show video clips of past classes' vignettes or role plays.

Extension: Ask students to create videos that depict appropriate classroom behavior.

Reviewing rules and procedures with students

Extra Support/Scaffolding: Record rule or procedure violations on video, and view them with the class prior to discussing how to get behavior back on track.

Extension: Ask students to use a problem-solving process to resolve situations in which students are violating or ignoring rules (define the problem, identify obstacles or constraints, find solutions, predict outcomes, try solutions).

Classroom meetings

Extra Support/Scaffolding: Create a poster or other visual that expresses the guidelines for classroom meetings using words and pictures.

Extension: Ask students to listen and respectfully point out errors in reasoning during classroom meetings.

Student self-assessment

Extra Support/Scaffolding: Explain to students (using pictures and words) what each level of the self-assessment scale looks and sounds like.

Extension: Ask students to track their adherence to classroom rules and procedures over time and make generalizations about what they did that helped them improve adherence.

Element 5: Organizing the physical layout of the classroom

Learning centers

Extra Support/Scaffolding: Provide illustrated directions at each learning center showing where materials are, what the procedure for the center is, and what the center should look like before students leave it.

Extension: Ask students to evaluate centers for ease of access to supplies, clarity of directions for the center activity, and their ability to focus while at the center.

Computers and technology equipment

Extra Support/Scaffolding: Provide illustrated directions for each computer or piece of technology equipment showing where materials are, what the procedures for using the equipment are, and what the technology equipment area should look like before students leave it.

Extension: Ask students to evaluate computer and technology equipment areas for ease of access, clarity of expectations, and their ability to focus while working with the technology equipment.

Lab equipment and supplies

Extra Support/Scaffolding: Provide illustrated directions for each area where lab equipment and supplies are stored showing where specific materials are, the procedure for handling and using equipment, and how equipment and supplies should look when returned to storage.

Extension: Ask students to evaluate storage areas for lab equipment and supplies for ease of access, clarity of directions, and their ability to find what they need.

Bookshelves

Extra Support/Scaffolding: Use color coding and/or pictures to indicate books on specific topics, materials for specific projects, or where books should be returned to on the shelves.

Extension: Ask students to write and display reviews of books they recently read or have enjoyed in the past.

Wall space

Extra Support/Scaffolding: Accompany text posted on the walls with pictures and diagrams.

Extension: Ask students to create learning resources to display on the walls, such as posters showing correct procedures or timelines of important dates.

Displaying student work

Extra Support/Scaffolding: Post small cards next to student work listing aspects of the displayed item that were done especially well.

Extension: Ask students to identify especially good aspects of their displayed work.

Classroom décor

Extra Support/Scaffolding: Provide extra support (pictures, diagrams) through the classroom décor without making students feel patronized (use graphics and color schemes that are appropriate for students' ages).

Extension: Ask students to evaluate the classroom décor regarding how welcoming it is, how it helps them learn, and if it has aspects that are distracting.

Classroom materials

Extra Support/Scaffolding: Label cabinets, drawers, and supply caddies with pictures and words so students can quickly find what they need.

Extension: Create a system that allows students to request supplies they need for individual projects or cognitively complex tasks.

Teacher's desk

Extra Support/Scaffolding: Create an area where students who need extra support can work that allows them to consult the teacher more frequently than if they were at their desks.

Extension: Create a system that allows students who need to confer with the teacher about independent projects or tasks to schedule a one-on-one interview with the teacher.

Student desks

Extra Support/Scaffolding: Seat students who need extra support closer to the teacher and in such a way that the teacher can interact with them if they are experiencing difficulty.

Extension: Seat students who often complete extra work or extensions close to each other so they can collaborate and confer without disturbing others.

Areas for whole-group instruction

Extra Support/Scaffolding: Place a word wall (with words and pictures) close to the whole-group instruction area, and point to terms and concepts that arise during whole-group instruction.

Extension: Ask students to evaluate how well they can hear, see, and participate during whole-group instruction.

Areas for group work

Extra Support/Scaffolding: Designate a prop (ball, stuffed animal) that is held by the person speaking during a group discussion and is passed to the next person when it is their turn to speak.

Extension: Create areas for larger group projects (making large posters, building prototypes, conducting experiments).

As indicated, the extra support/scaffolding techniques that might be used with this design question include using simple vocabulary, pictures, stories, and video to communicate classroom rules and procedures and using illustrations, color-coding, diagrams, and specific feedback to make the classroom more navigable. Extension activities include asking students to make decisions about classroom rules and procedures and to evaluate the classroom's setup for ease of use.

To illustrate how a coach can facilitate a teacher's move from Applying (3) to Innovating (4) for one of the elements from lesson segments involving routine events, consider the following vignette. The teacher is working on *learning centers*, a strategy associated with element 5—organizing the physical layout of the classroom. Notice that the coach draws the teacher's attention to a special population of students and provides information about ways to adapt strategies for that population. She then helps the teacher adapt the strategy to provide extra scaffolding and support for those students.

Mr. Russ's coach, Yvonne, has been helping him work on his growth goal of organizing the physical layout of the classroom for several months. He's done a lot of reorganization and experimentation with the furniture and traffic patterns in his classroom, and he has even added learning centers to his classroom as a result of his work. It's become one of his favorite strategies, and he uses it extensively. Yvonne recently observed his students while they worked at their centers, however, and she noticed several students who seemed disengaged and often misbehaved at their centers. When she meets with Mr. Russ next, she asks him about them.

"I know," he sighs, "and I think I know why those students keep causing problems. Most of them are English learners, and they can't read the directions at the centers yet. I don't have time to explain every center to them. I've tried asking the other students at the center to read the directions to them, but they're eighth graders, and even if they can't read the directions, they don't like having a peer read them to them. The other day, one of them said, 'I'm not in kindergarten. I don't need them read to me.' I don't want to embarrass them or make them feel belittled, but the centers are working really well for everybody else. I want my ELs to get to participate in them too."

"So," observes Yvonne, "your goal is for your ELs to be able to work effectively at the centers, and the problem is that they can't read the directions, so they don't know what to do."

"Right," replies Mr. Russ.

"Let me give you some background," says Yvonne, "and then we can talk about some alternative solutions."

She explains to Mr. Russ that everyone goes through a series of stages when learning a language. One of those stages involves matching spoken words to printed words, which is a precursor to reading, and which can be supported in specific ways.

"Students at that stage need pictures and visuals to help them make the link between their spoken vocabulary and their reading vocabulary," she explains. "What if you added pictures and visuals to your directions? Do you think you could create a more visual version of the directions for a center?"

"Hmmmm," murmurs Mr. Russ. "You know, I might be able to. Almost like a pictograph or a diagram for each center. I might be able to use a flowchart."

"Those are all good ideas," says Yvonne, "and it might encourage them to ask a peer for help reading things if they only need assistance with one word or sentence, rather than a page of directions."

Lesson Segments Addressing Content

Elements of lesson segments addressing content are organized into three design questions: What will I do to help students effectively interact with new knowledge?, What will I do to help students practice and deepen their understanding of new knowledge?, and What will I do to help students generate and test hypotheses about new knowledge?

What Will I Do to Help Students Effectively Interact With New Knowledge?

Elements 6 through 13 are associated with this design question. Here we present adaptations for the strategies for these elements.

Element 6: Identifying critical information

Identifying critical-input experiences

Extra Support/Scaffolding: Create a word wall (with pictures) that shows and categorizes important terms and concepts associated with each critical-input experience.

Extension: Create a list of the main ideas for a critical-input experience; ask students to categorize each idea as they learn about it and make generalizations about each idea after the critical-input experience.

Visual activities

Extra Support/Scaffolding: Take students on virtual or real-life field trips to locations where they can experience critical information.

Extension: Ask students to create their own storyboards, graphic organizers, or pictures that highlight critical content.

Narrative activities

Extra Support/Scaffolding: Use pictures, audio, and video clips while telling stories about critical information.

Extension: Ask students to tell stories that illustrate critical information.

Tone of voice, gestures, and body position

Extra Support/Scaffolding: Display a picture for each important idea or concept of the critical information, and point to the appropriate picture when talking about a particular idea or concept.

Extension: Ask students to create a gesture for each important idea or concept of the critical information, and have them make the gesture whenever that idea or concept is referred to.

Pause time

Extra Support/Scaffolding: Immediately before pausing, provide students with a picture representing critical content and ask them to consider why the picture is important.

Extension: Ask students to write down what they are thinking during pause time and then work in groups to organize their comments into categories.

Element 7: Organizing students to interact with new knowledge

Grouping for active processing

Extra Support/Scaffolding: Create protocols for groups to follow that prompt students to share their perspectives, ask and answer questions, and paraphrase what other students are saying.

Extension: Ask students to evaluate the extent to which they offered their perspectives, asked and answered questions, and paraphrased what other students were saying during group discussions.

Group norms

Extra Support/Scaffolding: Before asking students to write down norms that are important to them, provide personal stories or illustrations of the important aspects of group discussion (perspectives, questioning, paraphrasing).

Extension: After a group discussion, ask students to evaluate how well they adhered to their group's norms.

Fishbowl demonstration

Extra Support/Scaffolding: Create hand signals or signs that indicate important aspects of group discussions (perspectives, questioning, paraphrasing), and ask students in the fishbowl demonstration to use the hand signal or sign that indicates what they are doing during the demonstration.

Extension: Ask students to track how often students in the fishbowl demonstration shared their perspectives, asked or answered questions, and paraphrased what others said; ask students to make generalizations about the relative importance of each aspect based on their observations.

Job cards

Extra Support/Scaffolding: Add pictures that illustrate the responsibilities of a role to each job card.

Extension: Ask students to identify additional roles (other than those identified by the teacher) that they think would benefit their group's functioning and to make job cards for those roles.

Predetermined "buddies" to help form ad hoc groups

Extra Support/Scaffolding: Use charts with fewer blanks, and have students fill out new charts often so students don't feel "stuck" with their current set of partners.

Extension: Ask students to share something about themselves or their interests with the person signing up to be their partner.

Contingency plan for ungrouped students

Extra Support/Scaffolding: Explicitly teach students how to introduce themselves to a new partner, share something about themselves, and begin working.

Extension: Ask students to compare their experiences working with different partners to identify ways they can work effectively with a wide variety of partners.

Grouping students using preassessment information

Extra Support/Scaffolding: When grouping students homogeneously, identify specific knowledge that each group needs to focus on.

Extension: When grouping students heterogeneously, create guidelines to ensure that both high- and low-prior-knowledge students benefit from the experience.

Element 8: Previewing new content

What do you think you know?

Extra Support/Scaffolding: Give a short overview of a topic or show pictures of the topic before asking students to write down everything they know about it.

Extension: Ask students to select specific aspects of their prior knowledge for in-depth investigation.

Overt linkages

Extra Support/Scaffolding: Use graphic organizers and diagrams to illustrate links and connections between previous and new content.

Extension: Ask students to identify similarities and differences between previous and new content.

Preview questions

Extra Support/Scaffolding: Post preview questions in the classroom and, throughout a unit, point to the appropriate preview question while presenting information that will help answer it.

Extension: Ask students to write preview questions in their academic notebooks and add entries throughout a unit whenever they hear information they think applies to a specific question.

Brief teacher summary

Extra Support/Scaffolding: Use a graphic organizer or diagram to illustrate key ideas and patterns in information.

Extension: After presenting introductory information about a unit, ask students to write a summary that predicts what information will be presented during the unit.

Skimming

Extra Support/Scaffolding: Create a symbol for each main idea of a passage that students are going to skim, and teach them to jot the appropriate symbol next to information that applies to that idea while they skim.

Extension: Ask students to identify patterns in information that they skim and to make generalizations about the content based on their observations.

Teacher-prepared notes

Extra Support/Scaffolding: Use pictures and diagrams to express ideas in teacher-prepared notes.

Extension: Ask students to review a teacher-prepared outline of the content and select a topic they would like to investigate in greater detail than what will be presented in class.

K-W-L strategy (Ogle, 1986)

Extra Support/Scaffolding: Give a short overview of a topic before asking students what they already know about that topic.

Extension: Ask students to create individual K-W-L charts in their academic notebooks.

Advance organizers

Extra Support/Scaffolding: When creating graphic organizers, use pictures and text that show connections between previous and new content.

Extension: Ask students to add their personal interests to advance organizers and show how those interests relate to previous and new content.

Anticipation guides

Extra Support/Scaffolding: Give a short overview of a topic or show pictures of a topic before asking students to respond to statements about the topic.

Extension: Ask students to respond to statements about a topic in their academic notebooks and to revisit their responses throughout a unit to identify and correct errors in their thinking.

Word splash activity

Extra Support/Scaffolding: Use words and pictures when presenting new terms and phrases to students.

Extension: Ask students to make generalizations about the content based on the categories they created for each of the terms and phrases.

Preassessment

Extra Support/Scaffolding: Give a short overview of a topic or show pictures of a topic before asking students to complete a preassessment on the topic.

Extension: Ask students to select a topic from the preassessment for which they have a lot of prior knowledge and investigate it on a deeper level.

Element 9: Chunking content into digestible bites

Presenting content in small chunks

Extra Support/Scaffolding: Give a brief overview of each chunk or show pictures representing the chunk before presenting it in more detail.

Extension: Ask students to select a chunk of information they would like to investigate in greater detail.

Using preassessment data to vary the size of each chunk

Extra Support/Scaffolding: Use stories or video clips to build students' background knowledge for information about which they displayed misconceptions or little prior knowledge on the preassessment.

Extension: Ask students to select a topic from the preassessment that they would like to investigate in greater detail.

Chunk processing

Extra Support/Scaffolding: Use a storyboard to illustrate a procedure for summarizing information before asking students to engage in chunk processing.

Extension: Ask students to identify how each chunk of information presented relates to the main ideas of a unit or learning goal.

Element 10: Helping students process new information

Perspective analysis (Marzano, 1992)

Extra Support/Scaffolding: Review various prominent positions on a topic and the reasoning behind each one before asking students to engage in perspective analysis.

Extension: Ask students to identify multiple opposing positions to their own on a topic.

Thinking hats (de Bono, 1999)

Extra Support/Scaffolding: Create graphics for each thinking hat that remind students of the perspective they represent, and display the graphic for the thinking hat that students are currently using.

Extension: Ask students to wear the blue hat first in a discussion about a topic. This hat requires students to determine the order in which they would like to wear the other five hats.

Collaborative processing

Extra Support/Scaffolding: Create a protocol for students to use during group discussions that ensures each student summarizes, asks questions about, and makes predictions about new information. Also, illustrate the protocol using a storyboard or pictures.

Extension: Ask students to make generalizations about new information in their academic notebooks after collaborative processing.

Jigsaw cooperative learning

Extra Support/Scaffolding: Before asking students to investigate their expert topics, give a brief overview of each one, and ask students to generate questions they think will be important to answer about that topic.

Extension: After hearing about each expert topic, ask students to identify similarities and differences between each of the expert topics.

Reciprocal teaching

Extra Support/Scaffolding: If students are going to be discussion leaders, allow them to preview the content and generate questions ahead of time.

Extension: Ask students to respectfully identify and correct errors in thinking and reasoning that arise during their discussions.

Concept attainment

Extra Support/Scaffolding: Collect and display pictures of examples and nonexamples for the concept under investigation.

Extension: Ask students to explain why specific items are examples or nonexamples of a concept.

Element 11: Helping students elaborate on new information

General inferential questions

Extra Support/Scaffolding: Take students on virtual or real-life field trips or other background-knowledge-building experiences before asking default questions.

Extension: Ask students to identify the specific teacher-presented information that they are using as premises to respond to reasoned inference questions.

Elaborative interrogation

Extra Support/Scaffolding: Ask students to explain the reasoning behind specific parts of their responses to questions (rather than their whole response).

Extension: Ask students to make generalizations about categories of people, places, things, or ideas and predict the consequences of events based on the evidence they give for their responses to questions.

Element 12: Helping students record and represent knowledge

Informal outline

Extra Support/Scaffolding: Ask students to sketch small pictures or symbols next to each big idea in their informal outline.

Extension: Ask students to select a big idea on their outline that they would like to investigate further.

Combination notes, pictures, and summary

Extra Support/Scaffolding: Post examples of various kinds of pictures and diagrams that students can use in the "pictures" side of their notes.

Extension: Ask students to draw conclusions and make generalizations about the content in their summaries.

Graphic organizers

Extra Support/Scaffolding: Post pictures of specific graphic organizers and the informational patterns they correspond to in the classroom for students to refer to.

Extension: Ask students to create their own graphic organizers for specific informational patterns.

Free-flowing web

Extra Support/Scaffolding: Have students use different colors to show the topic, main ideas, and details on their free-flowing webs.

Extension: Ask students to include different perspectives about a topic in their free-flowing webs.

Academic notebooks

Extra Support/Scaffolding: Use loose-leaf notebooks as academic notebooks, and have students make entries on a different page each day so they can take pages out and rearrange them as necessary.

Extension: Ask students to select topics from their academic notebooks that they would like to investigate in greater depth.

Dramatic enactments

Extra Support/Scaffolding: Ask volunteers to participate in role plays or demonstrate body representations for the whole class before asking all students to participate.

Extension: Ask students to select important scenes, processes, events, or concepts from the content to be the subject of dramatic enactments and justify their selections.

Rhyming pegwords

Extra Support/Scaffolding: Ask students to draw pictures of the images they use to associate information with each pegword.

Extension: Ask students to use a decision-making matrix to decide which information is important enough to be memorized.

Link strategy

Extra Support/Scaffolding: Create video versions of students' linking narratives (involving symbols and substitutes).

Extension: Ask students to create video versions of their linking narratives and ask the class to guess what information the narrative is supposed to help them remember.

Element 13: Helping students reflect on their learning

Reflective journals

Extra Support/Scaffolding: Select a specific reflection question for students to respond to after each lesson and provide sample answers for each question.

Extension: Ask students to find connections between their answers to multiple reflection questions (for example, What information was difficult to understand? and What could you have done better today?).

Think logs

Extra Support/Scaffolding: Select a specific cognitive question for students to respond to after each lesson and provide sample answers for each question.

Extension: Ask students to find connections between their answers to multiple cognitive questions (for example, What part of the problem-solving process was most difficult? and What do you do when you encounter information you don't understand?).

Exit slips

Extra Support/Scaffolding: Select a specific reflective question for students to respond to on an exit slip and provide sample answers for each question.

Extension: Save students' exit slips over the course of a unit, then ask students to compare the slips at the end of the unit and make generalizations about their learning during the unit.

Knowledge comparison

Extra Support/Scaffolding: Create a list of strategies and techniques that students in the class found particularly useful in boosting their knowledge gain and post the list in a place where all students can see it.

Extension: Ask students to examine a graph showing their knowledge gain over a unit to identify strategies and techniques that were particularly useful in boosting their knowledge gain.

Two-column notes

Extra Support/Scaffolding: Quickly review the main ideas of a lesson before asking students to record and react to parts of the lesson they found interesting.

Extension: Ask students to select one of their reactions, questions, or extended ideas about the content to investigate in greater detail.

As indicated, the extra support/scaffolding techniques that might be used with this design question include categorizing and illustrating critical information with pictures and stories, helping students develop background knowledge about new information through firsthand experiences, and using media and dramatic instruction to enhance students' understanding of new information. Extension activities include asking students to make generalizations and identify patterns in new information and helping students make deeper connections between new information and what they already know.

What Will I Do to Help Students Practice and Deepen Their Understanding of New Knowledge?

Elements 14 through 20 are associated with this design question. Here we present adaptations for the strategies for these elements.

Element 14: Reviewing content

Cloze activities

Extra Support/Scaffolding: Use pictures, film clips, and audio clips in addition to text to present previously learned information with missing pieces.

Extension: Ask students to create cloze activities for their peers using previously learned information.

Summaries

Extra Support/Scaffolding: Create video or pictograph summaries in addition to written and oral summaries.

Extension: Ask students to create video, pictograph, written, or oral summaries about previously learned information.

Presented problems

Extra Support/Scaffolding: Post previously learned information about how to solve specific types of problems (expressed using words, pictures, diagrams, and charts) in the room where students can refer to it.

Extension: Ask students to create posters that express previously learned information about how to solve specific types of problems using words, pictures, diagrams, and charts.

Demonstration

Extra Support/Scaffolding: Post storyboards or pictorial representations of previously learned skills and procedures in the room where students can refer to them.

Extension: Ask students to create storyboards or pictorial representations of previously learned skills and procedures.

Brief practice test or exercise

Extra Support/Scaffolding: Post a list of correct answers to previous practice tests or exercises (expressed using words, pictures, diagrams, and charts) in the room where students can refer to it.

Extension: Ask students to create lists of previously learned information from practice tests or exercises using words, pictures, diagrams, and charts.

Questioning

Extra Support/Scaffolding: Accompany teacher questions about previously learned information with visuals that clarify important ideas or concepts in the question.

Extension: Ask students to categorize their peers' responses to questions about previously learned information and make generalizations about the content based on their categories.

Element 15: Organizing students to practice and deepen knowledge

Perspective analysis (Marzano, 1992)

Extra Support/Scaffolding: Review various prominent positions on a topic and the reasoning behind each before asking students to engage in perspective analysis.

Extension: Ask students to identify multiple opposing positions to their own on a topic.

Thinking hats (de Bono, 1999)

Extra Support/Scaffolding: Create graphics for each thinking hat that remind students of the perspective they represent, and display the graphic for the thinking hat students are currently using.

Extension: Ask students to wear the blue hat first in a discussion about a topic. This hat requires students to determine the order in which they would like to wear the other five hats.

Cooperative learning

Extra Support/Scaffolding: Make a list of answers that students arrived at on their own before asking them to confer with a partner.

Extension: Ask students to compare their approach to a problem with another student's approach to the same problem.

Cooperative comparisons

Extra Support/Scaffolding: Ask students to focus on one cooperative comparison question.

Extension: Ask students to make generalizations about how their group learns best based on their answers to cooperative comparison questions.

Pair-check (Kagan & Kagan, 2009)

Extra Support/Scaffolding: Pair high-background-knowledge students with low-background-knowledge students for pair-check.

Extension: Ask students to identify coaching techniques that were especially effective during pair-check.

Think-pair-share and think-pair-square (Kagan & Kagan, 2009)

Extra Support/Scaffolding: Create a protocol to ensure that both students share their ideas and the reasoning behind those ideas and illustrate the protocol using a storyboard or pictures.

Extension: Ask students to identify similarities and differences between their group's conclusions and other groups' conclusions.

Student tournaments

Extra Support/Scaffolding: Ensure that all groups contain students with high and low background knowledge.

Extension: In addition to giving tangible rewards to the top teams, give special awards for good sportsmanship, teamwork, or growth in understanding.

Error analysis and peer feedback

Extra Support/Scaffolding: Create a flowchart (with words and pictures) showing the correct procedure for a task that students can use to evaluate their partner's performance.

Extension: Ask students to create a flowchart (with words and pictures) showing the correct procedure for a task.

Performances and peer critiques

Extra Support/Scaffolding: Show video recordings of previous students' culminating performances to current students.

Extension: Ask students to identify similarities and differences between other students' culminating performances.

Inside-outside circle (Kagan & Kagan, 2009)

Extra Support/Scaffolding: Put tape on the carpet or floor so students understand where to stand and where to move to. Additionally, display a storyboard or pictures depicting student behavior during this strategy.

Extension: Ask students to identify similarities and differences between the perspectives of their different partners.

Element 16: Using homework

Preview homework

Extra Support/Scaffolding: Ask students to focus on listing questions, observations, or connections related to text or media about upcoming content.

Extension: Ask students to find additional sources of information about upcoming content.

Homework to deepen knowledge

Extra Support/Scaffolding: Create a study guide (with words and pictures/diagrams) that students can use to review content that is the focus of homework.

Extension: Ask students to compare, contrast, or classify aspects of current content with previous content or with content related to their interests.

Homework to practice a process or skill

Extra Support/Scaffolding: Create a flowchart (with words and pictures/diagrams) showing the correct procedure for a process or skill that is the focus of homework.

Extension: Ask students to explain techniques that helped them increase their fluency, speed, or accuracy with a process or skill.

Parent-assisted homework

Extra Support/Scaffolding: Create a list of specific reflective questions that parents can ask their student after he or she reads a text passage or views media related to the content.

Extension: Have students present an oral summary to their parents about a text passage or media related to the content; provide parents with a list of main ideas and details related to the content.

Element 17: Helping students examine similarities and differences

Sentence stem comparisons

Extra Support/Scaffolding: Ask students to create a list of what they know about each element of a sentence stem comparison before completing it.

Extension: Ask students to create and complete sentence stems related to the content.

Venn diagrams

Extra Support/Scaffolding: Ask students to create a list of what they know about each item or concept being compared before completing a Venn diagram.

Extension: Ask students to make generalizations about each item or concept being compared based on their Venn diagrams.

Double-bubble diagram

Extra Support/Scaffolding: Ask students to create a list of the attributes of each item or concept being compared before completing a double-bubble diagram.

Extension: Ask students to create double-bubble diagrams that compare three or four items or concepts.

Comparison matrix

Extra Support/Scaffolding: Provide the elements and attributes that students should use in their comparison matrices and provide a review of each element and attribute.

Extension: Ask students to identify the elements and attributes to use in their comparison matrices.

Classification chart

Extra Support/Scaffolding: List attributes associated with each category on a comparison chart and provide a review of each attribute.

Extension: Ask students to generate lists of attributes associated with each category on a comparison chart.

Student-generated classification patterns

Extra Support/Scaffolding: Create a concept wall with pictures of different concepts; allow students to use examples from the concept wall when generating classification patterns.

Extension: Ask students to make generalizations about a concept based on their classification patterns.

Similes

Extra Support/Scaffolding: Provide one element of a simile; ask students to provide the other and explain how the two are alike—for example, real numbers are like _____ because _____ .

Extension: Ask students to create similes using abstract concepts or ideas.

Metaphors

Extra Support/Scaffolding: Provide one element of a metaphor; ask students to provide the other and explain the connection between the two—for example, the British Empire was a(n) _____ because _____ .

Extension: Ask students to create metaphors using abstract concepts or ideas.

Sentence stem analogies

Extra Support/Scaffolding: Create sentence stem analogies that only require students to fill in one term.

Extension: Ask students to create sentence stem analogies for abstract concepts or ideas.

Visual analogies

Extra Support/Scaffolding: Use pictures and words to demonstrate visual analogies.

Extension: Ask students to create alternative ways to express analogies visually.

Element 18: Helping students examine errors in reasoning

Identifying errors of faulty logic

Extra Support/Scaffolding: Display written examples of each type of error of faulty logic along with pictures that symbolize each type.

Extension: Ask students to compose or find examples of errors of faulty logic.

Identifying errors of attack

Extra Support/Scaffolding: Display written examples of each type of error of attack along with pictures that symbolize each type.

Extension: Ask students to compose or find examples of errors of attack.

Identifying errors of weak reference

Extra Support/Scaffolding: Display written examples of each type of error of weak reference along with pictures that symbolize each type.

Extension: Ask students to compose or find examples of errors of weak reference.

Identifying errors of misinformation

Extra Support/Scaffolding: Display written examples of each type of error of misinformation along with pictures that symbolize each type.

Extension: Ask students to compose or find examples of errors of misinformation.

Practicing identifying errors in logic

Extra Support/Scaffolding: Give students fewer possibilities to select from when they are learning to identify errors in logic (for example, is this error of faulty logic an example of contradiction or evading the issue?).

Extension: Ask students to correct examples so they no longer contain errors in logic.

Finding errors in the media

Extra Support/Scaffolding: Highlight the section of media or text that contains errors in logic before asking students to identify the type of error being made.

Extension: Ask students to find media or texts that contain errors in logic and identify the type of errors being made.

Examining support for claims

Extra Support/Scaffolding: Highlight the elements of a claim and its support before asking students to examine the claim.

Extension: Ask students to find claims in advertising and the media and to examine the support provided for them to determine if they are valid or invalid.

Statistical limitations

Extra Support/Scaffolding: Tell stories that illustrate how ignoring or paying attention to specific types of statistical limitations led to good or bad conclusions.

Extension: Ask students to gather statistics about a topic and make conclusions about the topic based on the statistics, being careful to take statistical limitations into account.

Element 19: Helping students practice skills, strategies, and processes

Close monitoring

Extra Support/Scaffolding: Break strategies or skills into smaller chunks that students can practice separately before putting them together.

Extension: Ask students to compare different parts of a strategy or skill to make generalizations about the process.

Frequent structured practice

Extra Support/Scaffolding: Create a visual representation of the skill or process for students that explains each step using words and pictures.

Extension: Ask students to track their progress with a skill or strategy to determine when they are ready to move to varied practice.

Varied practice

Extra Support/Scaffolding: Warn students that they may encounter challenges during varied practice; describe common challenges and how to overcome them.

Extension: Ask students to describe how they overcame the challenges or obstacles they faced.

Fluency practice

Extra Support/Scaffolding: Help students set a series of small goals so they continue to experience success while improving their fluency, accuracy, and skill.

Extension: Ask students to describe techniques that helped them make large increases in their fluency, accuracy, and skill.

Worked examples

Extra Support/Scaffolding: Use pictures, diagrams, arrows, and labels to clearly illustrate the correct procedure for solving a problem.

Extension: Have students annotate problems (using pictures, diagrams, arrows, and labels) to show the procedure they used to solve them.

Practice sessions prior to testing

Extra Support/Scaffolding: Give individual students feedback about what specific part of a process or skill is most important for them to work on during their practice sessions.

Extension: Ask students to investigate new techniques for performing a process or skill that are as effective as the ones taught.

Element 20: Helping students revise knowledge

Academic notebook entries

Extra Support/Scaffolding: Have high understanding students help low understanding students revise their academic notebooks.

Extension: Ask students to revise academic notebook entries that relate to their interests by investigating those topics more deeply and adding information to them.

Academic notebook review

Extra Support/Scaffolding: Ask students to share important ideas, concepts, and vocabulary from their academic notebooks during a whole-class discussion; compile the information shared into a study guide for the class.

Extension: Prompt students to answer questions about the information in their academic notebooks by investigating specific topics in greater detail than what was presented in class.

Peer feedback

Extra Support/Scaffolding: Ask students to respond to one specific question only when looking at a peer's academic notebook.

Extension: Ask students to identify similarities and differences between peers' academic notebooks and their own.

Assignment revision

Extra Support/Scaffolding: Give concrete feedback that specifies exactly what students need to do to raise their grade.

Extension: Ask students to suggest the grade that they think they deserve on a revised assignment, and have them provide their rationale for deserving that grade.

As indicated, the extra support/scaffolding techniques that might be used with this design question include activities like creating visual displays and posters so students can reference information in the classroom, helping students focus on specific details or questions, and making directions for procedures more explicit. Extension activities include asking students to explain newly learned information in greater depth and to invent better ways to practice newly learned processes.

What Will I Do to Help Students Generate and Test Hypotheses About New Knowledge?

Elements 21 through 23 are associated with this design question. Here we present adaptations for the strategies for these elements.

Element 21: Organizing students for cognitively complex tasks

Student-designed tasks

Extra Support/Scaffolding: Explain and give examples of each type of task to students before asking them to identify which type of task best addresses their question or prediction.

Extension: Ask students to design two types of tasks that could address their question or prediction and to select the design that seems most likely to yield the best results.

Cooperative learning

Extra Support/Scaffolding: Explicitly teach interpersonal and group skills and the expectations for various group roles and depict those roles using storyboards or pictures.

Extension: Ask students to evaluate their use of interpersonal and group skills and their fulfillment of a role in a group.

Academic notebook charts, graphs, and tables

Extra Support/Scaffolding: Help students set small goals for their cognitively complex tasks so they experience success often.

Extension: Ask students to identify techniques or strategies that led to significant progress on their cognitively complex task.

Think logs

Extra Support/Scaffolding: Ask students to focus on one cognitive question only while reflecting on their cognitively complex tasks.

Extension: Ask students to compare their answers to cognitive questions to their future plans for approaching cognitively complex tasks, and have them decide if they should adjust their plans based on these answers.

Journals

Extra Support/Scaffolding: Ask students to focus on one reflection question only while reflecting on their cognitively complex tasks.

Extension: Ask students to compare their answers to reflection questions to their future plans for approaching cognitively complex tasks, and have them decide if they should adjust their plans based on these answers.

Peer response groups

Extra Support/Scaffolding: Ask students to give their peers feedback about one specific aspect only of their cognitively complex task.

Extension: Ask students to compare their peers' cognitively complex tasks to their own and draw conclusions about what they could do a better job on.

Self-evaluations

Extra Support/Scaffolding: Ask students to evaluate one aspect of their cognitively complex task at a time.

Extension: Ask students to provide evidence to support the grade they think they deserve on their cognitively complex task.

Peer tutoring

Extra Support/Scaffolding: Ask students to identify specific areas they would like a peer tutor to work with them on.

Extension: Ask students to identify specific techniques they think will help their peer improve his or her skills or knowledge.

Element 22: Engaging students in cognitively complex tasks involving hypothesis generation and testing

Experimental-inquiry tasks

Extra Support/Scaffolding: Create a diagram (with pictures and words) that shows the process that should be followed for an experimental-inquiry task, and post it in the classroom.

Extension: Ask students to research other experiments done on the same topic as their own task and compare their results with others'.

Problem-solving tasks

Extra Support/Scaffolding: Create a diagram (with pictures and words) that shows the process that should be followed for a problem-solving task, and post it in the classroom.

Extension: Ask students to research other problems similar to their own, and have them compare their results with the results of others.

Decision-making tasks

Extra Support/Scaffolding: Create a diagram (with pictures and words) that shows the process that should be followed for a decision-making task, and post it in the classroom.

Extension: Ask students to research other decisions made about the same topic as their own task, and have them compare their decisions with the decisions of others.

Investigation tasks

Extra Support/Scaffolding: Create a diagram (with pictures and words) that shows the process that should be followed for an investigation task, and post it in the classroom.

Extension: Ask students to research other investigations into the same topic as their own task and compare their results with others'.

Element 23: Providing resources and guidance

Providing support for claims

Extra Support/Scaffolding: Tell stories about famous claims, labeling the different kinds of support presented for them as grounds, backing, or qualifiers.

Extension: Ask students to find other people who have made claims similar to their own, and have them compare their support with other support given for that claim.

Examining claims for errors

Extra Support/Scaffolding: Ask students to identify the part of their claim they are most unsure about and help them articulate why they are unsure about it.

Extension: Ask students to explain which error in thinking led to an error in their claim.

Scoring scales

Extra Support/Scaffolding: Show examples of student artifacts (written work, recordings of performances, other products) from cognitively complex tasks that illustrate different levels of performance for a scale used to score a cognitively complex task.

Extension: Ask students to identify what they will need to do to meet and exceed their goal score for a cognitively complex task.

Interviews

Extra Support/Scaffolding: Anticipate parts of a student's cognitively complex task that will be particularly difficult, and prepare the student to deal with the challenge during an interview.

Extension: Ask the student which parts of his or her cognitively complex task will be most difficult, and help the student plan to deal with the challenge.

Circulating around the room

Extra Support/Scaffolding: Create an unobtrusive signal that students can use to alert the teacher that his or her attention is needed.

Extension: Ask students questions that prompt them to consider their cognitively complex task from a new perspective.

Expressions and gestures

Extra Support/Scaffolding: Draw pictures or diagrams while explaining concepts to students as they are working on their cognitively complex tasks.

Extension: Use the same gestures or verbal expressions consistently when referring to a concept or idea.

Collecting assessment information

Extra Support/Scaffolding: Procure and offer resources to specific students based on information from their assessments.

Extension: Confer with students about resources that will help them extend their cognitively complex tasks and about how to access them—for example, extending a task about weather by helping launch a weather balloon from a local weather station.

Feedback

Extra Support/Scaffolding: Focus feedback on one aspect of the student's cognitively complex task at a time and help the student make necessary changes.

Extension: Ask students to respond to the teacher's feedback by explaining what they want to do differently on their next cognitively complex task.

As indicated, the extra support/scaffolding techniques that might be used with this design question include activities such as clarifying steps and parts of cognitively complex tasks and providing detailed instruction and guidance about specific next steps. Extension activities include asking students to evaluate their own performance on cognitively complex tasks and create plans for future tasks based on their results.

To illustrate how a coach can facilitate a teacher's move from Applying (3) to Innovating (4) for one of the elements from lesson segments addressing content, consider the following vignette. The teacher is working on *graphic organizers*, a strategy associated with element 12—helping students record and represent knowledge. First, the coach prompts the teacher to select a strategy she'd like to adapt for a special population of students. The teacher has a good idea of what she'd like to work on, so the coach verifies that she has made a good choice, provides information on how to adapt strategies for advanced students, and helps her think about ways to provide further extensions in the future.

Ms. Countryman, an elementary school teacher, has been using a variety of strategies related to helping students record and represent knowledge over the past semester, and she feels comfortable using and monitoring students' responses to most of them. Her coach, Martin, has asked her to select a strategy related to her growth goal that she'd like to adapt in order to meet the unique needs of students in her class. When they meet, Ms. Countryman brings a handful of graphic organizers.

"From what I see, I'm guessing you've picked a strategy," says Martin, smiling.

"Yes," replies Ms. Countryman. "It was pretty easy to figure out which one I wanted. Here's why: you know our reading curriculum has all these great graphic organizers. I love using them, and my students love them too. I've made them a part of my students' regular seatwork. After they read a story, I work with them as a small group to select the best organizer for the story and then, independently, they summarize the story using the graphic organizer. They do a great job, and we review their organizers before digging deeper into the story the next day."

"Yes, that matches what I've seen in your room," Martin says.

"Well, anyway, here's the problem I've run into. I have seven advanced students, and they've started reading stories outside the normal curriculum because it's just too simple for them. But the chapter books they've started don't really work with my graphic organizer routine. For one thing, my students only read a chapter at a time, not the whole story, and for another, the patterns in the books my advanced students are reading are more sophisticated than the patterns in the normal curriculum. More and more I feel like I'm asking my advanced students to shoehorn themselves into a model that doesn't fit what they're learning."

"I'm glad you recognized that," says Martin. "Let's talk about what you can do to fix it."

He and Ms. Countryman spend the rest of the session talking about how to support advanced students' special needs, and Ms. Countryman decides to give her students a little more freedom.

"I have an idea," she says. "What if instead of offering them the premade graphic organizers, I work with their small group to identify a pattern in the information and make an organizer specific to it. Then they can use that organizer to summarize what they've read, and we can still use their work for review the next day."

"That sounds like a great way to start," replies Martin. "And keep this in mind for later on: once your students feel very comfortable identifying patterns in information and creating organizers for them, you might want to give them a bit more freedom and let them individually identify patterns and create organizers for them. I agree that it's probably too much to give them right away, but it's good to keep next steps in mind."

Lesson Segments Enacted on the Spot

Elements of lesson segments enacted on the spot are organized into four design questions: What will I do to engage students?, What will I do to recognize and acknowledge adherence or lack of adherence to rules and procedures?, What will I do to establish and maintain effective relationships with students?, and What will I do to communicate high expectations for all students?

What Will I Do to Engage Students?

Elements 24 through 32 are associated with this design question. Here we present adaptations for the strategies for these elements.

Element 24: Noticing when students are not engaged

Scanning the room

Extra Support/Scaffolding: Make note of students whose attention often wanders or who easily become disengaged, and check on those students frequently.

Extension: Ask students to signal the teacher if they find their attention is wandering or if they realize that they are disengaged.

Monitoring levels of attention

Extra Support/Scaffolding: Use a graph or chart on the board to periodically indicate the class's level of attention.

Extension: Ask students to track their own levels of attention and engagement through a class period or day.

Measuring engagement

Extra Support/Scaffolding: Use pictures, stories, or video clips to describe the concept of engagement and different levels of engagement.

Extension: Ask students to identify two to three personal strategies they can use to reengage if they find their attention wandering.

Element 25: Using academic games

What Is the Question?

Extra Support/Scaffolding: Incorporate pictures and media (like video and audio clips) into clues.

Extension: Ask students to design clues for What Is the Question?; use student-designed clues with other classes, or make student designers ineligible to respond to their own clues.

Name That Category

Extra Support/Scaffolding: Accompany category names with pictures that will help students remember important concepts or terms associated with that category.

Extension: Limit students to a specific number of words that they can say while trying to get their teammates to guess a category (for example, only five terms).

Talk a Mile a Minute

Extra Support/Scaffolding: Add pictures to lists of words that fit in a category.

Extension: Add a few difficult bonus words to the bottom of each card used in Talk a Mile a Minute; if a team guesses all the regular words, they can try to get bonus points by guessing the extra words.

Classroom Feud

Extra Support/Scaffolding: Incorporate pictures and media (like video and audio clips) into questions.

Extension: Ask students to design questions for Classroom Feud; use student-designed questions with other classes, or make student designers ineligible to answer their own questions.

Which One Doesn't Belong?

Extra Support/Scaffolding: Accompany words in word groups with pictures.

Extension: Create groups of five or six words where two don't belong or groups of seven words where three don't belong.

Inconsequential competition

Extra Support/Scaffolding: Track which students have been on a winning team over the course of the year and try to arrange teams so that all students have at least one experience on a winning team.

Extension: Ask students to create their own academic games based on the content and play them with the whole class.

Turning questions into games

Extra Support/Scaffolding: Explicitly teach students how to explain why they think their answer is correct and how to resolve disagreements if their whole team doesn't agree on the same answer.

Extension: Ask students to keep a list of questions they have during a lesson and use them for an impromptu game at the end of the lesson.

Vocabulary review games

Extra Support/Scaffolding: Accompany words in vocabulary games with pictures.

Extension: Ask students to invent their own vocabulary review games.

Element 26: Managing response rates

Random names

Extra Support/Scaffolding: If the student whose name is drawn can't answer the question, break it into smaller parts.

Extension: Draw several names after asking a question and ask the students whose names were drawn to discuss their answers in front of the class until they reach a consensus.

Hand signals

Extra Support/Scaffolding: Create and hang a poster in the classroom that shows (using words and pictures) the responses associated with different hand signals.

Extension: Tally students' hand-signal responses to questions, share the results with the class, ask students to defend their answers, and then have students answer the same question using hand signals again.

Response cards

Extra Support/Scaffolding: Ask students to respond to a question a second time after discussing students' initial responses.

Extension: Tally students' responses, share the results with the class, ask students to defend their answers, and then have students answer the same question again.

Response chaining

Extra Support/Scaffolding: Explicitly teach students how to paraphrase another student's answer to a question.

Extension: Ask students to identify similarities and differences between their answers to questions and other students' answers.

Paired response

Extra Support/Scaffolding: Pair students with higher and lower background knowledge together.

Extension: Ask students to describe errors they identified in their own answers after conferring with a partner.

Choral response

Extra Support/Scaffolding: Display the target information statement so the whole class can see it (poster, board, projection screen); add pictures to clarify vocabulary terms or abstract concepts.

Extension: Ask students to compose target information statements for a learning goal or unit.

Wait time

Extra Support/Scaffolding: If students don't know the answer to a question, ask them to use wait time to think about whether they can answer part of the question or what information they know that is related to the question.

Extension: Ask students who know the answer to a question right away to use wait time to think of support for their answer or to examine their initial answer for errors.

Elaborative interrogation

Extra Support/Scaffolding: Ask students to explain the reasoning behind specific parts of their responses to questions (rather than their whole response).

Extension: Ask students to make generalizations about categories of people, places, things, or ideas and predict the consequences of events based on the evidence they give for their responses to questions.

Multiple types of questions

Extra Support/Scaffolding: Explicitly teach students processes for determining how parts of information relate to the whole (analysis), forming conjectures about subsequent events (prediction), making and defending inferences (interpretation), and using criteria to make judgments (evaluation).

Extension: Ask students to explain the process they used to answer a specific type of question (analytical, predictive, interpretive, evaluative).

Element 27: Using physical movement

Stand up and stretch

Extra Support/Scaffolding: Explain the biological reasons for movement and stretching with students, and encourage them to stretch anytime they need to renew their focus.

Extension: Ask students to experiment by comparing their ability to focus when they take stretch breaks with their level of focus when they don't.

Give one, get one

Extra Support/Scaffolding: Encourage students to look in other students' notebooks for pictures or diagrams that they want to add to their notebooks.

Extension: Ask students to identify and correct errors in their own or other students' notebooks.

Vote with your feet

Extra Support/Scaffolding: Provide background knowledge related to a question immediately before asking students to vote.

Extension: Use a vote-discuss-revote sequence before announcing the right answer; ask students who change their answer when they revote to explain why they changed it.

Corners activities

Extra Support/Scaffolding: Post related background information with each corner question.

Extension: Ask students to select a corner question they would like to investigate further.

Stand and be counted

Extra Support/Scaffolding: Before asking students to stand and be counted, provide a list of the major ideas and concepts presented during the lesson.

Extension: Ask students who score themselves high on a rubric or scale to make a generalization about the topic based on the major ideas and concepts presented in the lesson.

Body representations

Extra Support/Scaffolding: Present students with a picture that represents a term or concept before asking students to create a body representation for it.

Extension: Ask students to create short skits that illustrate a concept or term.

Drama-related activities

Extra Support/Scaffolding: Show students a video clip related to an event or situation before asking them to act it out.

Extension: Ask students to record and review their dramatic enactment of an event or situation to compare it to the original event or situation.

Element 28: Maintaining a lively pace

Instructional segments

Extra Support/Scaffolding: Create graphics to represent each type of instructional segment and display the applicable one during each type of segment (that is, administrative tasks, presentation of new content, practicing and deepening understanding of key knowledge and skills, getting organized into groups, seat work, and transitions).

Extension: Track how quickly students transition from one segment to another; encourage them to improve their time.

Pace modulation

Extra Support/Scaffolding: Explicitly explain the concepts of *overwhelmed* and *bored* to students; establish signals so that students can communicate their comfort level with the current pace of the lesson.

Extension: Ask students to look for patterns in the pace of lessons, and have them suggest changes they think will help them learn better.

The parking lot

Extra Support/Scaffolding: Present and illustrate background information about parking lot issues and questions to students.

Extension: Ask students to bring background information about parking lot issues and questions to class.

Motivational hook/launching activity

Extra Support/Scaffolding: Use pictures and visual media during motivational hook/launching activities.

Extension: Ask students to bring anecdotes, video and audio clips, headlines, or other media to class to be used as motivational hook/launching activities.

Element 29: Demonstrating intensity and enthusiasm

Direct statements about the importance of content

Extra Support/Scaffolding: Ask guests to come to tell the class about their experiences using the content in the real world.

Extension: Ask students to find and bring examples of people or organizations that use the content in the real world.

Explicit connections

Extra Support/Scaffolding: Give background about local, national, or global events before connecting the content to them.

Extension: Ask students to describe connections between the content and their interests or local, national, or global events.

Nonlinguistic representations

Extra Support/Scaffolding: Create highly concrete nonlinguistic representations (using content familiar to students) that use pictures to show connections and patterns in the content.

Extension: Ask students to create nonlinguistic representations that show connections and patterns in the content they are excited about and want to investigate further.

Personal stories

Extra Support/Scaffolding: Play video or audio recordings of students telling personal stories about the content.

Extension: Ask students to tell or write about their interaction with the content (what excited them, what was difficult at first, important insights).

Verbal and nonverbal signals

Extra Support/Scaffolding: Use particular gestures consistently as a signal when referring to big ideas or important aspects of the content.

Extension: Ask students to give feedback on the teacher's use of verbal and nonverbal signals (helpful, distracting, detracting).

Humor

Extra Support/Scaffolding: Make sure that students have the background knowledge needed to understand jokes and humor used in the classroom.

Extension: Ask students to share teacher-approved jokes or funny sayings about the content with the class.

Quotations

Extra Support/Scaffolding: Explain and illustrate difficult vocabulary terms or concepts used in quotes.

Extension: Ask students to find quotes related to the content or their interests; post the quotes in the classroom.

Movie and film clips

Extra Support/Scaffolding: Provide background knowledge that students will need to understand a movie or film clip.

Extension: Ask students to suggest movie and film clips that are related to the content; screen them before showing them to the class.

Element 30: Using friendly controversy

Friendly controversy

Extra Support/Scaffolding: Ask a small group of students to demonstrate a discussion that follows friendly controversy guidelines, and discuss the demonstration with the class.

Extension: Ask students to conduct an investigation of a perspective they disagree with but are interested in.

Class vote

Extra Support/Scaffolding: Provide background knowledge about an issue before asking students to vote.

Extension: Ask students who were initially undecided or who changed their position about an issue to explain what convinced them to change their mind.

Seminars

Extra Support/Scaffolding: Help students summarize the text, video, or other resource being discussed before the seminar.

Extension: Ask students to investigate questions that arose but were not answered in their seminar groups.

Expert opinions

Extra Support/Scaffolding: Give students some background knowledge about different experts before asking them to select one to research.

Extension: Ask students to compare their own ideas and positions with an expert's ideas and positions on an issue.

Opposite point of view

Extra Support/Scaffolding: Have students interview or talk to someone with a point of view that is the opposite of their own.

Extension: Have students identify and compare several different points of view that are different from their own.

Diagramming perspectives

Extra Support/Scaffolding: Ask students to create a list of what they know about various points of view before creating a Venn diagram.

Extension: Ask students to make generalizations about various points of view based on their Venn diagrams.

Lincoln-Douglas debate

Extra Support/Scaffolding: Take students on a virtual or real-life field trip that highlights the policy or issue that will be the subject of a debate.

Extension: Ask students to predict the consequences of adopting a policy or a position on an issue that is the subject of a debate.

Town hall meeting (Hess, 2009)

Extra Support/Scaffolding: Invite guest speakers who have strong opinions on the subject of an upcoming town hall meeting to speak to the class.

Extension: Ask students to predict the consequences of a new policy or a change in policy that is the subject of a town hall meeting.

Legal model (Hess, 2009)

Extra Support/Scaffolding: Explain the stories behind legal cases that will be the focus of legal model discussions. (What conflict caused the case? How did lower courts rule? Why did the Supreme Court agree to hear the case?)

Extension: Ask students to investigate the consequences of the Supreme Court's ruling in a case.

Element 31: Providing opportunities for students to talk about themselves

Interest surveys

Extra Support/Scaffolding: Ask students to record their responses to interest surveys (audio or video).

Extension: Ask students to tell about projects or investigations they have already completed related to their interests.

Student learning profiles

Extra Support/Scaffolding: Ask students to describe (written or orally) the best learning experiences they've had.

Extension: Ask students to investigate their learning styles to identify activities that help them learn best.

Life connections

Extra Support/Scaffolding: Invite guest speakers to speak to students about how they use content in the real world.

Extension: Ask students to identify how learning content has affected their lives.

Informal linkages during class discussion

Extra Support/Scaffolding: Alert students ahead of time that the class will be learning about something related to their interests, and invite them to share their knowledge about the topic as a part of the discussion. Help them prepare to share with the class.

Extension: Invite students to complete independent investigations of topics related to their interests and present their findings to the class.

Element 32: Presenting unusual or intriguing information

Teacher-presented information

Extra Support/Scaffolding: Use video and audio clips to present unusual or intriguing information.

Extension: Invite students to investigate unusual or intriguing information that interests them in more depth.

Webquests

Extra Support/Scaffolding: Create a list of links related to the content for students to explore and allow students to explore these links in class.

Extension: Ask students to look for errors in information they find on the Internet.

One-minute headlines

Extra Support/Scaffolding: Show video clips of previous students' one-minute headlines.

Extension: Record students' one-minute headlines to show to other classes.

Believe it or not

Extra Support/Scaffolding: Collect and archive pictures that illustrate unusual or little-known information related to the content.

Extension: Ask students to categorize unusual information related to the content and make generalizations about the content based on their categorization.

History files

Extra Support/Scaffolding: Create and archive a list of historical perceptions related to the content from which students can pick one perception to study.

Extension: Ask students to compare historical perceptions of a concept or idea at different points throughout history.

Guest speakers and firsthand consultants

Extra Support/Scaffolding: Ask guest speakers to bring visuals and media that explain how they use the content in the real world.

Extension: Ask students to suggest people they know who use the content in the real world and who might be willing to speak to the class.

As indicated, the extra support/scaffolding techniques that might be used with this design question include using pictures when giving directions or working with content vocabulary, explaining the rationale behind different classroom activities in more depth, and using more detailed tracking systems to monitor specific students' engagement levels. Extension activities include asking students to help design and lead games and classroom activities and asking students to think about and adjust their own levels of engagement and attention.

What Will I Do to Recognize and Acknowledge Adherence or Lack of Adherence to Rules and Procedures?

Elements 33 through 35 are associated with this design question. Here we present adaptations for the strategies for these elements.

Element 33: Demonstrating withitness

Being proactive

Extra Support/Scaffolding: Check in with students who may cause problems throughout the day or class period to see how they are doing.

Extension: Ask students who may cause problems to check in with the teacher throughout the day or class period to let him or her know how they are doing.

Occupying the whole room physically and visually

Extra Support/Scaffolding: Make eye contact more frequently and spend extra time near students who may need extra help or who are likely to cause a problem.

Extension: Ask students to compare their behavior in different classes and explain any differences they notice.

Noticing potential problems

Extra Support/Scaffolding: Note combinations of students who tend to cause problems and avoid grouping them together or seating them near each other.

Extension: Ask students to identify classmates they work well with, and allow them to work with or sit near those students.

Series of graduated actions

Extra Support/Scaffolding: Create a list of consequences for not following classroom behaviors and display them using storyboards or symbols so that students clearly understand what will happen if they choose not to stop inappropriate behavior.

Extension: Brainstorm a list of actions that students can take if they feel that other students are influencing them to behave inappropriately (move away, not respond, confer with the teacher).

Element 34: Applying consequences for lack of adherence to rules and procedures

Verbal cues

Extra Support/Scaffolding: Refer to the learning goal when reminding a student that his or her behavior is counterproductive—for instance, "Becky, is what you are doing helping you write a more engaging introduction to your essay? How can I help you get back on track?"

Extension: Ask students to describe the consequences of their current behavior.

Pregnant pause

Extra Support/Scaffolding: Explain to students the purpose of the pregnant pause and model how you will use it. Explain that it is a signal to indicate that student behavior must be modified immediately.

Extension: Follow up with students after making them the subject of a pregnant pause to explain what they were doing wrong and how fixing it facilitated the class's learning.

Nonverbal cues

Extra Support/Scaffolding: Describe and post gestures that will be used to indicate inappropriate behavior.

Extension: Ask students to use nonverbal cues to signal to their peers that they are acting inappropriately.

Time-out

Extra Support/Scaffolding: Post the graduated time-out process in the room with pictures to indicate each step.

Extension: Follow up with students who have been in time-out to hear how well they think they are adhering to their action plan for changing their behavior.

Overcorrection

Extra Support/Scaffolding: Tell students stories about people in the real world or in literature who compensated for wrongdoing through overcorrection.

Extension: Ask students to suggest ways that they could overcorrect for their destructive behavior.

Interdependent group contingency

Extra Support/Scaffolding: Create and post a list of ways that students can respectfully remind their peers to adhere to behavioral standards.

Extension: Ask students to describe positive and negative group behaviors exhibited by the class.

Home contingency

Extra Support/Scaffolding: Record comments about a student's behavior in school in a notebook that he takes home to show to his or her parents/guardians each night.

Extension: Ask a student's parents/guardians to alert the teacher to unusual events or situations that may make it more difficult for the student to behave appropriately in school.

Planning for high-intensity situations

Extra Support/Scaffolding: Alert administrators or counselors if a student seems on edge or if there is a possibility that the student might lose control.

Extension: Follow up by asking students to identify why they lost control and what helped them calm down.

Overall disciplinary plan

Extra Support/Scaffolding: Track disciplinary incidents in the classroom related to different areas of the disciplinary plan.

Extension: Evaluate the effectiveness of different aspects of the disciplinary plan, and make adjustments as necessary.

Element 35: Acknowledging adherence to rules and procedures

Verbal affirmations

Extra Support/Scaffolding: Track one's verbal affirmations to ensure that all well-behaved students receive recognition from the teacher.

Extension: Have students identify ways to recognize positive contributions to the class with verbal affirmations.

Nonverbal affirmations

Extra Support/Scaffolding: Track one's nonverbal affirmations to ensure that all well-behaved students receive recognition from the teacher.

Extension: Have students identify ways to recognize positive contributions to the class with nonverbal affirmations.

Tangible recognition

Extra Support/Scaffolding: Use pictures and words to clearly explain what is required to earn tangible recognitions.

Extension: Ask students to explain how they changed their behavior to earn tangible recognitions.

Token economies

Extra Support/Scaffolding: Use pictures and words to clearly explain how a token economy works.

Extension: Ask students to explain how a token economy motivated them to adhere to rules and procedures.

Daily recognition forms

Extra Support/Scaffolding: Use small symbols to represent each category in which students can earn points.

Extension: Ask students to explain how daily recognition forms motivated them to adhere to rules and procedures.

Color-coded behavior

Extra Support/Scaffolding: Give concrete examples and illustrations of behavior that warrants a negative or positive color change.

Extension: Ask students to explain why their color was changed.

Certificates

Extra Support/Scaffolding: Have preprinted certificates translated into the language a student's parents/guardians speak so they can understand and celebrate their student's positive behavior.

Extension: Ask students to describe the behavior for which they received a certificate.

Phone calls, emails, and notes

Extra Support/Scaffolding: Have positive emails or notes translated into the language a student's parents/guardians speak so they can understand and celebrate the student's positive behavior.

Extension: Visit a student's home to explain to his or her parents/guardians how their student's behavior positively influenced the class.

As indicated, the extra support/scaffolding techniques that might be used with this design question include activities like closely monitoring specific students in class, clearly communicating consequences using pictures and diagrams, and giving concrete examples of desired and undesired behaviors. Extension activities include helping students self-regulate their own behavior and explore the rationale of why specific behaviors are undesirable in the classroom.

What Will I Do to Establish and Maintain Effective Relationships With Students?

Elements 36 through 38 are associated with this design question. Here we present adaptations for the strategies for these elements.

Element 36: Understanding students' interests and backgrounds

Student background surveys

Extra Support/Scaffolding: Allow students to record (audio or video) their responses to background survey questions if they aren't comfortable writing them.

Extension: Ask students to create artwork, musical compositions, written pieces, films, or other media to express their background, interests, and goals.

Opinion questionnaires

Extra Support/Scaffolding: Allow students to record (audio or video) their responses to opinion questionnaire questions.

Extension: Ask students to create artwork, musical compositions, written pieces, films, or other media that express their opinions on classroom topics.

Individual teacher-student conferences

Extra Support/Scaffolding: Begin a teacher-student conference by providing information about your own life and interests.

Extension: Ask students to identify interests or perspectives they would like to investigate in more depth.

Parent-teacher conferences

Extra Support/Scaffolding: Mark important student events or transitions on a calendar and ask students about them when they occur.

Extension: Ask students to describe how events or transitions in their lives are affecting their learning at school.

School newspaper, newsletter, or bulletin

Extra Support/Scaffolding: Ask students whose names and activities do not appear in a school publication what they are involved in.

Extension: Ask students to briefly report to the class about the success of events they were involved in.

Informal class interviews

Extra Support/Scaffolding: Focus informal class interviews on various subgroups represented in a class (social groups, racial groups, interest groups) for whom little information has been previously provided.

Extension: Attend school functions that students attend (pep rallies, athletic games, dances, or social functions).

Investigating student culture

Extra Support/Scaffolding: Investigate elements of student culture associated with various subgroups in a class (social groups, racial groups, interest groups).

Extension: Ask students to explain a specific aspect of their culture using media of their choice (written composition, music, art, film, drama).

Autobiographical metaphors and analogies

Extra Support/Scaffolding: Show students examples of autobiographical metaphors and analogies written by previous students.

Extension: Ask students to make generalizations about themselves based on their autobiographical metaphors and analogies.

Six-word autobiographies

Extra Support/Scaffolding: Show students examples of six-word autobiographies written by previous students.

Extension: Ask students to make and present autobiography bags (collections of belongings and items that help students explain who they are and what is important to them).

Independent investigations

Extra Support/Scaffolding: Encourage students to select reporting methods that they prefer (written or oral, live or recorded) to report the results of their independent investigations.

Extension: Ask students to make generalizations about the subject of their investigations based on their findings.

Quotes

Extra Support/Scaffolding: Share examples of quotes that previous students selected to describe themselves.

Extension: Ask students to investigate the authors of their quotes and compare the authors' lives to their own.

Commenting on student achievements or areas of importance

Extra Support/Scaffolding: Keep track of which students often receive recognition for their accomplishments and which seldom receive recognition; seek out accomplishments of seldom-recognized students and make a point of recognizing them.

Extension: Ask students how they prefer to be recognized (certificate, social recognition, one-on-one recognition, recommendation).

Lineups

Extra Support/Scaffolding: Use questions for lineups that take into account different ethnic and socioeconomic cultural norms.

Extension: Allow students to suggest questions to use for lineups; screen these questions for appropriateness before using them.

Individual student learning goals

Extra Support/Scaffolding: Conduct individual interviews with students who are having trouble identifying their interests or connecting their interests to the learning goal.

Extension: Ask students to give a presentation to the class at the end of a unit explaining what they learned by studying their individual learning goal.

Element 37: Using verbal and nonverbal behaviors that indicate affection for students

Greeting students at the classroom door

Extra Support/Scaffolding: Give students a high five, handshake, or hug as they enter the classroom.

Extension: Ask students about recent events in their lives (athletics games, drama activities, competitions) as they enter the room.

Informal conferences

Extra Support/Scaffolding: Track informal interactions with students, and seek out students who don't naturally initiate interaction.

Extension: Designate a recurring day (once a week, once a month) when students can come and spend time, ask questions, or get help from the teacher before or after school.

Attending after-school functions

Extra Support/Scaffolding: Take pictures at a student's after-school function and post them in the classroom.

Extension: Write notes to students commenting on specific positive aspects of your experience at their after-school function.

Greeting students by name outside of school

Extra Support/Scaffolding: Show interest in students by referring to having seen them outside of school—for instance, "Good morning, Greta. It was fun to see you at the mall yesterday!"

Extension: Greet students' parents by name when seeing them outside of school.

Giving students special responsibilities or leadership roles in the classroom

Extra Support/Scaffolding: Give specific instructions to students, and check on them frequently to make sure they understand and are fulfilling their responsibilities or roles appropriately.

Extension: If students need help with their responsibility or role, ask them to suggest another student to help them, and have them explain why they think that student would be a good helper.

Scheduled interaction

Extra Support/Scaffolding: Solicit compliments about students' accomplishments from their other teachers.

Extension: Keep track of what you talked about with a student on previous occasions, and follow up on the topic when you interact with them again.

Photo bulletin board

Extra Support/Scaffolding: Help students draw a picture, write a sentence, select a quote, or create some other small representation of themselves to hang beside their picture.

Extension: Ask students to bring in a favorite photo of themselves for the photo bulletin board (screen these before displaying them).

Physical behaviors

Extra Support/Scaffolding: Study different cultural norms for physical contact, and be sensitive to students' individual preferences for physical contact.

Extension: Find alternative ways to express affection to students for whom physical contact is unpleasant or awkward.

Humor

Extra Support/Scaffolding: Make sure that students have the background knowledge needed to understand jokes and humor used in the classroom.

Extension: Invite students to share teacher-approved jokes or funny sayings about the content with the class.

Element 38: Displaying objectivity and control

Self-reflection

Extra Support/Scaffolding: Chart your consistency in applying positive and negative consequences to different groups of students (ethnic groups, socioeconomic groups, gender groups, expectancy groups).

Extension: Examine the extent to which students are self-regulating their own behavior; the number of teacher reminders or reprimands should steadily decline over the course of the year.

Self-monitoring

Extra Support/Scaffolding: Find out more about the backgrounds of students who trigger negative thoughts and emotions in you (home visit, informal conversations, other teachers).

Extension: Compare one's attitude toward a specific student over time to evaluate how successful reframing has been.

Identifying emotional triggers

Extra Support/Scaffolding: On difficult days, set small, achievable, short-term goals for yourself and for students; celebrate when these goals are accomplished.

Extension: Track your mood for several weeks to determine which days of the week are easiest and hardest for you; schedule important conversations or complex activities for days when you tend to feel more positive.

Self-care

Extra Support/Scaffolding: Break tedious or big tasks into smaller parts, and celebrate the completion of each part with a small reward.

Extension: Identify tasks, activities, or people that are difficult to deal with, and give yourself positive consequences whenever you handle those circumstances well.

Assertiveness

Extra Support/Scaffolding: Pause before responding to communication that feels threatening or uncomfortable; when possible, wait overnight to answer emails, and let difficult phone calls go to voicemail.

Extension: When confronted with a difficult situation, list your legitimate rights in the situation, various possible responses to the situation, and pros and cons for each response.

Maintaining a cool exterior

Extra Support/Scaffolding: Select one element of maintaining a cool exterior to focus on at a time; when you feel confident with it, select another to practice.

Extension: Record conflict management experiences in a journal; periodically read previous entries to compare your past abilities with your current abilities, and identify areas where you've improved and can still improve.

Active listening and speaking

Extra Support/Scaffolding: If you don't understand what a student is trying to say, ask clarifying questions and offer short summaries of what you think they are trying to say.

Extension: After a conversation with a student, ask the student to reflect on how the conversation helped them think more clearly about an issue.

Communication styles

Extra Support/Scaffolding: Discuss and post the characteristics of assertive communication in the classroom (using pictures and words).

Extension: Publicly recognize students who communicate assertively; ask them to compare their communication to less effective communication styles.

Unique student needs

Extra Support/Scaffolding: Keep track of students who have unique needs and anticipate how specific activities, assignments, or classroom events will affect them.

Extension: Help students with unique needs identify strengths and weaknesses of their specific personality type; help them proactively plan to counteract their weaknesses.

As indicated, the extra support/scaffolding techniques that might be used with this design question include allowing students to use audio or visual media to communicate with the teacher and telling personal stories about the content. Extension activities include asking students to make generalizations about themselves and their interests and asking students to share further details about themselves with the class.

What Will I Do to Communicate High Expectations for All Students?

Elements 39 through 41 are associated with this design question. Here we present adaptations for the strategies for these elements.

Element 39: Demonstrating value and respect for low-expectancy students

Identifying expectation levels for all students

Extra Support/Scaffolding: Use more levels to classify students in terms of your expectations, such as low, low-average, average, high-average, and high.

Extension: Identify your expectation levels for students in specific subject areas.

Identifying differential treatment of low-expectancy students

Extra Support/Scaffolding: Select one affective tone area and one quality of interaction area to track.

Extension: Learn more about groups for whom you have biased patterns of thought; seek out information that contradicts current biases and beliefs.

Nonverbal and verbal indicators of respect and value

Extra Support/Scaffolding: Select one nonverbal and one verbal indicator to focus on using.

Extension: Track your use of specific nonverbal and verbal indicators with the goal of using them more frequently with low-expectancy students.

Element 40: Asking questions of low-expectancy students

Question levels

Extra Support/Scaffolding: Break complex questions into small parts, and ask a different student to answer each part.

Extension: Ask one student to summarize his or her peers' answers to different parts of a question and synthesize them into one answer to the whole question.

Response opportunities

Extra Support/Scaffolding: Formally track how often each low-expectancy student is asked to answer a question.

Extension: Track how often each low-expectancy student attempts to answer a question when called on.

Follow-up questioning

Extra Support/Scaffolding: Use pictures or other media when giving hints or cues to students.

Extension: Ask students to explain how their thinking about a question changed because of the teacher's follow-up questioning.

Evidence and support for student answers

Extra Support/Scaffolding: Provide possible answers when asking students to supply evidence or support.

Extension: Ask students to explain how their thinking about a question changed because they had to provide evidence and support for their answer.

Encouragement

Extra Support/Scaffolding: Track positive comments and encouragement given to students.

Extension: Evaluate tracking data to determine if certain groups receive more or less encouragement.

Wait time

Extra Support/Scaffolding: If students don't have an answer, have them identify a part of the question about which they do know something and describe it. Then use that scaffolding to help build their knowledge base.

Extension: Ask students who know the answer to a question right away to use wait time to think of support for their answer or examine their initial answer for errors.

Tracking responses

Extra Support/Scaffolding: Let students know that you want them to answer more questions and are planning to start calling on them more often.

Extension: Check in with students to see how they feel about being called on to answer questions more often.

Avoiding inappropriate reactions

Extra Support/Scaffolding: With students, generate a list of inappropriate reactions to student answers, as well as ways to help and encourage fellow students. Post the list where all students can see it.

Extension: Ask students to predict consequences for appropriate and inappropriate reactions to student answers.

Element 41: Probing incorrect answers with low-expectancy students

Using an appropriate response process

Extra Support/Scaffolding: Post a list of the types of help students can access if they don't know the answer to a question.

Extension: Help students design an appropriate response process to use when students ask and answer questions during small-group work.

Letting students "off the hook" temporarily

Extra Support/Scaffolding: Track how often specific students opt out of answering a question. Meet with these students individually to encourage them and help them fill in holes in their understanding of the content.

Extension: Help students who have trouble answering questions in front of the class use specific strategies to gradually feel more comfortable answering in front of the class.

Answer revision

Extra Support/Scaffolding: Ask students to revise specific parts of their responses to questions (rather than their whole response).

Extension: Ask students to explain how revising one part of their answer to a question caused them to think about other parts of the question differently.

Think-pair-share (Lyman, 2006)

Extra Support/Scaffolding: Create a protocol to ensure that both students share their answers and the reasoning behind them.

Extension: Ask students to identify similarities and differences between their answer and their partner's answer.

As indicated, the extra support/scaffolding techniques that might be used with this design question include focusing on very specific indicators of value and respect and using simpler vocabulary to explain the desired response to a question. Extension activities include asking students to provide fuller answers with more support and tailoring gestures of value and respect to specific students' preferences.

To illustrate how a coach can facilitate a teacher's move from Applying (3) to Innovating (4) for one of the elements from lesson segments enacted on the spot, consider the following vignette. The teacher is working on *tracking responses*, a strategy associated with element 40—asking questions of low-expectancy students. The coach identifies a strategy that has worked well for the teacher and asks her to adapt it for a special population of students. The coach listens to the teacher's idea and verifies that it is manageable and sustainable. He also prompts the teacher to explain the adaptation to students and helps the teacher think about how to gradually remove the support once students no longer need it.

Miss Wessel teaches French at Westview High, and her coach, Chad, has been very pleased with her progress toward her growth goal—asking questions of low-expectancy students—over the past few months. During his observations, he's watched her call on every student several times, and she's reached a point where she gets a satisfactory response from most of her students most of the time. Chad knows that tracking responses has been a helpful strategy for Miss Wessel thus far, and he's asked her to think about how she can give her students even more support as she uses it.

"I've noticed that your struggling students still cringe when you call on them," he tells her. "I feel like they haven't quite bought in to the idea that you're going to call on them whether they raise their hand or not."

"I know what you're talking about," replies Miss Wessel, "and I admit, it's hard to keep calling on them when I know that they don't want me to. I wish there was some way for me to make it less scary for them."

"There probably is," replies Chad. "Let's see if we can think of some ideas."

After rejecting several ideas as unmanageable or unreasonable, Miss Wessel has a thought.

She says, "What if I create a set of specific questions and give them to that group of students before class? I'll let them know that I am going to call on them, and that I'll be asking them one of those questions. That will give them a bit more time to prepare an answer, and then maybe they can stop worrying about whether I'm going to call on them, and focus on finding an answer to the question."

"Is it manageable for you to create a question list like that?" asks Chad.

"Yes," she says, "I think it is. Here's why. I already prepare most of my questions before class. All I would have to do is cut and paste a few of those questions into a different document and print out several copies before class. I think that would work."

"OK," says Chad, "and remember that this is support, not a permanent system. It would probably be good if you explain that to your students too. In a few weeks, I'll want us to have another conversation about how you can slowly remove this support but still sustain your students' participation in answering questions."

Miss Wessel agrees to keep that in mind and revisit the issue in a few weeks.

Summary

This chapter provided examples of ways that a coach can help a teacher move beyond the Applying (3) level to the Innovating (4) level. This can be accomplished by integrating several strategies to create a macrostrategy or adapting strategies related to a specific element for students' unique needs and situations. After reviewing how to integrate several strategies to create a macrostrategy, we provided research about how to adapt strategies for special populations. Finally, we provided ways that a teacher can adapt strategies associated with each of the forty-one elements of the model for students who need extra support or scaffolding and for students who need extra challenges or extensions.

Chapter 5: Comprehension Questions

1. What must a teacher do to grow from the Applying (3) level to the Innovating (4) level? As described in chapter 2 and in this chapter, what can a coach do to support that growth?

2. What is a macrostrategy, and how should a teacher go about creating one?

3. What special populations of students might require adaptations of strategies for their unique needs and situations?

Role-Play

With a partner, role-play a situation (like those in the vignettes) where a teacher and coach are meeting to adapt a strategy for unique student needs and situations. If you are playing the teacher, choose a strategy. If you are playing the coach, guide the teacher from the Applying (3) level to the Innovating (4) level for the strategy.

After role-playing once, switch roles and repeat the process. The "teacher" should select a different strategy than the one used the first time.

Chapter 6

ASPECTS OF COACHING

The model of coaching presented in chapters 2 through 5 forms a foundation for coaching interactions. Using the recommendations in those chapters, a coach can help a teacher move from virtually no knowledge about a specific element of effective teaching to adapting strategies related to that element for unique student needs. The level of detail presented in chapters 2 through 5 forms a basis for coaching that will generate changes in teacher pedagogical skill and, consequently, student achievement. However, in addition to the specific coaching moves explained in previous chapters, there are four additional considerations we think are important to address. In this chapter, we provide direction related to the following areas: (1) coaching systems, (2) differentiating coaching, (3) coaching behaviors, and (4) virtual coaching.

Coaching Systems

Coaching can be used within a school in many ways:

- **Teacher-initiated coaching**—A teacher asks for a coach, and the administrator or district provides one. Alternatively, a teacher might independently arrange to be coached by another teacher or administrator.

- **Administrator-initiated coaching**—An administrator requires a teacher to work with a coach (for example, a first-year teacher or a teacher whose evaluation shows that he or she needs improvement).

- **District-initiated coaching**—A district requires a specific group of teachers to work with a coach (for example, first-year teachers, teachers whose evaluations show they need improvement, teachers who are new to the district, or specialist teachers [special education or literacy]).

- **School- or districtwide coaching programs**—Every teacher in a district or school is required to work with a coach.

Each of these approaches has advantages and disadvantages. In teacher-initiated coaching, the teacher is self-motivated and invested in the change, making it likely that he or she will practice strategies and incorporate them into his or her classroom repertoire. Additionally, teacher-initiated coaching relationships are usually quite positive and productive. However, in schools where teacher-initiated coaching is the norm, the teachers who most need coaching may not seek out the coach. Administrator-initiated and district-initiated coaching allow administrators and district leaders to assign coaches to teachers most in need of support. Assigning coaches to teachers can sometimes make it difficult for the coach to build trust, especially if the teacher views the coach as someone who will evaluate them or share the content of coaching sessions with an administrator. School- or districtwide coaching programs provide the most support for teachers' professional development and can foster a culture of collegiality and cooperation. This type of coaching program, however, may only allow each teacher a small portion of a coach's time and can be costly to implement. The following vignette illustrates how a districtwide coaching program might be used to support growth for all teachers.

> Lakeview School District's superintendent, Marty Holland, is in the process of implementing a districtwide coaching program. Although coaching has been used informally in the district for some time, and a few schools have hired coaches to work with their staff, Marty wants to provide support for all teachers. The coaching program is one element of the district's comprehensive professional development plan, which also includes workshops and trainings for teachers on research-based best practices. All teachers are required to participate in the coaching program, and each teacher works with a coach for one trimester of the year. For that trimester, the teacher is expected to select one growth-goal area, and the coaches are trained in a process that allows them to guide each teacher through the levels of a scale for their growth goal. During a meeting with administrators, Marty says, "I realize that this is a large investment of our resources, but coaching has been shown to be the most effective way to help teachers transfer the knowledge and skills they learn in trainings and workshops to the classroom." He goes on to explain how administrators can support the work of the coaches by consistently using the district's adopted model of effective teaching when talking about classroom practice.

Coaching Guidelines

As stated previously, school- or districtwide coaching programs can and should be designed to support teachers' professional development and growth. If a district or school establishes, or already has, a coaching program, specific guidelines can be used to guide the selection of coaches. For example:

- The coach is a master teacher with the proven ability to increase student achievement in his or her own classroom.

- The coach has a wide knowledge of curriculum and instruction and the interpersonal skills necessary to interact with others respectfully and professionally.

- The coach agrees with the goals of the coaching program.

- The coach understands and can describe and demonstrate what performance looks and sounds like at each level of the scale.

A district or school might also create a set of expectations for coaching relationships. For example:

- Teachers will meet with their coach at least once every two weeks.

- Coaches will spend more than 50 percent of their time in classrooms, either observing, modeling, or co-teaching.

- Coaches will help teachers identify and work on at least one growth goal every three months.

The following vignette shows how these guidelines might guide a coaching relationship.

Mrs. Hetzel is the principal of an urban high school with several instructional coaches on staff. Before Mrs. Hetzel became principal, the coaches at the school spent most of their time gathering materials and writing lesson plans for a select group of teachers. To ensure that coaches are better utilized in the future, Mrs. Hetzel has created a set of guidelines to guide each coach's interactions with teachers. First, each coach is assigned to specific teachers and is expected to meet with those teachers on a biweekly basis. Second, Mrs. Hetzel arranges for each coach to be trained in a process they can use to help teachers establish growth goals and guide each teacher through the levels of a scale that measures performance. Finally, Mrs. Hetzel asks coaches to track how much time they spend doing various coaching activities, such as meeting with teachers, modeling, co-teaching, reviewing video, and observing in classrooms.

As the coaching program continues from year to year, and teachers show consistent professional growth, coaches from other schools and teachers from Mrs. Hetzel's school develop interest in becoming coaches. Mrs. Hetzel designs a set of guidelines that aspiring coaches must meet. To be considered for a coaching position, a candidate must have proven his or her ability to improve student achievement in the classroom and must be able to demonstrate a wide knowledge of curriculum and instruction. Additionally, each candidate must have been trained in interpersonal communication skills. When she interviews candidates, Mrs. Hetzel asks them to describe each element of the school's model of effective teaching and asks them to explain what performance for that element looks and sounds like at each level of the school's performance scale.

Differentiating Coaching

Coaches can use the process outlined in this book with any teacher in any school to improve performance. However, there are aspects of the coaching relationship that can be tailored to a teacher's specific situation. Here we present three ways in which a coach can differentiate his or her work with a teacher: (1) using different types of coach-teacher conversations, (2) taking into account a teacher's level of experience, and (3) gauging a teacher's readiness for change.

Coach-Teacher Conversations

Robyn Jackson (2008) describes four different kinds of conversations that coaches might have with teachers: (1) reflecting, (2) facilitating, (3) coaching, and (4) directing.

Reflecting conversations are designed to guide a teacher in identifying behaviors and beliefs and understanding how those behaviors and beliefs affect events in his or her classroom. The coach uses paraphrasing and active listening to help the teacher express his or her thoughts. The desired outcome of a reflecting conversation is *realization*.

Facilitating conversations are designed to aid a teacher in clarifying goals. The coach uses clarifying questions to help the teacher identify goals whose achievement will result in growth for the teacher. The desired outcome of a facilitating conversation is *goals*.

Coaching conversations are designed to help the teacher understand why he or she is or isn't making progress. The coach might suggest specific strategies to use or identify corrections or additions that need to be made to current strategies. The desired outcome of a coaching conversation is *growth*.

Directing conversations are designed to give a teacher clear instructions, as well as consequences that will ensue if they are not followed. The coach uses specific language, such as "I would like you to use response chaining to increase the complexity of your students' answers. If you don't, you will continue to receive superficial responses." The desired outcome of a directing conversation is *action*.

The following vignette illustrates how a coach might use the directing conversation with a teacher.

> Mr. Hitchens has been working with his coach, Sarah, for two months, and he is still at the Beginning (1) level for his growth goal of managing response rates. Sarah has provided feedback and recommendations, but he continues to call only on students who raise their hands and to accept students' initial answers to a question, without discussion or further elaboration. Sarah sits down with him after school one day to discuss the situation.
>
> "Thanks for meeting with me," she begins. "I want to talk to you today about some concerns I have about your growth-goal progress. We've talked about several different strategies related to managing response rates, but you're not using them in your classroom. If you don't start using strategies for this growth goal, you won't progress beyond the Beginning (1) level, and you'll continue to receive superficial answers from a small group of students."
>
> "I know," he replies, "I just don't feel like those strategies fit my style."
>
> "If that's the case," Sarah replies, "I am happy to try other strategies with you, but right now, you are not practicing any of the strategies we've discussed. If you continue to refuse to work on your growth goal, I can't help you grow professionally."
>
> Although Mr. Hitchens seems uncomfortable at times during the conversation, he agrees to try the random names strategy in his classroom the next day, and Sarah agrees to come and observe.

Level of Experience

Although a coach can use the process described in this book with any teacher, regardless of his or her experience level, there are several issues that a coach should be aware of when working with new or experienced teachers. Table 6.1 presents these considerations.

Table 6.1: Considerations for Working With New and Experienced Teachers

New Teachers	Experienced Teachers
• Schedule shorter coaching sessions to keep the teacher from being overwhelmed. • Co-teach rather than model. • Explain how small chunks of information fit together (for example, learning goal, assessment, track progress, assessment, track progress, assessment, celebration).	• Ask the teacher to share his or her history with you. • Ask the teacher about his or her role in the school community. • Ask the teacher to describe his or her areas of particular strength.

As shown in table 6.1, new teachers may need the coach to take a more directive teaching role in the coaching relationship, while more experienced teachers may benefit from a coach who listens and helps them reflect on ways to improve their current practices. The following vignette illustrates how a coach might interact with two teachers who have different levels of experience.

Cynthia has been a coach for three years, and she has worked with many different teachers with many different levels of experience. This semester, she is working with Miss Burch, a first-year teacher, and with Mrs. Fabian, who has taught for thirty years. When she meets with Miss Burch the first time, Cynthia schedules only half an hour. She and Miss Burch go over the personal profile, and Miss Burch fills it out as Cynthia describes each area. She knows that Miss Burch is feeling overwhelmed, so she's careful not to give her any extra "homework" from their coaching sessions. During their next session, Miss Burch looks back at her personal profile.

"There sure are a lot of zeroes and ones," she observes.

"Don't worry," says Cynthia. "We're only going to work on one thing at a time."

During the remainder of the session, they talk about Miss Burch's interests and decide to start with providing clear learning goals and scales (rubrics), since Miss Burch is taking a professional development class on the same topic.

When Cynthia meets with Mrs. Fabian, she begins by asking her about her teaching history. Mrs. Fabian tells her about the different schools she's taught in, from Singapore to California to New York. Realizing that Mrs. Fabian has experience in a wide variety of urban, suburban, rural, and foreign schools, Cynthia asks Mrs. Fabian how her current students compare to previous classes and what roles she most enjoys taking in the school community. Finally, Cynthia and Mrs. Fabian examine Mrs. Fabian's personal profile, and Cynthia asks Mrs. Fabian to elaborate on the areas where she's rated herself as a 3 or 4. As Mrs. Fabian describes her classroom practice, she brings up areas she would like to work on, and Cynthia offers to provide support in the form of research, theory, and strategies that Mrs. Fabian can use to work on those areas.

Readiness for Change

In schools and districts where teachers are required to work with a coach, coaches may encounter teachers with different levels of receptiveness to coaching. To describe this dichotomy, Jackson (2008) created a categorization system based on teachers' willingness to learn. She identifies will (motivation to learn and change) and skill (ability to learn and change) as two factors that determine a teachers' receptiveness to coaching. She used these two factors to create four categories, as shown in figure 6.1.

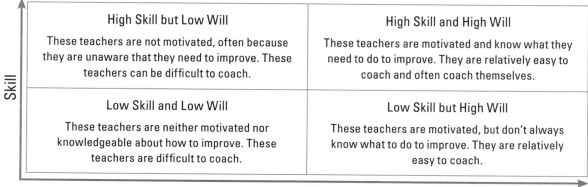

Figure 6.1: Teacher's skill and will.

Source: Adapted from Jackson, 2008. Used with permission.

As shown in figure 6.1 and in chapter 1, the motivation level of a teacher is one of the most important elements in determining the success of a coaching relationship. Al Burr (1993) also categorized teachers, but in a slightly different way:

- **Superstars**—These are the best teachers at a school. These teachers are often considered "irreplaceable" by their administrators, and parents often request that their children be assigned to these teachers' classes. Superstars are deeply respected by their colleagues and usually go above and beyond what is asked or required of them.

- **Backbones**—These are the good, solid teachers at a school. These teachers are less difficult to replace than superstar teachers, and parents are usually satisfied with having their child in these teachers' classes. These teachers work hard and do what is asked or required of them.

- **Mediocres**—These are teachers for whom a replacement would probably be an improvement. Parents are often dissatisfied with having their child in these teachers' classes. These teachers are resistant to change and do not consistently do what is asked or required of them.

However a coach chooses to classify teachers, the fact remains that some are less enthusiastic about coaching than others. The following list of techniques is useful for coaches working with reluctant teachers:

- **Monitor one's own behaviors closely**—Using a neutral expression and positive nonverbal signals (such as gestures, tone of voice, and eye movement) can help defuse tension.

- **Meet in a neutral location**—If a teacher is reluctant, it may be more comfortable to meet in a neutral location, like the library, rather than in the coach's office or the teacher's classroom.

- **Honor confidentiality**—In any coaching relationship, but especially in one with a reluctant teacher, explain what information is confidential and keep it confidential (for example, feedback, performance levels, and observation data).

- **Ask questions**—Rather than being directive, ask questions to find out why the teacher might be reluctant about coaching.

- **Avoid arguing**—Do not get emotionally involved or argue with a reluctant teacher. Maintain emotional objectivity by paraphrasing what a teacher is saying and verifying that you understand.

- **Involve administrators when necessary**—Reluctant teachers should not treat a coach disrespectfully. If this occurs, the coach should let the reluctant teacher know that disrespect will not be tolerated.

The following vignette illustrates how a coach might work with a reluctant teacher.

Mara is meeting today with Mrs. Murdock. Mrs. Murdock has made it clear that she does not need coaching and that she is only complying because the principal requires it. Mara arranges for them to meet in the school's library to go over Mrs. Murdock's personal profile. Before she asks to see the profile, Mara explains that the information in Mrs. Murdock's profile is confidential and will not be shared with the principal, district administrators, or other teachers.

"I should hope NOT!" says Mrs. Murdock.

Mara keeps her expression and tone neutral as she asks Mrs. Murdock about areas for which she scored herself as a 3 or 4. When Mara asks about areas for which Mrs. Murdock scored herself as a 1 or 0, Mrs. Murdock says that those are none of Mara's business.

Staying calm, Mara paraphrases Mrs. Murdock, saying, "So you don't want to share those areas with me?"

Mrs. Murdock nods her head and starts gathering her things to go.

Mara stays calm and looks Mrs. Murdock directly in the eye as she says, "Mrs. Murdock, I won't argue with you, but for me to do my job, we need to discuss your growth-goal areas. If you don't want to do that, I'll need to let the principal know."

After a few moments of silence, Mrs. Murdock replies, "Well, fine."

They examine her personal profile and identify helping students reflect on their learning as a good growth-goal area for Mrs. Murdock. The session progresses more smoothly after that, as Mara explains the research and theory behind that element and Mrs. Murdock selects a strategy to work on. After the session, Mara checks in with her administrator to let him know that she just met with Mrs. Murdock and, although the session was not ideal, they did identify a growth-goal element and a strategy for her to try. Mara explains that Mrs. Murdock was confrontational but also says she thinks the session ended respectfully.

Coaching Behaviors

As shown in chapter 1, there are several behaviors that are crucial to effective coaching. Here we provide strategies and suggestions for three of them: (1) modeling, (2) feedback, and (3) trust.

Modeling

Modeling is an important element of coaching, according to Knight (2007):

> Educators have known for decades that modeling is an important component of learning, and numerous research studies have demonstrated the power of modeling. . . . Modeling, observation, and feedback, then, are important, sometimes essential, for learning. We wouldn't teach someone to drive by giving them a lecture, tossing them a book, and then turning them loose on the freeway. . . . [Coaches enable] teachers to master new teaching practices by going into the classroom and showing the teacher exactly how a practice works with their children. (pp. 110–111)

There are several guidelines that a coach should keep in mind when modeling teaching.

- **Model in authentic environments**—Whenever possible, model a strategy with the teacher's own class. If that is not possible, model the strategy using the same content and at the same grade level that the teacher teaches.

- **Video record the coach modeling a strategy during a lesson**—This allows the teacher to watch the coach's use of the strategy multiple times.

- **Model a strategy multiple times**—Ask the teacher to compare the different uses of the strategy. Ask him or her to describe what stayed the same and what changed.

By following guidelines such as these, a coach can help a teacher see what a strategy looks like when used effectively in the classroom.

Feedback

Effective feedback should be timely and specific. While positive feedback is important, feedback should also highlight specific areas where improvement is needed. There are several ways that a coach can give feedback: informal verbal, informal written, formal verbal, and formal written.

Informal verbal feedback is usually unplanned and brief. A coach might stop by a teacher's classroom after school to give him a quick positive comment about an observation earlier in the day. *Informal written* feedback is also brief. A coach might send a quick email or leave a short note in a teacher's mailbox highlighting a positive teaching practice that the coach observed the teacher using.

Formal verbal feedback is more extensive and is usually given during a coaching session with the teacher. The coach should give the feedback and describe specific examples of the teacher's practice that illustrate either something a teacher did well, or something the teacher needs to work on. *Formal written* feedback, like formal verbal feedback, is detailed and specific about what the teacher did that was effective and what the teacher did that was not effective or needs to be adjusted. Formal written feedback might be given in a longer email or by memo. The coach normally retains a copy of formal written feedback to inform future discussions.

Trust

As described in chapter 1, trust must be present in a coaching relationship. The coach can build trust in many ways. Here we present three that are especially useful: (1) spending time together, (2) active listening, and (3) personal stories.

Spending time with a teacher does not need to involve activities outside of the school day. The simplest way for a coach to accomplish this is to invite the teacher to eat lunch together in the teacher's lounge or in the teacher's classroom. Alternatively, the coach might offer to help the teacher with a classroom task such as grading papers. Conversations during such interactions need not focus specifically on coaching or teaching topics, but they do need to provide ways for teachers and coaches to establish common interests and learn about each other's background.

Active listening has long been shown to be an important aspect of trusting relationships. Active listening communicates to the person speaking that he or she is important and that what he or she is saying is worth listening to. To listen actively, a coach should:

- **Look at the speaker while he or she is talking**—Eye contact communicates that the speaker has the listener's full attention.

- **Allow a pause of several seconds after the speaker stops speaking**—This allows the speaker to continue an unfinished thought, if necessary, and prevents the listener from jumping in too quickly.

- **Paraphrase what has been said**—By repeating the content of the speaker's message in his or her own words, a listener communicates that the message has been understood and gives the speaker an opportunity to correct any misunderstandings.

- **Ask clarifying questions**—If the listener doesn't understand what the speaker is saying, it is most respectful to say so and ask a question that will help clear up the misunderstanding.

Finally, a coach might volunteer *personal stories* about his or her experiences in the classroom or in life. Although coaches should not overuse this technique, it can help establish a personal connection between a coach and teacher.

The following vignette illustrates how a coach might use the behaviors of modeling, feedback, and trust to establish a coaching relationship with a teacher.

Claire has just found out that she will be working with three teachers at Juniper Elementary this trimester. Although Claire has worked with two of the teachers before, she doesn't know Ms. Dunstable, who is new there this year. To kick off their coaching relationship, Claire invites Ms. Dunstable to eat lunch with her in the teacher's lounge.

"Oh, I don't know if I can," says Ms. Dunstable. "I have a mountain of quizzes to grade, and I was going to do it while I ate my lunch."

"Would you mind if I ate with you in your classroom and helped grade?" asks Claire.

"Would you?" replies Ms. Dunstable. "That would be great!"

As they eat and grade, Claire gets a better idea of the sort of assessments Ms. Dunstable is using in her class and is introduced to the content she teaches. At their next coaching session, Ms. Dunstable thanks Claire for her help and explains that she's been busy with her twin daughters lately, and she's feeling a little behind with grading. Claire asks about Ms. Dunstable's daughters and listens actively while Ms. Dunstable explains that they were born premature and are still having trouble gaining weight.

"I'm a twin too, you know," says Claire.

"Really?" says Ms. Dunstable.

After a bit more conversation about siblings and families, Claire directs the conversation toward Ms. Dunstable's growth-goal element, previewing new content. Ms. Dunstable has selected the strategy of anticipation guides and Claire agrees to model it in her room. Later that week, as Claire models the strategy, Ms. Dunstable video records the lesson. Before their next coaching session, Claire video records Ms. Dunstable using the same strategy, and when they meet, they compare the two videos.

"The statements you created about the upcoming content were very insightful," says Claire. "They really gave your students something to think about."

Claire goes on to explain that Ms. Dunstable needs to focus her effort on discussing students' opinions about the statements rather than just hearing individual answers and moving on. To close the session, they watch the video of Claire using that part of the strategy and talk about what Ms. Dunstable can do to make her discussions more engaging.

Virtual Coaching

As seen in chapter 1, research has shown that bug-in-ear technology can be an effective way to provide teachers with feedback and coaching while they are teaching. Here we discuss the logistics involved with setting up virtual coaching and present different ways that coaches can structure their real-time feedback.

Logistics

In a recent article, Rock and her colleagues (2011) described the equipment they used to effectively implement virtual coaching using BIE technology. Table 6.2 (page 220) summarizes the equipment needed for the teacher and coach.

Table 6.2: Hardware for Virtual Coaching

Teacher Needs	Coach Needs
A wide-angle webcam	An external hard drive
A Bluetooth adapter	A headset with microphone
A Bluetooth headset	A webcam and microphone, if these are not built into the coach's computer

Source: Adapted from Rock et al., 2011.

The coach views the teacher's classroom remotely using Skype, a software program that is free to users of the Internet. The teacher wears a Bluetooth headset, and the coach can talk to her during the lesson without the students being aware. When engaging in virtual coaching, it may help for teachers and coaches to follow predetermined routines. For example, when the teacher answers the coach's call via Skype, the coach might take a moment to greet the students in the classroom. Then the teacher could minimize the Skype window or turn the computer screen away from students to avoid distracting them. Although the technology has proven to be very reliable, teachers and coaches might also decide how they will address dropped calls, audio or video issues, or other technical difficulties, in order to avoid wasting instructional time.

Real-Time Feedback

Rock and her colleagues (2011) also suggest that "the virtual coach and the teacher need to decide how feedback will be provided. Sometimes a running dialogue . . . is best; other coaches . . . use codes" (p. 46). For example, a coach might simply speak to a teacher as needed, providing short tidbits of timely feedback on the teacher's use of a specific strategy. Another coach might use codes, saying words like *summarize* or *predict* to remind a coach of specific steps in a strategy. The vignette that follows illustrates how a coach and teacher might use BIE technology during a lesson.

Jennifer, a coach in Connecticut, is conducting a virtual coaching session with Miss Becker, a teacher in Oregon. At the scheduled time, Jennifer initiates the Skype call to Miss Becker's computer, and Miss Becker's students perk up as they hear the familiar ring tone. Miss Becker slips her Bluetooth headset over her ear and answers the call. Jennifer briefly greets the students before Miss Becker minimizes the window on her computer screen.

Miss Becker, who teaches fifth grade, is just beginning a lesson on multiplying and dividing decimals. She is working on reviewing content, specifically using presented problems and demonstrations. Jennifer and Miss Becker have created a set of problems that require the students to use what they learned about multiplying decimals yesterday, and as Miss Becker passes the problems out and starts to give her students instructions about how long they have to work on them, Jennifer gives her some feedback: "I like the way you jumped right into the lesson, but you need to activate their background knowledge before you ask them to get to work. Why don't you ask them to describe the process for multiplying decimals to a partner before they start working?" Miss Becker does, and a quiet buzz fills the room.

Jennifer adds, "That's great. Now, why don't you have a few of them demonstrate the process? As you walk around, can you identify one or two students who understand it well?"

Miss Becker asks two students to come and demonstrate the process before everyone starts working on the presented problems.

After they've been working for several minutes, Jennifer gives Miss Becker some more advice: "You're doing great, and I can tell that they are really engaged. However, I see a few students who still look confused. You could either check in with them individually, or you could ask everyone to take a break and check what they've done so far with a partner. Which do you think would be best?"

Miss Becker decides to help the students individually, and Jennifer continues to provide feedback and suggestions as the lesson proceeds.

As Miss Becker is wrapping up the lesson, and the students are preparing to go out to recess, Jennifer cues her: "Remember that review is important at the end of a lesson too. After the students line up, review the main ideas of today's lesson with them."

Miss Becker does and, after the students leave for recess, she and Jennifer talk about what she did well and what she wants to work on next time before Jennifer signs off.

Summary

In this chapter, we presented additional aspects of coaching that coaches should be aware of as they guide teachers' professional growth. We discussed different systems that schools and districts can use to provide coaching to teachers, along with advantages and disadvantages associated with each option. We also provided guidelines that administrators and district leaders can use to guide the selection of coaches and the functioning of a coaching program. Then we reviewed ways to differentiate coaching, including several different types of coach-teacher conversations, ways to interact with teachers that take into account differences in experience and expertise, and tips for working with reluctant teachers. Next we provided practical strategies that coaches can use to model effective teaching, give feedback, and build trust. Finally, we discussed the logistical pieces necessary for virtual coaching and provided different ways that teachers can structure their feedback during a virtual coaching session.

Chapter 6: Comprehension Questions

1. Which coaching system most closely resembles the current coaching situation in your school or district?

2. Explain the purpose of each of the four types of coach-teacher conversations reviewed in the chapter. When during a coaching relationship might you use each type of conversation?

3. Of the six behaviors recommended for working with reluctant teachers, which do you already use? Which are you currently not using but would like to start using?

4. Which system for providing real-time feedback via BIE technology do you prefer: running dialogue or codes? Why?

Appendix

ANSWERS TO COMPREHENSION QUESTIONS

Answers to Chapter 2: Comprehension Questions

1. Describe the model of effective teaching presented in this chapter. How do the lesson segments, design questions, and elements fit together?

    The model of effective teaching presented in chapter 2 contains forty-one elements organized according to the design questions outlined in *The Art and Science of Teaching* (Marzano, 2007). These elements and design questions are sorted into three categories of classroom events, called lesson segments. Lesson segments involving routine events are those that occur on a regular basis. Lesson segments addressing content are those that involve students' interaction with academic content. Lesson segments enacted on the spot are those that occur on an as-needed basis.

2. Explain the key differences between each level of the scale presented in this chapter. What does a teacher need to do to move from Not Using (0) to Beginning (1)? Beginning (1) to Developing (2)? Developing (2) to Applying (3)? Applying (3) to Innovating (4)?

    To move from Not Using (0) to Beginning (1), a teacher must become aware of and try strategies related to an element. To move from Beginning (1) to Developing (2), a teacher must correct errors or omissions in his or her use of strategies related to an element. To move from Developing (2) to Applying (3), a teacher must monitor students' responses to strategies related to an element. To move from Applying (3) to Innovating (4), a teacher must either integrate several strategies related to an element to create a macrostrategy or adapt strategies for unique student needs and situations.

3. List teacher actions and coach actions for each of the four steps of the self-audit. What type of feedback should the coach offer during each step?

    First, the teacher completes a profile that indicates his or her current levels of performance for each of the forty-one elements of effective teaching, with the coach explaining each element. Then the teacher selects growth goals from the elements scored as 0 or 1. Next the coach verifies the teacher's selections and gives feedback about strategies that the teacher is using effectively, strategies that the teacher is using with errors or omissions, and strategies that the teacher should or could use, but isn't. Finally, the coach and teacher work together to write each growth goal.

4. For each level of the scale, describe actions that a coach can take to help a teacher move to the next level and teacher responses that show they have progressed to the next level.

    Not Using (0) to Beginning (1): The coach tells the teacher about research and theory related to his or her growth-goal element, provides or develops a list of strategies for the element, and explains the steps of the strategy a teacher chooses. When the teacher has tried the strategy in his or her classroom, he or she has moved to the Beginning (1) level.

    Beginning (1) to Developing (2): The coach identifies errors or omissions in the teacher's use of a strategy and helps the teacher correct them. The coach might identify

Coaching Classroom Instruction © 2013 Marzano Research Laboratory • marzanoresearch.com
Visit **marzanoresearch.com/classroomstrategies** to download this page.

such errors by observing the teacher, gauging student responses, or watching video recordings of the teacher. When the teacher performs the strategy without errors or omissions, he or she has moved to the Developing (2) level.

Developing (2) to Applying (3): The coach prompts the teacher to monitor students' responses to a strategy and helps the teacher adjust his or her instruction to achieve the desired student responses. When the teacher is monitoring students' responses and making adjustments to achieve the desired outcomes, he or she has moved to the Applying (3) level.

Applying (3) to Innovating (4): The coach helps the teacher integrate several strategies to create a macrostrategy or helps the teacher adapt a strategy for unique student needs and situations. When the teacher successfully uses a macrostrategy or adapts a strategy for unique student needs and situations, he or she has moved to the Innovating (4) level.

Answers to Chapter 3: Comprehension Questions

1. What must a teacher do to grow from the Not Using (0) level to the Beginning (1) level? As described in chapter 2 and in this chapter, what can a coach do to support that growth?

   To move from Not Using (0) to Beginning (1), a teacher must learn about research and theory associated with his or her growth-goal element, learn about strategies related to the element, select a strategy to work on, and try the strategy in his or her classroom. To guide a teacher from Not Using (0) to Beginning (1), the coach should review the research and theory that support the teacher's growth-goal element with the teacher. Then the coach should provide or develop a list of strategies for that element and help the teacher select one to try in his or her classroom. Finally, the coach should explain the steps of the selected strategy to the teacher and help him or her try it in the classroom.

2. Choose one of the forty-one elements, and find the following information for it:

   • Which lesson segment and design question are associated with the element?

   • What research and theory are associated with the element?

   • What strategies are associated with the element?

   Answers will vary according to the element chosen.

Answers to Chapter 4: Comprehension Questions

1. What must a teacher do to grow from the Beginning (1) level to the Developing (2) level? As described in chapter 2 and in this chapter, what can a coach do to support that growth?

   To move from Beginning (1) to Developing (2), a teacher must correct errors or omissions in his or her use of the strategy. A coach can help a teacher move from the Beginning (1) level to the Developing (2) level by alerting him or her to errors or omissions in the use of a strategy and giving him or her feedback about how to correct them. The coach might identify such errors by observing the teacher, examining students' responses to the strategy, talking to students about the teacher's use of the strategy, or watching video recordings of the teacher using the strategy.

2. What must a teacher do to grow from the Developing (2) level to the Applying (3) level? As described in chapter 2 and in this chapter, what can a coach do to support that growth?

   To move from Developing (2) to Applying (3), a teacher must monitor students' responses to a strategy and adjust instruction so the strategy achieves the desired student responses or outcomes. A coach can help a teacher move from the Developing (2) level to the Applying (3) level by prompting the teacher to pay attention to students' responses to a strategy and helping him or her make adjustments to achieve the desired student responses. The coach might do this by observing the teacher and providing cues, watching video recordings of the teacher using the strategy and examining students' responses, or by using bug-in-ear technology.

Answers to Chapter 5: Comprehension Questions

1. What must a teacher do to grow from the Applying (3) level to the Innovating (4) level? As described in chapter 2 and in this chapter, what can a coach do to support that growth?

   To move from Applying (3) to Innovating (4), the teacher can integrate several strategies related to an element to create a macrostrategy or adapt a strategy for unique student needs and situations. To guide a teacher from Applying (3) to Innovating (4), the coach can help the teacher identify several strategies that he or she has already used successfully that can be combined to create a macrostrategy. Alternatively, the coach can help the teacher identify his or her students' unique needs and adapt strategies to meet those needs or other unique situations.

2. What is a macrostrategy, and how should a teacher go about creating one?

   A macrostrategy is a set of instructional strategies used together for a specific purpose. A teacher can create one by combining several strategies associated with an element to create a larger strategy that directs students throughout an activity.

3. What special populations of students might require adaptations of strategies for their unique needs and situations?

   English learners, special education students, students from impoverished backgrounds, and gifted education students are all special populations who might benefit from strategies adapted for their unique needs and situations.

Answers to Chapter 6: Comprehension Questions

1. Which coaching system most closely resembles the current coaching situation in your school or district?

   Answers will vary. While teacher-initiated coaching requires the least amount of administrator support or financial resources, school- or districtwide coaching can ensure that all teachers receive support for their professional growth. Administrator-initiated coaching can provide targeted help to a struggling teacher, but it may require the coach to overcome reluctance in the teacher.

2. Explain the purpose of each of the four types of coach-teacher conversations reviewed in the chapter. When during a coaching relationship might you use each type of conversation?

   Reflecting conversations are designed to help teachers recognize the beliefs and behaviors that affect their classroom practice. Facilitating conversations are designed to help teachers set goals. Coaching conversations are designed to move teachers closer to accomplishing their goals, and directing conversations are designed to prompt a teacher to action.

3. Of the six behaviors recommended for working with reluctant teachers, which do you already use? Which are you currently not using but would like to start using?

   Answers will vary.

4. Which system for providing real-time feedback via BIE technology do you prefer: running dialogue or codes? Why?

   Answers will vary. Running dialogue allows a coach to provide more information and feedback, while codes may be less intrusive.

REFERENCES AND RESOURCES

Acheson, A. A., & Gall, M. D. (1992). *Techniques in the clinical supervision of teachers: Preservice and inservice applications* (3rd ed.). New York: Longman.

Ackland, R. (1991). A review of the peer coaching literature. *Journal of Staff Development, 12*(1), 22–27.

Adams, A., & Glickman, C. D. (1984). Does clinical supervision work? A review of research. *Tennessee Educational Leadership, 11*(11), 38–40.

Adler, N. J. (2006). Coaching executives. In M. Goldsmith & L. S. Lyons (Eds.), *Coaching for leadership: The practice of leadership coaching from the world's greatest coaches* (2nd ed., pp. 237–244). San Francisco: Pfeiffer.

Alexander, P. A., White, C. S., Haensly, P. A., & Crimmins-Jeanes, M. (1987). Training in analogical reasoning. *American Educational Research Journal, 24*(3), 387–404.

Allington, R. (1980). Teacher interruption behaviors during primary-grade oral reading. *Journal of Educational Psychology, 72*, 371–377.

Alseike, B. U. (1997). Cognitive Coaching: Its influences on teachers (Doctoral dissertation, University of Denver, 1997). *Dissertation Abstracts International, 58*, 183 (UMI No. 9804083)

Anderman, E. M., & Wolters, C. A. (2006). Goals, values, and affect: Influences on student motivation. In P. Alexander & P. Winne (Eds.), *Handbook of educational psychology* (pp. 369–389). Mahwah, NJ: Erlbaum.

Anderson, J. R. (1982). Acquisition of cognitive skills. *Psychological Review, 89*, 369–406.

Anderson, J. R. (1995). *Learning and memory: An integrated approach.* New York: Wiley.

Anderson, L., Evertson, C., & Emmer, E. (1980). Dimensions in classroom management derived from recent research. *Journal of Curriculum Studies, 12*, 343–356.

Anderson, R. H., & Snyder, K. J. (Eds.). (1993). *Clinical supervision: Coaching for higher performance.* Lancaster, PA: Technomic.

Arlin, M. (1979). Teacher transitions can disrupt time flow in classrooms. *American Educational Research Journal, 16,* 42–56.

Armento, B. J. (1978, February). *Teacher behavior and effective teaching of concepts.* Paper presented at the annual meeting of the American Association of Colleges for Teacher Education, Chicago. (ERIC Document Reproduction Service No. ED153949)

Auerbach, J. E. (2006). Cognitive coaching. In D. R. Stober & A. M. Grant (Eds.), *Evidence-based coaching handbook: Putting best practices to work for your clients* (pp. 103–127). Hoboken, NJ: Wiley.

Babad, E., Inbar, J., & Rosenthal, R. (1982). Pygmalion, Galatea, and the Golem: Investigations of biased and unbiased teachers. *Journal of Educational Psychology, 74,* 459–474.

Bachkirova, T., Cox, E., & Clutterbuck, D. (2010). Introduction. In E. Cox, T. Bachkirova, & D. Clutterbuck (Eds.), *The complete handbook of coaching* (pp. 1–20). Thousand Oaks, CA: SAGE.

Baker, W. P., & Lawson, A. E. (1995). *Effect of analogical instruction and reasoning level on achievement in general genetics.* Tempe: Department of Zoology, Arizona State University. (ERIC Document Reproduction Service No. ED390713)

Bangert-Drowns, R. L., Hurley, M. M., & Wilkinson, B. (2004). The effects of school-based writing-to-learn interventions on academic achievement: A meta-analysis. *Review of Educational Research, 74*(1), 29–58.

Bangert-Drowns, R. L., Kulik, C. C., Kulik, J. A., & Morgan, M. (1991). The instructional effects of feedback in test-like events. *Review of Educational Research, 61*(2), 213–238.

Bangert-Drowns, R. L., Kulik, J. A., & Kulik, C. C. (1991). Effects of classroom testing. *Journal of Educational Research, 85*(2), 89–99.

Becker, W. C. (Ed.). (1988). Direct instruction: Special issue. *Education and Treatment of Children, 11,* 297–402.

Bettencourt, E. M., Gillett, M. H., Gall, M. D., & Hull, R. E. (1983). Effects of teacher enthusiasm training on student on-task behavior and achievement. *American Educational Research Journal, 20*(3), 435–450.

Biancarosa, G., Bryk, A. S., & Dexter, E. R. (2010). Assessing the value-added effects of literacy collaborative professional development on student learning. *Elementary School Journal, 111*(1), 7–34.

Black, P., & Wiliam, D. (1998). Assessment and classroom learning. *Assessment in Education, 5*(1), 7–75.

Bloom, M. S. (1976). *Human characteristics and school learning.* New York: McGraw-Hill.

Bloom, M. S. (1984). The search for methods of group instruction as effective as one-to-one tutoring. *Educational Leadership, 41*(8), 4–18.

Bluckert, P. (2010). The Gestalt approach to coaching. In E. Cox, T. Bachkirova, & D. Clutterbuck (Eds.), *The complete handbook of coaching* (pp. 80–93). Thousand Oaks, CA: SAGE.

Bourne, A. (2007). Using psychometrics in coaching. In S. Palmer & A. Whybrow (Eds.), *Handbook of coaching psychology: A guide for practitioners* (pp. 385–403). New York: Routledge.

Bowen, C. W. (2000). A quantitative review of cooperative learning effects on high school and college chemistry achievement. *Journal of Chemical Education, 77*(1), 116–119.

Bowles, E. P., & Nelson, R. O. (1976). Training teachers as mediators: Efficacy of a workshop versus the bug-in-the-ear technique. *Journal of School Psychology, 14*(1), 15–25.

BrainyQuote. (n.d.). *Isaac Newton quotes.* Accessed at www.brainyquote.com/quotes/authors/i/isaac _newton.html on August 1, 2012.

Brekelmans, M., Wubbels, T., & Creton, H. A. (1990). A study of student perceptions of physics teacher behavior. *Journal of Research in Science Teaching, 27*, 335, 350.

Broadhurst, A., & Darnell, D. (1965). An introduction to cybernetics and information theory. *Quarterly Journal of Speech, 51*, 442–453.

Brockbank, A., & McGill, I. (2006). *Facilitating reflective learning through mentoring & coaching.* Philadelphia: Kogan Page.

Brophy, J. (Ed.). (2004). *Advances in research on teaching: Vol. 10—Using video in teacher education.* Oxford, England: Elsevier.

Brophy, J. E. (1983). Research on the self-fulfilling prophecy and teacher expectations. *Journal of Educational Psychology, 75*(5), 631–661.

Brophy, J. E. (1996). *Teaching problem students.* New York: Guilford Press.

Brophy, J. E. (2006). History of research in classroom management. In C. M. Evertson & C. S. Weinstein (Eds.), *Handbook of classroom management: Research, practice, and contemporary issues* (pp. 3–43). Mahwah, NJ: Erlbaum.

Brophy, J. E., & Evertson, C. M. (1976). *Learning from teaching: A developmental perspective.* Boston: Allyn & Bacon.

Brophy, J. E., & Good, T. L. (1970). Teacher's communication of differential expectations for children's classroom performance: Some behavioral data. *Journal of Educational Psychology, 61*(5), 365–374.

Brown, J. S., & Burton, R. R. (1978). Diagnostic models for procedural bugs in basic mathematical skills. *Cognitive Science, 2*, 155–192.

Bryk, A. S., & Schneider, B. (2002). *Trust in schools: A core resource for improvement.* New York: Russell Sage Foundation.

Buckingham, M. (2007). *Go put your strengths to work: 6 powerful steps to achieve outstanding performance.* New York: Free Press.

Burley, S., & Pomphrey, C. (2011). *Mentoring and coaching in schools: Collaborative professional learning inquiry for teachers.* New York: Routledge.

Burr, A. (1993, September). *Being an effective principal.* Paper presented at the regional satellite meeting of the Missouri Leadership Academy, Columbia, MO.

Bush, R. N. (1984). Effective staff development. In *Making our schools more effective: Proceedings of three state conferences* (pp. 223–239). San Francisco: Far West Laboratory for Educational Research and Development. (ERIC Document Reproduction Service No. ED249576)

Butler, D. L., & Winne, P. H. (1995). Feedback and self-regulated learning: A theoretical synthesis. *Review of Educational Research, 65*(3), 245–281.

Cahill, L., Prins, B., Weber, M., & McGaugh, J. (1994). Adrenergic activation and memory of emotional events. *Nature, 371*(6499), 702–704.

Calandra, B., Gurvitch, R., & Lund, J. (2008). An exploratory study of digital video editing as a tool for teacher preparation. *Journal of Technology and Teacher Education, 16*(2), 137–153.

Canter, L. (2010). *Lee Canter's assertive discipline: Positive behavior management for today's classroom* (4th ed.). Bloomington, IN: Solution Tree Press.

Cantrell, S. C., & Hughes, H. K. (2008). Teacher efficacy and content literacy implementation: An exploration of the effects of extended professional development with coaching. *Journal of Literacy Research, 40*(1), 95–127.

Chaikin, A., Sigler, E., & Derlega, V. (1974). Nonverbal mediators of teacher expectancy effects. *Journal of Personality and Social Psychology, 30*(1), 144–149.

Clement, J., Lockhead, J., & Mink, G. (1979). Translation difficulties in learning mathematics. *American Mathematical Monthly, 88*, 3–7.

Clutterbuck, D. (2010). Team coaching. In E. Cox, T. Bachkirova, & D. Clutterbuck (Eds.), *The complete handbook of coaching* (pp. 271–283). Thousand Oaks, CA: SAGE.

Coats, W., & Smidchens, V. (1966). Audience recall as a function of speaker dynamism. *Journal of Educational Psychology, 57*, 189–191.

Cogan, M. L. (1973). *Clinical supervision*. Boston: Houghton Mifflin.

Cooper, H. (1989). *Homework*. White Plains, NY: Longman.

Cooper, H. M. (1979). Pygmalion grows up: A model for teacher expectation communication and performance influence. *Review of Educational Research, 49*(3), 389–410.

Cooper, H., & Baron, R. (1977). Academic expectations and attributed responsibility as predictors of professional teachers' reinforcement behavior. *Journal of Educational Psychology, 69*, 409–418.

Cooper, H., Robinson, J. C., & Patall, E. A. (2006). Does homework improve academic achievement? A synthesis of research, 1987–2003. *Review of Educational Research, 76*(1), 1–62.

Cornbleth, C., Davis, O., & Button, C. (1972). *Teacher-pupil interaction and teacher expectations for pupil achievement in secondary social studies class.* Paper presented at the annual meeting of the American Educational Research Association, Chicago.

Costa, A. L., & Garmston, R. (1985). Supervision for intelligent teaching. *Educational Leadership, 42*(5), 70–80.

Costa, A. L., & Garmston, R. J. (2002). *Cognitive coaching: A foundation for Renaissance schools* (2nd ed.). Norwood, MA: Christopher-Gordon.

Coulter, G. A., & Grossen, B. (1997). The effectiveness of in-class instructive feedback versus after-class instructive feedback for teachers learning direct instruction teaching behaviors. *Effective School Practices, 16*(4), 21–35.

Crismore, A. (Ed.). (1985). *Landscapes: A state-of-the-art assessment of reading comprehension research: 1974–1984—Final report.* Washington, DC: U.S. Department of Education. (ERIC Document Reproduction Service No. ED261350)

Cross, K. P. (1998). Classroom research: Implementing the scholarship of teaching. In T. Angelo (Ed.), *Classroom assessment and research: An update on uses, approaches, and research findings* (pp. 5–12). San Francisco: Jossey-Bass.

Csikszentmihalyi, M. (1990). *Flow: The psychology of optimal experience.* New York: Harper & Row.

Darnell, D. (1970). "Clozentropy": A procedure for testing English language proficiency of foreign students. *Speech Monographs, 37,* 36–46.

Darnell, D. (1972). Information theory: An approach to human communication. In R. Budd & B. Ruben (Eds.), *Approaches to human communication* (pp. 156–169). New York: Spartan.

de Bono, E. (1999). *Six thinking hats.* New York: Back Bay Books.

Deci, E., Koestner, R., & Ryan, R. (2001). Extrinsic rewards and intrinsic motivation in education: Reconsidered once again. *Review of Educational Research, 71,* 1–27.

Deci, E. L., Ryan, R. M., & Koestner, R. (2001). The pervasive effects of rewards on intrinsic motivation: Response to Cameron (2001). *Review of Educational Research, 71*(1), 43–51.

Dutton, M. M. (1990). *An investigation of the relationship between training in cooperative learning and teacher job satisfaction.* Accessed at http://diexpress.umi.com/dxweb on May 11, 2012.

Dwyer, T., Blizzard, L., & Dean, K. (1996). Physical activity and performance in children. *Nutrition Review, 54*(4), 27–31.

Dwyer, T., Sallis, J., Blizzard, L., Lazarus, R., & Dean, K. (2001). Relation of academic performance to physical activity and fitness in children. *Pediatric Exercise Science, 13,* 225–237.

Ebbinghaus, H. (1987). Regarding a new application of performance testing and its use with school children. *Journal of Psychology and Physiology, 13,* 225–237.

Edwards, J. L., Green, K., Lyons, C. A., Rogers, M. S., & Swords, M. (1998). *The effects of Cognitive Coaching and nonverbal classroom management on teacher efficacy and perceptions of school culture.* Paper presented at the annual meeting of the American Educational Research Association, San Diego, CA.

Eisenhart, M. (1977, May). *Maintaining control: Teacher competence in the classroom.* Paper presented at the American Anthropological Association, Houston, TX.

El-Nemr, M. A. (1980). Meta-analysis of outcomes of teaching biology as inquiry. *Dissertation Abstracts International, 40,* 5813A.

Emler, N., & Heather, N. (1980). Intelligence: An ideological bias of conventional psychology. In P. Salmon (Ed.), *Coming to know* (135–151). London: Routledge.

Emmer, E. T., Evertson, C., & Anderson, L. (1980). Effective classroom management at the beginning of the school year. *Elementary School Journal, 80*(5), 219–231.

Emmer, E. T., Evertson, C. M., & Worsham, M. E. (2003). *Classroom management for secondary teachers* (6th ed.). Boston: Allyn & Bacon.

Emmer, E. T., & Gerwels, M. C. (2006). Classroom management in middle and high school classrooms. In C. Evertson, C. M. Weinstein, & C. S. Weinstein (Eds.), *Handbook of classroom management: Research, practice, and contemporary issues* (pp. 407–437). Mahwah, NJ: Erlbaum.

Emmer, E. T., Sanford, J. P., Clements, B. S., & Martin, J. (1982). *Improving classroom management and organization in junior high schools: An experimental investigation* (R & D Report No. 6153). Austin: Research and Development Center for Teacher Education, University of Texas. (ERIC Document Reproduction Service No. ED261053)

Emmer, E. T., Sanford, J. P., Evertson, C. M., Clements, B. S., & Martin, J. (1981). *The classroom management improvement study: An experiment in elementary school classrooms* (R & D Report No. 6050). Austin: Research and Development Center for Teacher Education, University of Texas. (ERIC Document Reproduction Service No. ED226452)

Epstein, J. L., & Harackiewicz, J. (1992). Winning is not enough: The effects of competition and achievement orientation on intrinsic interest. *Personality and Social Psychology Bulletin, 18,* 128–138.

Evertson, C. M., & Emmer, E. T. (1982). Preventive classroom management. In D. Duke (Ed.), *Helping teachers manage classrooms* (pp. 2–31). Alexandria, VA: Association for Supervision and Curriculum Development.

Evertson, C. M., Emmer, E. T., Sanford, J. P., & Clements, B. S. (1983). Improving classroom management: An experiment in elementary classrooms. *Elementary School Journal, 84*(2), 173–188.

Evertson, C. M., Emmer, E. T., & Worsham, M. E. (2003). *Classroom management for elementary teachers* (6th ed.). Boston: Allyn & Bacon.

Evertson, C. M., & Weinstein, C. S. (Eds.). (2006). *Handbook of classroom management: Research, practice, and contemporary issues.* Mahwah, NJ: Erlbaum.

Feltz, D. L., & Landers, D. M. (1983). The effects of mental practice on motor skill learning and performance: A meta-analysis. *Journal of Sport Psychology, 5,* 25–57.

Fillery-Travis, A., & Lane, D. (2007). Research: Does coaching work? In S. Palmer & A. Whybrow (Eds.), *Handbook of coaching psychology: A guide for practitioners* (pp. 57–70). New York: Routledge.

Firestone, G., & Brody, N. (1975). Longitudinal investigation of teacher-student interactions and their relationship to academic performance. *Journal of Educational Psychology, 67*(4), 544–550.

Fitts, P. M., & Posner, M. I. (1967). *Human performance.* Belmont, CA: Brooks/Cole.

Folkman, J. (2006). Coaching others to accept feedback. In M. Goldsmith & L. S. Lyons (Eds.), *Coaching for leadership: The practice of leadership coaching from the world's greatest coaches* (2nd ed., pp. 71–76). San Francisco: Pfeiffer.

Fraser, B. J., Walberg, H. J., Welch, W. W., & Hattie, J. A. (1987). Synthesis of educational productivity research [Special issue]. *International Journal of Educational Research, 11*(2), 145–252.

Frederick, W. C. (1980). Instructional time. *Evaluation in Education, 4,* 117–118.

Gallwey, W. T. (2000). *The inner game of work*. New York: Random House.

Ganske, L. (1981). Note-taking: A significant and integral part of learning environments. *Education Communication and Technology Journal, 29*(3), 155–175.

Garet, M. S., Cronen, S., Eaton, M., Kurki, A., Ludwig, M., Jones, W., et al. (2008). *The impact of two professional development interventions on early reading instruction and achievement* (NCEE 2008–4030). Washington, DC: National Center for Education Evaluation and Regional Assistance.

Garvey, B. (2010). Mentoring in a coaching world. In E. Cox, T. Bachkirova, & D. Clutterbuck (Eds.), *The complete handbook of coaching* (pp. 341–354). Thousand Oaks, CA: SAGE.

Gauthier, R., & Giber, D. (2006). Coaching business leaders. In M. Goldsmith & L. S. Lyons (Eds.), *Coaching for leadership: The practice of leadership coaching from the world's greatest coaches* (2nd ed., pp. 116–125). San Francisco: Pfeiffer.

Gawande, A. (2011). Personal best: Top athletes and singers have coaches. Should you? *The New Yorker, 87*(30). Accessed at www.newyorker.com/reporting/2011/10/03/111003fa_fact _gawande on October 19, 2011.

Gettinger, M., & Kohler, K. M. (2006). Process-outcome approaches to classroom management and effective teaching. In C. Evertson, C. M. Weinstein, & C. S. Weinstein (Eds.), *Handbook of classroom management: Research, practice, and contemporary issues* (pp. 73–95). Mahwah, NJ: Erlbaum.

Gick, M. L., & Holyoak, K. J. (1980). Analogical problem solving. *Cognitive Psychology, 12*, 306–353.

Gick, M. L., & Holyoak, K. J. (1983). Schema induction and analogical transfer. *Cognitive Psychology, 15*, 1–38.

Giebelhaus, C. R., & Cruz, J. (1992). The third ear mechanical device: A supervision alternative. *Journal of Early Childhood Teacher Education, 42*(13), 8–12.

Giebelhaus, C. R., & Cruz, J. (1994). The mechanical third ear device: An alternative to traditional student teaching supervision strategies. *Journal of Teacher Education, 45*(5), 365–373.

Giebelhaus, C. R., & Cruz, J. (1995). *Final report: Implementing the BIE intervention strategy with early field experience student teachers*. Columbus: The Ohio State University. (ERIC Document Reproduction Service No. ED393808)

Gijbels, D., Dochy, J., Van den Bossche, P., & Segers, M. (2005). Effects of problem-based learning: A meta-analysis from the angle of assessment. *Review of Educational Research, 75*(1), 27–61.

Glickman, C. D. (2002). *Leadership for learning: How to help teachers succeed*. Alexandria, VA: Association for Supervision and Curriculum Development.

Goldhammer, R. (1969). *Clinical supervision: Special methods for the supervision of teachers*. New York: Holt, Rinehart, & Winston.

Goldhammer, R., Anderson, R. H., & Krajewski, R. J. (1993). *Clinical supervision: Special methods for the supervision of teachers* (3rd ed.). Fort Worth, TX: Harcourt Brace Jovanovich College.

Goldsmith, M. (2006). Coaching for behavioral change. In M. Goldsmith & L. S. Lyons (Eds.), *Coaching for leadership: The practice of leadership coaching from the world's greatest coaches* (2nd ed., pp. 37–42). San Francisco: Pfeiffer.

Good, T. L., & Brophy, J. E. (2003). *Looking in classrooms* (9th ed.). Boston: Allyn & Bacon.

Good, T. L., Cooper, H., & Blakey, S. (1980). Classroom interaction as a function of teacher expectations, student sex, and time of year. *Journal of Educational Psychology, 72,* 378–385.

Good, T. L., Sikes, J., & Brophy, J. (1973). Effects of teacher sex and student sex on classroom interaction. *Journal of Educational Psychology, 65,* 74–87.

Gorby, C. B. (1937). Everyone gets a share of the profits. *Factory Management and Maintenance, 95,* 82–83.

Grant, A. M. (2005a). *Workplace, executive and life coaching: An annotated bibliography from the behavioral science literature.* Unpublished manuscript, Coaching Psychology Unit, University of Sydney, Australia.

Grant, A. M. (2005b). What is evidence-based executive, workplace and life coaching? In M. Cavanagh, A. M. Grant, & T. Kemp (Eds.), *Evidence-based coaching: Volume 1—Theory, research and practice from the behavioural sciences* (pp. 1–12). Bowen Hills, Australia: Australian Academic Press.

Grant, A. M. (2006). Workplace and executive coaching: A bibliography from the scholarly business literature. In D. R. Stober & A. M. Grant (Eds.), *Evidence based coaching handbook: Putting best practices to work for your clients* (pp. 367–388). Hoboken, NJ: Wiley.

Grant, A. M., Green, L. S., & Rynsaardt, J. (2010). Developmental coaching for high school teachers: Executive coaching goes to school. *Consulting Psychology Journal: Practice and Research, 62*(3), 151–168.

Grant, A. M., & Stober, D. R. (2006). Introduction. In D. R. Stober & A. M. Grant (Eds.), *Evidence based coaching handbook: Putting best practices to work for your clients* (pp. 1–14). Hoboken, NJ: Wiley.

Graue, M. E., Weinstein, T., & Walberg, H. J. (1983). School-based home instruction and learning: A quantitative synthesis. *Journal of Educational Research, 76,* 351–360.

Griffith, C. R. (1926). *Psychology of coaching; A study of coaching methods from the point of view of psychology.* New York: Scribner.

Guzzetti, B. J., Snyder, T. E., Glass, G. V., & Gamas, W. S. (1993). Promoting conceptual change in science: A comparative meta-analysis of instructional interventions from reading education and science education. *Reading Research Quarterly, 28*(2), 117–155.

Haas, M. (2005). Teaching methods for secondary algebra: A meta-analysis of findings. *NASSP Bulletin, 89*(642), 24–46.

Hall, L. E. (1989). The effects of cooperative learning on achievement: A meta-analysis. *Dissertation Abstracts International, 50,* 343A.

Haller, E. P., Child, D. A., & Walberg, H. J. (1988). Can comprehension be taught? A quantitative synthesis of "metacognitive studies." *Educational Researcher, 17*(9), 5–8.

Halpern, D. F., Hansen, C., & Reifer, D. (1990). Analogies as an aid to understanding and memory. *Journal of Educational Psychology, 82*(2), 298–305.

Hamaker, C. (1986). The effects of adjunct questions on prose learning. *Review of Educational Research, 56,* 212–242.

Harris, M. J., & Rosenthal, R. (1985). *Mediation of interpersonal expectancy effects: 31 meta-analyses. Psychological Bulletin, 97*(3), 363–386.

Hattie, J. A. (1992). Measuring the effects of schooling. *Australian Journal of Education, 36*(1), 5–13.

Hattie, J., Biggs, J., & Purdie, N. (1996). Effects of learning skills interventions on student learning: A meta-analysis. *Review of Educational Research, 66*(2), 99–136.

Henk, W. A., & Stahl, N. A. (1985). *A meta-analysis of the effect of notetaking on learning from lecture.* Paper presented at the 34th annual meeting of the National Reading Conference, St. Petersburg Beach, FL. (ERIC Document Reproduction Service No. ED258533)

Hennessy, S., & Deaney, R. (2009). The impact of collaborative video analysis by practitioners and researchers upon pedagogical thinking and practice: A follow-up study. *Teachers and Teaching: Theory and Practice, 15*(5), 617–638.

Herold, P. L., Ramirez, M., & Newkirk, J. (1971). A portable radio communication system for teacher education. *Educational Technology, 11,* 30–32.

Hess, D. E. (2009). *Controversy in the classroom: The democratic power of discussion.* New York: Routledge.

Hill, J. D., & Flynn, K. M. (2006). *Classroom instruction that works with English language learners.* Alexandria, VA: Association for Supervision and Curriculum Development.

Hofstetter, C. R., Sticht, T. G., & Hofstetter, C. H. (1999). Knowledge, literacy, and power. *Communication Research, 26*(1), 58–80.

Jackson, R. (2008). *The instructional leader's guide to strategic conversations with teachers.* Washington, DC: Mindsteps.

Jensen, E. (2005). *Teaching with the brain in mind* (2nd ed.). Alexandria, VA: Association for Supervision and Curriculum Development.

Jensen, E. (2009). *Teaching with poverty in mind: What being poor does to kids' brains and what schools can do about it.* Alexandria, VA: Association for Supervision and Curriculum Development.

Jeter, J., & Davis, O. (1973). *Elementary school teachers' differential classroom interaction with children as a function of differential expectations of pupil achievements.* Paper presented at the annual meeting of the American Educational Research Association, New Orleans, LA.

Johnson, D., Maruyama, G., Johnson, R., Nelson, D., & Skon, L. (1981). Effects of cooperative, competitive, and individualistic goal structures on achievement: A meta-analysis. *Psychological Bulletin, 89*(1), 47–62.

Johnson-Laird, P. N. (1983). *Mental models.* Cambridge, MA: Harvard University Press.

Johnson-Laird, P. N., & Byrne, R. M. J. (1991). *Deduction.* Hillsdale, NJ: Erlbaum.

Jonas, P. M. (2004). *Secrets of connecting leadership and learning with humor.* Lanham, MD: Scarecrow Education.

Joyce, B., & Showers, B. (2002). *Student achievement through staff development* (3rd ed.). Alexandria, VA: Association for Supervision and Curriculum Development.

Kagan, S., & Kagan, M. (2009). *Kagan cooperative learning.* San Clemente, CA: Kagan.

Kahan, D. (2002). The effects of a bug-in-the-ear device in intralesson communication between a student teacher and a cooperating teacher. *Journal of Teaching in Physical Education, 22*(1), 86–104.

Kauffman, C., Boniwell, I., & Silberman, J. (2010). The positive psychology approach to coaching. In E. Cox, T. Bachkirova, & D. Clutterbuck (Eds.), *The complete handbook of coaching* (pp. 158–171). Thousand Oaks, CA: SAGE.

Kee, K., Anderson, K., Dearing, V., Harris, E., & Shuster, F. (2010). *RESULTS coaching: The new essential for school leaders.* Thousand Oaks, CA: Corwin Press.

Kester, S., & Letchworth, G. (1972). Communication of teacher expectations and their effects on achievement and attitudes of secondary school students. *Journal of Educational Research, 66,* 51–55.

Kinnucan-Welsch, K., Rosemary, C., & Grogan, P. (2006). Accountability by design in literacy professional development. *Reading Teacher, 59*(5), 426–435.

Kirsch, I. (1999). The response expectancy: An introduction. In I. Kirsch (Ed.), *How expectancies shape experiences* (p. 7). Washington, DC: American Psychological Association.

Knight, J. (2007). *Instructional coaching: A partnership approach to improving instruction.* Thousand Oaks, CA: Corwin Press.

Knight, J. (2011). What good coaches do. *Educational Leadership, 69*(2), 18–22.

Korner, I. N., & Brown, W. H. (1952). The mechanical third ear. *Journal of Counseling Psychology, 16*(1), 81–84.

Kounin, J. S. (1983). *Classrooms: Individual or behavior settings? Micrographs in teaching and learning* (General Series No. 1). Bloomington: Indiana University, School of Education. (ERIC Document Reproduction Service No. ED240070)

Kouzes, J. M., & Posner, B. Z. (2006). When leaders are coaches. In M. Goldsmith & L. S. Lyons (Eds.), *Coaching for leadership: The practice of leadership coaching from the world's greatest coaches* (2nd ed., pp. 136–144). San Francisco: Pfeiffer.

Kretlow, A. G., & Bartholomew, C. C. (2010). Using coaching to improve the fidelity of evidence-based practices: A review of studies. *Teacher Education and Special Education, 33*(4), 279–299.

Kumar, D. D. (1991). A meta-analysis of the relationship between science instruction and student engagement. *Education Review, 43*(1), 49–66.

Land, M. L. (1980, February). *Joint effects of teacher structure and teacher enthusiasm on student achievement.* Paper presented at the annual meeting of the Southwest Educational Research Association, San Antonio, TX. (ERIC Document Reproduction Service No. ED182310)

Lee, A. Y. (n.d.). *Analogical reasoning: A new look at an old problem.* Boulder: University of Colorado, Institute of Cognitive Science.

Linden, D. E., Bittner, R. A., Muckli, L., Waltz, J. A., Kriegekorte, N., Goebel, R., Singer, W., & Munk, M. H. (2003). Cortical capacity constraints for visual working memory: Dissociation of FMRI load effects in a fronto-parietal network. *Neuroimage, 20*(3), 1518–1530.

Lipsey, M. W., & Wilson, D. B. (1993). The efficacy of psychological, educational, and behavioral treatment. *American Psychologist, 48*(12), 1181–1209.

Lott, G. W. (1983). The effect of inquiry teaching and advanced organizers upon student outcomes in science education. *Journal of Research in Science Teaching, 20*(5), 437–451.

Lou, Y., Abrami, P. C., Spence, J. C., Paulsen, C., Chambers, B., & d'Apollinio, S. (1996). Within-class grouping: A meta-analysis. *Review of Educational Research, 66*(4), 423–458.

Lovelace, M. K. (2005). Meta-analysis of experimental research based on the Dunn & Dunn model. *Journal of Educational Research, 98*(3), 176–183.

Luiten, J., Ames, W., & Ackerson, G. (1980). A meta-analysis of the effects of advance organizers on learning and retention. *American Educational Research Journal, 17*(2), 211–218.

Lundeberg, M., Koehler, M. J., Zhang, M., Karunaratne, S., McConnell, T. J., & Eberhardt, J. (2008, March). *"It's like a mirror in my face": Using video-analysis in learning communities of science teachers to foster reflection in teaching dilemmas.* Paper presented at the annual meeting of the American Educational Research Association, New York. Accessed at http://pbl.educ.msu.edu/wp-content/uploads/2008/04/lundeberg_et_al_march_2008.pdf on February 16, 2012.

Lyman, F. (2006). *Think-pair-share SmartCard* [Reference Card]. San Clemente, CA: Kagan.

Lysakowski, R. S., & Walberg, H. J. (1981). Classroom reinforcement in relation to learning: A quantitative analysis. *Journal of Educational Research, 75*, 69–77.

Lysakowski, R. S., & Walberg, H. J. (1982). Instructional effects of cues, participation, and corrective feedback: A quantitative synthesis. *American Educational Research Journal, 19*(4), 559–578.

Marsh, J. A., Sloan McCombs, J., Lockwood, J. R., Martorell, F., Gershwin, D., Naftel, S., et al. (2008). *Supporting literacy across the sunshine state: A study of Florida middle school reading coaches.* Santa Monica, CA: RAND Education.

Martinek, T., & Johnson, S. (1979). Teacher expectations: Effects on dyadic interaction and self-concept in elementary-age children. *Research Quarterly, 50*, 60–70.

Marzano, R. J. (1992). *A different kind of classroom: Teaching with dimensions of learning.* Alexandria, VA: Association for Supervision and Curriculum Development.

Marzano, R. J. (with Marzano, J. S., & Pickering, D. J.). (2003). *Classroom management that works: Research-based strategies for every teacher.* Alexandria, VA: Association for Supervision and Curriculum Development.

Marzano, R. J. (2006). *Classroom assessment and grading that work.* Alexandria, VA: Association for Supervision and Curriculum Development.

Marzano, R. J. (2007). *The art and science of teaching: A comprehensive framework for effective instruction.* Alexandria, VA: Association for Supervision and Curriculum Development.

Marzano, R. J. (with Boogren, T., Heflebower, T., Kanold-McIntyre, J., & Pickering, D.). (2012). *Becoming a reflective teacher*. Bloomington, IN: Marzano Research Laboratory.

Marzano, R. J., & Brown, J. L. (2009). *A handbook for the art and science of teaching*. Alexandria, VA: Association for Supervision and Curriculum Development.

Marzano, R. J., Frontier, T., & Livingston, D. (2011). *Effective supervision: Supporting the art and science of teaching*. Alexandria, VA: Association for Supervision and Curriculum Development.

Marzano, R. J., Gaddy, B. B., Foseid, M. C., Foseid, M. P., & Marzano, J. S. (2005). *A handbook for classroom management that works*. Alexandria, VA: Association for Supervision and Curriculum Development.

Marzano, R. J., Gnadt, J., & Jesse, D. M. (1990). *The effects of three types of linguistic encoding strategies on the processing of information presented in lecture format*. Unpublished manuscript, University of Colorado at Denver.

Marzano, R. J., Pickering, D. J., & Pollock, J. E. (2001). *Classroom instruction that works: Research-based strategies for increasing student achievement*. Alexandria, VA: Association for Supervision and Curriculum Development.

Mastin, V. (1963). Teacher enthusiasm. *Journal of Educational Research, 56*, 385–386.

Mayer, R. E. (1979). Can advance organizers influence meaningful learning? *Review of Educational Research, 49*, 371–383.

Mayer, R. E. (1989). Models of understanding. *Review of Educational Research, 59*, 43–64.

Mayer, R. E. (2003). *Learning and instruction*. Upper Saddle River, NJ: Merrill/Prentice Hall.

McCaslin, M., Bozack, A. R., Napoleon, L., Thomas, A., Vasquez, V., Wayman, V., & Zhang, J. (2006). Self-regulated learning and classroom management: Theory, research, and consideration for classroom practice. In C. Evertson, C. M. Weinstein, & C. S. Weinstein (Eds.), *Handbook of classroom management: Research, practice, and contemporary issues* (pp. 223–252). Mahwah, NJ: Erlbaum.

McCombs, B. L. (2001). Self-regulated learning and academic achievement: A phenomenological view. In B. J. Zimmerman & D. H. Schunk (Eds.), *Self-regulated learning and academic achievement: Theoretical perspectives* (2nd ed., pp. 67–124). Mahwah, NJ: Erlbaum.

McConnell, J. W. (1977, April). *The relationship between selected teacher behaviors and attitudes and achievement of algebra classes*. Paper presented at the annual meeting of the American Educational Research Association, New York. (ERIC Document Reproduction Service No. ED141118)

McDaniel, M. A., & Donnelly, C. M. (1996). Learning with analogy and elaborative interrogation. *Journal of Educational Psychology, 88*(3), 508–519.

McVee, M. B., Dunsmore, K., & Gavalek, J. R. (2005). Schema theory revisited. *Review of Educational Research, 75*(4), 531–566.

Meichenbaum, D., Bowers, K., & Ross, R. (1969). A behavioral analysis of teacher expectancy effect. *Journal of Personality and Social Psychology, 13*, 306–316.

Mendoza, S., Good, T., & Brophy, J. (1972). *Who talks in junior high classrooms?* (Report No. 68). Austin: Research and Development Center for Teacher Education, University of Texas at Austin.

Moriarity, B., Douglas, G., Punch, K., & Hattie, J. (1995). The importance of self-efficacy as a mediating variable between learning environments and achievement. *British Journal of Educational Psychology, 65,* 73–84.

Moskowitz, G., & Hayman, J. L. (1976). Success strategies of inner-city teachers: A year-long study. *Journal of Educational Research, 69,* 283–289.

Nelson, J. R., Martella, R., & Galand, B. (1998). The effects of teaching school expectations and establishing a consistent consequence on formal office disciplinary actions. *Journal of Emotional and Behavioral Disorders, 4*(3), 153–161.

Nesbit, J. C., & Adesope, O. O. (2006). Learning with concept and knowledge maps: A meta-analysis. *Review of Educational Research, 76*(3), 413–448.

Neuman, S. B., & Wright, T. S. (2010). Promoting language and literacy development for early childhood educators: Mixed-methods study of coursework and coaching. *Elementary School Journal, 111*(1), 63–86.

Nolan, J., Hawkes, B., & Francis, P. (1993). Case studies: Windows onto clinical supervision. *Educational Leadership, 51*(2), 52–56.

Norwood, K., & Burke, M. A. (2011). Education. In L. Wildflower & D. Brennan (Eds.), *The handbook of knowledge-based coaching: From theory to practice* (pp. 211–220). San Francisco: Jossey-Bass.

Nuthall, G. (1999). The way students learn: Acquiring knowledge from an integrated science and social studies unit. *Elementary School Journal, 99*(4), 303–341.

Nuthall, G., & Alton-Lee, A. (1995). Assessing classroom learning: How students use their knowledge and experience to answer classroom achievement test questions in science and social studies. *American Educational Research Journal, 32*(1), 185–223.

Nye, B., Konstantopoulos, S., & Hedges, L. V. (2004). How large are teacher effects? *Educational Evaluation and Policy Analysis, 26*(3), 237–257.

Oades, L. G., Caputi, P., Robinson, P. M., & Partridge, B. (2005). A contemporary coaching theory to integrate work and life in changing times. In M. Cavanagh, A. M. Grant, & T. Kemp (Eds.), *Evidence-based coaching: Volume 1—Theory, research and practice from the behavioural sciences* (pp. 69–82). Bowen Hills, Australia: Australian Academic Press.

O'Reilly, M. F., Renzaglia, A., Hutchins, M., Koterba-Bass, L., Clayton, M., Halle, J. W., et al. (1992). Teaching systematic instruction competencies to special education student teachers: An applied behavioral supervision model. *Journal of the Association for Persons With Severe Handicaps, 17,* 104–111.

O'Reilly, M. F., Renzaglia, A., & Lee, S. (1994). An analysis of acquisition, generalization and maintenance of systematic instruction competencies by preservice teachers using behavioral supervision techniques. *Education and Training in Mental Retardation and Developmental Disabilities, 29,* 22–23.

Ogle, D. (1986). K-W-L: A teaching model that develops active reading of expository text. *Reading Teacher, 39*(6), 564–570.

Page, S. (1971). Social interaction and experimenter effects in a verbal conditioning experiment. *Canadian Journal of Educational Psychology, 25,* 463–475.

Pajak, E. (1993). *Approaches to clinical supervision: Alternatives for improving instruction.* Norwood, MA: Christopher-Gordon.

Pajak, E. (2002). Clinical supervision and psychological functions: A new direction for theory and practice. *Journal of Curriculum and Supervision, 17*(3), 189–205.

Palincsar, A. S., & Brown, A. L. (1984). Reciprocal teaching of comprehension-fostering and comprehension-monitoring activities. *Cognition and Instruction, 1*(2), 117–175.

Palmer, P. J. (2007). *The courage to teach: Exploring the inner landscape of a teacher's life.* San Francisco: Jossey-Bass.

Palmer, S., & Szymanska, K. (2007). Cognitive behavioural coaching: An integrative approach. In S. Palmer & A. Whybrow (Eds.), *Handbook of coaching psychology: A guide for practitioners* (pp. 86–117). New York: Routledge.

Palmer, S., & Whybrow, A. (2007). Coaching psychology: An introduction. In S. Palmer & A. Whybrow (Eds.), *Handbook of coaching psychology: A guide for practitioners* (pp. 1–20). New York: Routledge.

Parsloe, E. (1995). *Coaching, mentoring, and assessing: A practical guide to developing competence* (Rev. ed.). New York: Kogan Page.

Paschal, R. A., Weinstein, T., & Walberg, H. J. (1984). The effects of homework on learning: A quantitative synthesis. *Journal of Educational Research, 78,* 97–104.

Passmore, J. (2007). Behavioral coaching. In S. Palmer & A. Whybrow (Eds.), *Handbook of coaching psychology: A guide for practitioners* (pp. 73–85). New York: Routledge.

Pavan, B. N. (1985, April). *Clinical supervision: Research in schools utilizing comparative measures.* Paper presented at the annual meeting of the American Educational Research Association, Chicago.

Perry, N. E., Turner, J. C., & Meyer, D. K. (2006). Classrooms as contexts for motivating learning. In P. Alexander & P. Winne (Eds.), *Handbook of educational psychology* (pp. 327–348). Mahwah, NJ: Erlbaum.

Pflaum, S. W., Walberg, H. J., Karegianes, M. L., & Rasher, S. P. (1980). Reading instruction: A quantitative analysis. *Educational Researcher, 9*(7), 12–18.

Piercy, T. D. (2006). *Compelling conversations: Connecting leadership to student achievement.* Englewood, CO: Advanced Learning Press.

Plax, T. G., & Kearney, P. (1990). Classroom management: Structuring the classroom for work. In J. Daly, G. Friedrich, & A. Vangelesti (Eds.), *Teaching communication: Theory, research, and methods* (pp. 223–236). Hillsdale, NJ: Erlbaum.

Powell, G. (1980, December). *A meta-analysis of the effects of "imposed" and "induced" imagery upon word recall.* Paper presented at the annual meeting of the National Reading Conference, San Diego, CA. (ERIC Document Reproduction Service No. ED199644)

Prochaska, J. O., DiClemente, C. C., & Norcross, J. C. (1992). In search of how people change: Applications to addictive behaviors. *American Psychologist, 47*(9), 1102–1114.

Raphael, R. E., & Kirschner, B. M. (1985). *The effects of instruction in compare/contrast text structure in sixth-grade students' reading comprehension and writing products* [Research Series No. 161]. Lansing, MI: Institute for Research on Teaching.

Redfield, D. L., & Rousseau, E. W. (1981). A meta-analysis of experimental research on teacher questioning behavior. *Review of Educational Research, 51*(2), 237–245.

Reeve, J. (2006). Extrinsic rewards and inner motivation. In C. Evertson, C. M. Weinstein, & C. S. Weinstein (Eds.), *Handbook of classroom management: Research, practice, and contemporary issues* (pp. 645–664). Mahwah, NJ: Erlbaum.

Reeve, J., & Deci, E. (1996). Elements of competitive situations that affect intrinsic motivation. *Personality and Social Psychology Bulletin, 22*, 24–33.

Reeves, D. B. (2007). Coaching myths and realities. *Educational Leadership, 65*(2), 89–90.

Rejeski, W., Darracott, C., & Hutslar, S. (1979). Pygmalion in youth sport: A field study. *Journal of Sports Psychology, 1*, 311–319.

Rist, R. (1970). Student social class and teacher expectations: The self-fulfilling prophecy in ghetto education. *Harvard Educational Review, 40*, 411–451.

Rock, M. L., Gregg, M., Thead, B. K., Acker, S. E., Gable, R. A., & Zigmond, N. P. (2009). Can you hear me now? Evaluation of an online wireless technology to provide real-time feedback to special education teachers-in-training. *Teacher Education and Special Education, 32*(1), 64–82.

Rock, M. L., Zigmond, N. P., Gregg, M., & Gable, R. A. (2011). The power of virtual coaching. *Educational Leadership, 69*(2), 42–48.

Roeser, R. W., Peck, S. C., & Nasir, N. S. (2006). Self and identity processes in school motivation, learning, and achievement. In P. Alexander & P. Winne (Eds.), *Handbook of educational psychology* (pp. 391–424). Mahwah, NJ: Erlbaum.

Rogers, C. R., & Farson, R. E. (2006). Active listening. In J. S. Osland, M. E. Turner, D. A. Kolb, & I. M. Rubin (Eds.), *The organizational behavior reader* (8th ed., pp. 279–290). Upper Saddle River, NJ: Pearson.

Rogers, J. (2011). Afterword: Challenges ahead. In L. Wildflower & D. Brennan (Eds.), *The handbook of knowledge-based coaching: From theory to practice* (pp. 341–344). San Francisco: Jossey-Bass.

Rosenshine, B. (1970). Enthusiastic teaching: A research review. *School Review, 78*, 499–514.

Rosenshine, B. (2002). *Converging findings on classroom instruction.* Accessed at http://nepc.colorado.edu/files/Chapter09-Rosenshine-Final.pdf on May 21, 2012.

Rosenshine, B., & Furst, N. (1973). The use of direct observation to study teaching. In R. Traverss (Ed.), *Handbook of research on teaching* (2nd ed., pp. 263–298). Chicago: Rand McNally.

Rosenshine, B., Meister, C., & Chapman, S. (1996). Teaching students to generate questions: A review of the intervention studies. *Review of Educational Research, 66*(2), 181–221.

Rosenshine, B., & Meister, C. C. (1994). Reciprocal teaching: A review of the research. *Review of Educational Research, 64*(4), 479–530.

Ross, J. A. (1988). Controlling variables: A meta-analysis of training studies. *Review of Educational Research, 58*(4), 405–437.

Rovee-Collier, C. (1995). Time windows in cognitive development. *Developmental Psychology, 31*(2), 147–169.

Rubovits, P., & Maehr, M. (1971). Pygmalion analyzed: Toward an explanation of the Rosenthal-Jacobson findings. *Journal of Personality and Social Psychology, 19,* 197–203.

Sanford, J. P., & Evertson, C. M. (1981). Classroom management in a low SES junior high: Three case studies. *Journal of Teacher Education, 32*(1), 34–38.

Scheeler, M. C., & Lee, D. L. (2002). Using technology to deliver immediate corrective feedback to preservice teachers. *Journal of Behavioral Education, 11*(4), 231–241.

Scheeler, M. C., McAfee, J. K., Ruhl, K. L., & Lee, D. L. (2006). Effects of corrective feedback delivered via wireless technology on preservice teacher performance and student behavior. *Teacher Education and Special Education, 29*(1), 12–25.

Scheeler, M. C., Ruhl, K. L., & McAfee, J. K. (2004). Providing performance feedback to teachers: A review. *Teacher Education and Special Education, 27*(4), 396–407.

Schein, E. H. (2006). Coaching and consultation revisited: Are they the same? In M. Goldsmith & L. S. Lyons (Eds.), *Coaching for leadership: The practice of leadership coaching from the world's greatest coaches* (2nd ed., pp. 17–25). San Francisco: Pfeiffer.

Schön, D. A. (1987). *Educating the reflective practitioner: Toward a new design for teaching and learning in the professions.* San Francisco: Jossey-Bass.

Schunk, D. H., & Cox, P. D. (1986). Strategy training and attributional feedback with learning disabled students. *Journal of Educational Psychology, 73*(3), 201–209.

Schwanenflugel, P. J., Stahl, S. A., & McFalls, E. L. (1997). *Partial word knowledge and vocabulary growth during reading comprehension* (Research Report No. 76). Athens: University of Georgia, National Reading Research Center.

Skiffington, S., & Zeus, P. (2000). *The complete guide to coaching at work.* New York: McGraw-Hill.

Skinner, C. H., Fletcher, P. A., & Hennington, C. (1996). Increasing learning rates by increasing student response rates. *School Psychology Quarterly, 11,* 313–325.

Skinner, M. E., & Welch, F. C. (1996). Peer coaching for better teaching. *College Teaching, 44*(4), 153–156.

Smith, F., & Luginbuhl, J. (1976). Inspecting expectancy: Some laboratory results of relevance for teacher training. *Journal of Educational Psychology, 68,* 265–272.

Smith, H. (1985). The marking of transitions by more and less effective teachers. *Theory Into Practice, 24,* 57–62.

Smith, M. C. (1997). Self-reflection as a means of increasing teacher efficacy through Cognitive Coaching (Master's thesis, California State University at Fullerton, 1997). *Dissertation Abstracts International, 58* (01-A). (UMI No. 1384304)

Smollett, T. (Trans.). (1997). *The adventures of Telemachus, the son of Ulysses.* Athens: University of Georgia Press.

Soar, R. S., & Soar, R. M. (1979). Emotional climate and management. In P. L. Peterson & H. J. Walberg (Eds.), *Research on teaching: Concepts, findings, and implications* (pp. 97–119). Berkeley, CA: McCutchan.

Stage, S. A., & Quiroz, D. R. (1997). A meta-analysis of interventions to decrease disruptive classroom behavior in public education settings. *School Psychology Review, 26*(3), 333–368.

Stahl, S. A. (1999). *Vocabulary development.* Cambridge, MA: Brookline.

Stahl, S. A., & Fairbanks, M. M. (1986). The effects of vocabulary instruction: A model-based meta-analysis. *Review of Educational Research, 56*(1), 72–110.

Stipek, D. J., & Weisz, J. R. (1981). Perceived personal control and academic achievement. *Review of Educational Research, 51*(1), 101–137.

Stone, C. L. (1983). A meta-analysis of advanced organizer studies. *Journal of Experimental Education, 51*(7), 194–199.

Sullivan, C. G. (1980). *Clinical supervision: A state of the art review.* Alexandria, VA: Association for Supervision and Curriculum Development.

Sweitzer, G. L., & Anderson, R. D. (1983). A meta-analysis of research in science teacher education practices associated with inquiry strategy. *Journal of Research in Science Teaching, 20,* 453–466.

Taylor, M. (1979). Race, sex, and the expression of self-fulfilling prophecies in a laboratory teaching situation. *Journal of Personality and Social Psychology, 37,* 897–912.

Taylor, W. (1953). "Cloze procedure": A new tool for measuring readability. *Journalism Quarterly, 30,* 415–433.

Tennenbaum, G., & Goldring, E. (1989). A meta-analysis of the effect of enhanced instruction: Cues, participation, reinforcement, and feedback and correctives on motor skill learning. *Journal of Research and Development in Education, 22*(3), 53–64.

Tennyson, R. D., & Cocchiarella, M. J. (1986). An empirically based instructional design theory for teaching concepts. *Review of Educational Research, 56,* 40–71.

Thomson, C. L., Holmberg, M. C., Baer, D. M., Hodges, W. L., & Moore, S. G. (1978). An experimental analysis of some procedures to teacher primary and reinforcement skills to preschool teachers. *Monographs of the Society for Research in Child Development, 43*(4), 1–86.

Tomlinson, C. A., & Imbeau, M. B. (2010). *Leading and managing a differentiated classroom.* Alexandria, VA: Association for Supervision and Curriculum Development.

Toulmin, S., Rieke, R., & Janik, A. (1981). *An introduction to reasoning.* New York: Macmillan.

Tschannen-Moran, B., & Tschannen-Moran, M. (2010). *Evocative coaching: Transforming schools one conversation at a time*. San Francisco: Jossey-Bass.

Tschannen-Moran, M. (2004). *Trust matters: Leadership for successful schools*. San Francisco: Jossey-Bass.

van der Mars, H. (1988). The effects of audio-cueing on selected teaching behaviors of an experienced elementary physical education specialist. *Journal of Teaching in Physical Education, 8*(1), 64–72.

van Es, E. A. (2009). Participants' roles in the context of a video club. *Journal of the Learning Sciences, 18*, 100–137.

Vanderburg, M., & Stephens, D. (2010). The impact of literacy coaches. *Elementary School Journal, 111*(1), 141–163.

Walberg, H. J. (1982). What makes schooling effective? A synthesis and critique of three national studies. *Contemporary Education Review, 1*, 23–34.

Walberg, H. J. (1999). Productive teaching. In H. C. Waxman & H. J. Walberg (Eds.), *New directions for teaching practice research* (pp. 75–104). Berkeley, CA: McCutchan.

Weiner, N. (1967). *The human use of human beings*. New York: Avon.

Weinstein, C. (1977). Modifying student behavior in an open classroom through changes in the physical design. *American Educational Research Journal, 14*, 249–262.

West, L. H. T., & Fensham, P. J. (1976). Prior knowledge or advance organizers as affective variables in chemical learning. *Journal of Research in Science Teaching, 13*, 297–306.

Whitmore, J. (2009). *Coaching for performance: GROWing human potential and purpose* (4th ed.). Boston: Brealey.

Williams, R. G., & Ware, J. E., Jr. (1976). Validity of student ratings of instruction under different incentive conditions: A further study of the Dr. Fox effect. *Journal of Educational Psychology, 68*, 48–56.

Williams, R. G., & Ware, J. E., Jr. (1977). An extended visit with Dr. Fox: Validity of student ratings of instruction after repeated exposure to a lecturer. *American Educational Research Journal, 14*, 449–457.

Willis, B. (1970). The influence of teacher expectation on teachers' classroom interaction with selected children. *Dissertation Abstracts International, 30*, 5072A.

Wise, K. C., & Okey, J. R. (1983). A meta-analysis of the effects of various science teaching strategies on achievement. *Journal of Research in Science Teaching, 20*(5), 415–425.

Wubbels, T., Brekelmans, M., den Brok, P., & van Tartwijk, J. (2006). An interpersonal perspective on classroom management in secondary classrooms in the Netherlands. In C. Evertson & C. S. Weinstein (Eds.), *Handbook of classroom management: Research, practice, and contemporary issues* (pp. 1161–1191). Mahwah, NJ: Erlbaum.

Wubbels, T., Brekelmans, M., van Tartwijk, J., & Admiral, W. (1999). Interpersonal relationships between teachers and students in the classroom. In H. C. Waxman & H. J. Walberg (Eds.), *New directions for teaching practice and research* (pp. 151–170). Berkeley, CA: McCutchan.

Wubbels, T., & Levy, J. (1993). *Do you know what you look like? Interpersonal relationships in education.* London: Falmer Press.

Wyckoff, W. L. (1973). The effect of stimulus variation on learning from lecture. *Journal of Experimental Education, 41,* 85–96.

Zeus, P., & Skiffington, S. (2002). *The coaching at work toolkit: A complete guide to techniques and practices.* Sydney, Australia: McGraw-Hill.

INDEX

A

Adler, N., 9
administrator-initiated coaching, 211–212
advanced students, differentiation strategies for,
    156–157
Anderson, R., 4–5
Applying (3) to Innovating (4) lesson segments
    coaching perspective, 33–34
    content lesson segments, 165–185
    differentiation strategies for advanced and
        struggling students, 156–157
    enacted on the spot lesson segments, 186–207
    macrostrategy, creating a, 155–156
    routine events lesson segments, 157–164
    vignettes, 35, 208
Art and Science of Teaching, The (Marzano), 18, 19,
    32, 35, 58, 153
assessment
    formative, 13, 38, 65, 158
    individual score-level, 65, 158
Auerbach, J., 12

B

Bachkirova, T., 4
Bartholomew, C., 6, 7, 11
Becoming a Reflective Teacher (Marzano), 18, 19,
    32, 38, 40, 43, 45, 51, 53, 54, 56
Beginning (1) to Developing (2) and Developing
    (2) to Applying (3) lesson segments
    coaching perspective, 33
    content lesson segments, 75–112

enacted on the spot lesson segments, 112–153
    relationship between teacher actions and student
        responses, 63–63
    routine events lesson segments, 63–75
    vignettes, 34–35, 63
behaviors, coaching, 13, 217–219
Biancarosa, G., 7
BIE (bug-in-ear) technology, 16, 17, 219–220
Big Four model, 13
Bluckert, P., 9
Bourne, A., 11
Brockbank, A., 8, 11
Brophy, J., 37
Brown, W., 17
Bryk, A., 7, 10
Buckingham, M., 9
Burke, M. A., 12, 15–16
Burley, S., 9
Burr, A., 216
Bush, R., 6

C

Cantrell, S., 7
Caputi, P., 4
change, teachers and readiness for, 215–217
Chapman, S., 155
choice, 11
clinical supervision, 4–5, 12
Clinical Supervision (Cogan), 5
Clinical Supervision (Goldhammer), 5
cloze activities, 90, 173
Clutterbuck, D., 4, 16

coach, use of term, 4
coaching
    aspects of, 7–8
    behaviors, 217–219
    benefits of, 5–7
    clinical supervision, 4–5
    continuum model, 15–16
    conversations, 213
    differentiating, 213–217
    goals, 6
    guidelines, 212–213
    history of, 3–4
    nonevaluative nature of, 8–9
    requirements for effective, 9–11
    research and theory, putting into practice, 18
    student achievement and, 7
    systems, 211–213
    teacher knowledge and skills, 7
Coaching for Performance (Whitmore), 14
coaching models
    Big Four model, 13
    coaching continuum model, 15–16
    Cognitive Coaching, 12–13
    GROW model, 14–15
    Inner Game model, 13–14
    team coaching, 16
    virtual, 16–17, 219–221
coaching perspective, establishing a, 30–35
coaching relationships
    coaching perspective, establishing a, 30–35
    establishing a model of effective teaching, 19–23
    measuring teachers' progress, scale for, 23–24
    self-audit, conducting a, 24–30
coach-teacher conversations, 213–214
Cogan, M., 4–5, 12
Cognitive Coaching, 12–13
collaborative processing, 31, 84, 170
concept attainment, 32, 86, 170
content, strategies for helping students process new, 31–32
content addressing, Applying (3) to Innovating (4) lesson segments
    chunking content, 169
    cooperative learning, 174–175, 181
    elaborating on new content, 170
    homework, using, 176
    hypothesis generation and testing of new content, 181–183
    identifying critical information, 165–166
    interacting with new content, grouping students

for, 165–173
    knowledge, revising, 180–181
    practice understanding of new content, 174–176, 179–180
    practicing skills, 179–180
    previewing new, 167–169
    processing strategies, 169–170
    questioning strategies, 170
    reasoning, identifying errors in, 178–179
    recording and representing information, 171–172
    resources and guidance, providing, 183–184
    reviewing content, 173–174
    similarities and differences, identifying, 176–178
    student reflection, 172–173
    vignette, 185
content addressing, Beginning (1) to Developing (2) and Developing (2) to Applying (3) lesson segments
    chunking content, 82–83
    cooperative learning, 92, 105–106
    elaborating on new content, 85–86
    homework, using, 95–96
    hypothesis generation and testing of new content, 105–111
    identifying critical information, 76–77
    interacting with new content, grouping students for, 76–90
    knowledge, revising, 103–105
    practice understanding of new content, 77–79, 90–105
    practicing skills, 102–103
    previewing new, 79–82
    processing strategies, 83–85
    questioning strategies, 85–86
    reasoning, identifying errors in, 99–101
    recording and representing information, 86–88
    resources and guidance, providing, 109–111
    reviewing content, 90–91
    similarities and differences, identifying, 96–99
    student reflection, 88–89
    vignette, 112
content addressing, description of lesson segments for, 20, 21, 22, 23, 25–26
content addressing, Not Using (0) to Beginning (1) lesson segments
    chunking content, 42, 43
    cognitive dissonance, 48
    cooperative learning, 42, 43, 44–45, 46, 47, 48
    homework, using, 45, 46
    hypothesis generation and testing of new

content, 47–48
  identifying critical information, 41, 43
  interacting with new content, grouping students
    for, 41–44
  knowledge, revising, 45, 47
  practice understanding of new content, 44–47
  practicing skills, 45, 47
  previewing new, 42, 43
  processing strategies, 42, 44
  questioning strategies, 42, 44
  reasoning, identifying errors in, 45, 47
  resources and guidance, providing, 48
  reviewing content, 44, 46
  similarities and differences, identifying, 45, 46
  student reflection, 42–43, 44
  vignette, 49
content knowledge, 13
conversations, coach-teacher, 213–214
Costa, A., 9, 12
Cox, E., 4

D

de Bono, E., 31, 84, 92, 169, 174
Developing (2) to Applying (3). *See* Beginning (1)
    to Developing (2) and Developing (2) to
    Applying (3) lesson segments
Dexter, E., 7
DiClemente, C., 10
differentiating coaching, 213–217
differentiation strategies for advanced and
    struggling students, 156–157
directing conversations, 213–214
direct instruction, 13
district-initiated coaching, 211, 212
double-bubble diagrams, 97, 177

E

Effective Supervision (Marzano), 19
effective teaching model, establishing, 19–23
Emler, N., 3
enacted on the spot, Applying (3) to Innovating (4)
    lesson segments
  academic games, using, 186–187
  behaviors that indicate affection for students,
    202–203
  controversy/competition, use of mild, 192–194
  engagement, indicators of, 186
  engaging students, 186–195

  expectations for low-expectancy students,
    communicating high, 205–207
  instructional pace, 190–191
  objectivity and control, displaying, 203–205
  personal information relevant to students, 194
  physical activity, using, 189–190
  presenting unusual or intriguing information,
    194–195
  relationships with students, establishing and
    maintaining, 199–201
  response rates, monitoring, 188–189
  rules and procedures, recognizing, 195–199
  student interests and backgrounds,
    understanding, 199–201
  teacher intensity and enthusiasm, 191–192
  vignette, 208
  withitness, demonstrating, 196
enacted on the spot, Beginning (1) to Developing
    (2) and Developing (2) to Applying (3) lesson
    segments
  academic games, using, 113–116
  behaviors that indicate affection for students,
    142–144
  controversy/competition, use of mild, 124–127
  engagement, indicators of, 113
  engaging students, 112–130
  expectations for low-expectancy students,
    communicating high, 147–152
  instructional pace, 121–122
  objectivity and control, displaying, 144–147
  personal information relevant to students,
    127–128
  physical activity, using, 119–121
  presenting unusual or intriguing information,
    128–130
  relationships with students, establishing and
    maintaining, 137–147
  response rates, monitoring, 116–119
  rules and procedures, recognizing, 130–137
  student interests and backgrounds,
    understanding, 137–141
  teacher intensity and enthusiasm, 122–124
  vignette, 153
  withitness, demonstrating, 130–131
enacted on the spot, description of lesson segments
    for, 20–21, 22, 27–28
enacted on the spot, Not Using (0) to Beginning
    (1) lesson segments
  academic games, using, 49–50, 51
  behaviors that indicate affection for students,

54, 55
controversy/competition, use of mild, 50, 52
engagement, indicators of, 49, 51
engaging students, 49–52
expectations for low-expectancy students,
	communicating high, 56–57
instructional pace, 50, 52
objectivity and control, displaying, 54, 55
personal information relevant to students, 50, 52
physical activity, using, 50, 51
presenting unusual or intriguing information,
	50, 52
relationships with students, establishing and
	maintaining, 54–55
response rates, monitoring, 50, 51
rules and procedures, recognizing, 53–54
student interests and backgrounds,
	understanding, 54, 55
teacher intensity and enthusiasm, 50, 52
vignette, 57–58
withitness, demonstrating, 53
English learners, differentiation strategies for,
	156–157
experience levels, teachers and, 214–215

F

facilitating conversations, 213
Farson, R., 8–9
feedback
	effective coaching and, 10–11
	nonevaluative, 8–9
	peer, 104, 175, 181
	role of, 217–218
	verbal, 67, 159, 218
	virtual coaching and real-time, 16–17, 220
	written, 218
Fénelon, F., 4
Fillery-Travis, A., 9
fishbowl demonstration, 77–78, 166
Flynn, K., 156
Folkman, J., 10
formative assessment, 13, 38, 65, 158

G

Gable, R., 17
Gallwey, W. T., 11, 13–14
Garmston, R., 9, 12
Garvey, B., 3

Gauthier, R., 4
Gawande, A., 3, 7
Giber, D., 4
Goldhammer, R., 4–5, 12
Goldsmith, M., 9
Good, T., 37
Gorby, C. B., 3–4
Grant, A., 3–4, 6, 8
Green, L. S., 6
Gregg, M., 17
Griffith, C. R., 3
Grogan, P., 7
GROW model, 14–15

H

Handbook for the Art and Science of Teaching, A
	(Marzano and Brown), 19
Heather, N., 3
Herold, P., 17
Hess, D. E., 126–127, 193–194
Hill, J., 156
Hughes, H., 7

I

Imbeau, M., 156
information processing strategies, 21–32
Inner Game model, 13–14
inside-outside circle, 94–95, 176

J

Jackson, R., 213–214, 215
Jensen, E., 156
jigsaw cooperative learning, 32, 84, 170
Joyce, B., 5–6, 9

K

Kagan, M., 93, 94–95, 175, 176
Kagan, S., 93, 94–95, 175, 176
Kinnucan-Welsch, K., 7
Knight, J., 6, 10, 11, 13, 217
Korner, I., 17
Kouzes, J., 11
Kretlow, A., 6, 7, 11
K-W-L strategy, 80–81, 168

L

Lane, D., 9
learning centers, 71, 162
Lee, D., 16
legal model, 127, 194
Les Aventures de Telemaque (Fénelon), 4
lesson segments, 19–23
    See also under type of
listening, active, 218
Lyman, F., 152, 207

M

macrostrategy, creating a, 155–156
Marzano, R., 5, 18, 19–21, 31, 83, 91–92, 169, 174
Mayer, R., 37
McAfee, J., 16–17
McGill, I., 8, 11
"Mechanical Third Ear, The" (Korner and Brown), 17
Meister, C., 155
mentor, use of term, 4
modeling, 217

N

Neuman, S., 7
Newkirk, J., 17
Newton, I., 3
nonevaluative feedback, 8–9
Norcross, J., 10
Norwood, K., 12, 15–16
Not Using (0) level to Beginning (1) level lesson segments
    coaching perspective, 30–33
    content lesson segments, 41–49
    enacted on the spot lesson segments, 49–58
    routine events lesson segments, 38–41
    vignette, 34

O

Oades, L., 4
Ogle, D., 80–81, 168

P

pair-check, 93, 175
Palmer, P., 10

Palmer, S., 3, 13
Parsloe, E., 8
Partridge, B., 4
Passmore, J., 14–15
peer feedback, 104, 175, 181
peer response groups, 107, 182
peer tutoring, 107, 182
perspective analysis, 31, 83, 91–92, 169, 174
Piercy, T., 9
Pomphrey, C., 9
Posner, B., 11
Prochaska, J., 10
Psychology of Coaching (Griffith), 3

R

Ramirez, M., 17
real-time feedback, 16–17, 220
reciprocal teaching, 32, 85, 155, 170
Reeves, D., 9, 10
reflecting conversations, 213
reflection-in-action, 16
reflective journals, 88, 106, 172, 182
Robinson, P., 4
Rock, M., 17, 219–220
Rogers, C., 8–9
Rogers, J., 9
role-playing, 59, 154, 209
Rosenshine, B., 37, 155
Rosemary, C., 7
routine events, Applying (3) to Innovating (4) lesson segments
    celebrating success, 159
    classroom layouts, organizing, 162–163
    classroom rules and procedures, establishing and maintaining, 159–160–161
    goal-setting strategies (rubrics), 157–158
    student progress, tracking, 158–159
    vignette, 164
routine events, Beginning (1) to Developing (2) and Developing (2) to Applying (3) lesson segments
    celebrating success, 67
    classroom layouts, organizing, 71–74
    classroom rules and procedures, establishing and maintaining, 68–71
    goal-setting strategies (rubrics), 64–65
    student progress, tracking, 65–67
    vignette, 75
routine events, description of lesson segments for,

19–20, 21, 22, 24–25
routine events, Not Using (0) to Beginning (1) lesson segments
  celebrating success, 38, 39
  classroom layouts, organizing, 39, 40
  classroom rules and procedures, establishing and maintaining, 39, 40
  goal-setting strategies (rubrics), 38, 39
  student progress, tracking, 38, 39
  vignette, 41
Ruhl, K., 16–17
Rynsaardt, J., 6

S

scale for measuring teachers' progress, 23–24
  See also under type of
Scheeler, M. C., 16–17
Schein, E., 9
Schneider, B., 10
Schön, D., 16
school- or districtwide coaching programs, 211, 212
self-audit, conducting a, 24–30
self-evaluations, 107, 182
Showers, B., 5–6, 9
Skiffington, S., 3, 16
Stephens, D., 6–7
Stober, D., 8
struggling students, differentiation strategies for, 156–157
student achievement
  Cognitive Coaching and, 12–13
  relationship of coaching to, 7
supervision, clinical, 4–5, 12
Szymanska, K., 13

T

teacher
  experience levels, 214–215

-initiated coaching, 211
  knowledge and skills, relationship of coaching to, 7
  readiness for change, 215–217
teachers' progress, scale for measuring, 23–24
teaching model, establishing an effective, 19–23
team coaching, 16
thinking hats, 31, 84, 92, 169, 174
think logs, 88–89, 106, 172, 182
think-pair-share, 93, 152, 175, 207
think-pair-square, 93, 175
Tomlinson, C. A., 156
town hall meeting, 126–127, 193
trust, 10
  methods for building, 218
Trust in Schools (Bryk and Schneider), 10
Tschannen-Moran, B., 10
Tschannen-Moran, M., 10

V

Vanderburg, M., 6–7
Venn diagrams, 96–97, 177
verbal feedback, 67, 159, 218
virtual coaching, 16–17, 219–221

W

Whitmore, J., 14
Whybrow, A., 3
withitness, demonstrating, 53, 130–131, 196
Wright, T., 7
written feedback, 218

Z

Zeus, P., 3, 16
Zigmond, N., 17

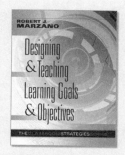